Danish Yearbook of Musicology
39 · 2012

Danish Yearbook of Musicology
Volume 39 · 2012

PUBLISHED BY

Danish Musicological Society

EDITED BY

Michael Fjeldsøe, Peter Hauge, and
Thomas Holme Hansen

Distributed by Aarhus University Press
Århus 2012

Danish Yearbook of Musicology • Volume 39 • 2012
Dansk Årbog for Musikforskning

EDITORS
Michael Fjeldsøe • fjeldsoe@hum.ku.dk
Peter Hauge • ph@kb.dk
Thomas Holme Hansen • musthh@hum.au.dk

PRODUCTION
Layout by Hans Mathiasen
Printed by Werks Offset A/S

Danish Yearbook of Musicology is published with support from
the Danish Council for Independent Research | Humanities.

ADDRESS
Danish Yearbook of Musicology
From 15 Dec. 2012:
c/o Department of Arts and Cultural Studies
Section of Musicology
University of Copenhagen
Karen Blixens Vej 1, DK-2300 København S
E-mail: editors e-mail-addresses
Website: www.dym.dk

Distributed by Aarhus University Press, www.unipress.dk

ISBN 978-87-88328-30-1
ISSN 1604-9896

Printed in Denmark 2012

Contents

The present issue of *Danish Yearbook of Musicology* includes three articles all of which treat aspects of musical life in Copenhagen: Niels Krabbe's 'Kurt Weill's *Deadly Sins* in Copenhagen: a thistle in the Danish kitchen garden of 1936' deals with the reception history of Weill's *Deadly Sins* staged at The Royal Theatre, also taking into consideration areas such as the cultural and political mood at the institution forming the performances of the work. Arne Spohr's article, '"This Charming Invention Created by the King": Christian IV and his invisible music', presents a refreshing view on Christian IV's Chapel Royal arguing that it was custom that musicians ('instrumentalists') were divided into smaller ensembles, first of all emphasizing different performance traditions but also creating a fertile space for experimentation and innovation. The popular mannerism of the time – the invisible music or the idea of hiding the 'producers' of music focusing on sound presentation – was indeed also popular at the Danish court. Finally, also Kristin Rygg focuses on sides of music performance at the court of Christian IV in 'When Angels Dance for Kings: the beginning of Scandinavian music theatre'. Rygg deals with a *ballet de cour*, to which Schütz most likely composed the music and which was performed at the Great Wedding in 1634; she explores how this ballet reveals traditions of courtly music theatre in Northern Europe. Rygg concludes that it was most likely inspired by the French *ballet de cour* with concepts of rulership related to alchemy and perhaps also Rosicrucianism.

In addition to the three articles, this year's volume also presents an array of scholarly reviews of new publications covering subjects ranging from Byzantine neumes of the Middle Ages to the Egyptian singer, Umm Kulthum who died in 1975, as well as abstracts of ongoing research projects. Tore Tvarnø Lind opens the volume with the viewpoint, 'Whose Musicology? Response to critique of musicology in Denmark', which is a contribution to the debate arguing that musicology today embraces a cornucopia of different methodologies and approaches to the subject of music.

The editorial team would like to take this opportunity to thank the Danish Council for Independent Research in the Humanities for its support for the publication and Aarhus University Press for excellent collaboration. Our thanks are also due to the contributors, to the editorial board, and to Axel Teich Geertinger for help with the German proofreading.

Copenhagen and Århus, November 2012
Michael Fjeldsøe, Peter Hauge & Thomas Holme Hansen

Viewpoint

Whose Musicology? Response to critique of musicology in Denmark

Tore Tvarnø Lind

Something's rotten in the state of musicology: musicology students who don't know Vivaldi's work! Students who don't read music! Musicologists who don't do musicology! Over the last year or so, musicology in Denmark has been subject to harsh critique launched by German professor in musicology, Linda Koldau from the Department of Aesthetics and Communication, Musicology, at Aarhus University.

Koldau's critique has received lengthy attention in Danish news media in 2011 and 2012, for example in the newspapers *Politiken*, *Information*, and *Weekendavisen*, and on blogs on the Internet. Even after announcing her resignation that will happen at the end of 2012, Koldau has continued to publish her critique, which in my view seriously calls for reactions from musicologists who have another view on the matter. This viewpoint should be seen as one such reaction.

Musicology isn't that appealing to the average news media consumer, I guess, but Koldau's critique of musicology has been blended with scandalous accusations, serious cooperation- and communication issues with her colleagues, alongside a critique of the university's board of directors, whom she accused of violating her freedom of speech.[1] Then even musicology becomes a subject sexy enough for journalistic storytelling. Koldau played the victim and the media took the bait.

Koldau has taken full advantage of her freedom of speech in public media – any discussion about violation in that connection is nonsense; rather, the problems might just as well be related to her unwillingness on to engage in face-to-face dialogue about music and musicology with her colleagues at the Aarhus department. This is the clear impression one gets from reading a comment from one of her colleagues.[2] By reference to incompatibilities between the department's idea of musicology and her own, Koldau was released from her duty to participate in staff meetings. On top of the freedom of speech issue, Koldau accused her colleagues for bullying her. These accusations have been dismissed by the university itself, and the

---

1   See for example Danish PEN, 21 Feb. 2012: http://danskpen.dk/2012/02/21/videnskabsministeren-ma-sikre-musikprofessors-ytringsfrihed/.
2   Steen Kaargaard Nielsen's comment, 22 Feb. 2012, appears at the Danish PEN site as the second comment on the same reference as the above, further down the page.

Ombudsman dismissed the case with reference to the agreement achieved between Koldau and the university.[3] Also musicology students at Aarhus University have reacted to Koldau's critique, which in their view is 'insubstantial' and based on a 'misunderstanding'.[4]

KOLDAU'S DIAGNOSIS

On the blog *Forskningsfrihed?* (*Freedom of Research?*), Koldau has lately re-published her critique under the title 'The Discipline of Musicology and Its Special Issues' (the original Danish title is 'Faget musikvidenskab og dets særlige problematik', 22 April 2012).[5] In summarizing parts of the critique previously published in newspapers in June 2011, Koldau presents a rather one-sided and undifferentiated diagnosis of the state of musicology.

Koldau claims that it is internationally accepted that musicology is to be divided into three distinct categories: historical musicology, which is musicology proper; systematic musicology; and ethnomusicology. According to Koldau, this division was part of the very foundation of musicology in the nineteenth century, and nothing will ever change that. In Aarhus, accordingly, musicology is not historical but of the systematic kind, dominated by popular music culture, sound culture, and culture theory – implying that popular music studies are only rarely dealing with historical contextualization. I feel the need to emphasize that I know quite a few colleagues in Aarhus, who are dealing with music history and historiography in relation to many different kinds of music and musical culture.

One of Koldau's primary claims is that not a single scholar from outside the borders of Denmark will identify musicology in Denmark as musicology. According to Koldau, Danish students have no knowledge of the great musical masterpieces (that is, from the canon of West European art music) and they do not read music. Moreover, research and teaching at Danish departments *is not* musicology proper – it is sociology and culture theory and so on and so forth. Of course, this is a fight over definitions. What is musicology? I would maintain that not a single scholar in Denmark is able to identify with Koldau's version of Danish musicology. If there is any possible conclusion to be made here it is that *nobody* seems to be able to identify with the musicology that Koldau talks about, other than herself. This makes me wonder: either Koldau doesn't have a clue about what is going on or she is right, and we are all a bunch of great pretenders believing in our ignorance to be doing musicology while we in fact are doing something entirely different.

---

3   See the remark of the Ombudsman at: www.ombudsmanden.dk/find/nyheder/alle/koldau-sag/.
4   Published in *Politiken*, 21 Feb. 2012, see: http://politiken.dk/debat/ECE1546506/studerende-koldaus-kritik-beror-paa-en-misforstaaelse/.
5   See Koldau's diagnosis here: http://professorvaelde.blogspot.dk/2012/04/faget-musikvidenskab-og-dets-srlige.html.

METHODOLOGICAL PLURALISM

In her diagnosis, Koldau feels compelled to enlighten her readers by describing ethnomusicology – which isn't taught at Aarhus – as the study of 'other [non-European] cultures and European folk music'.[6] Somebody, please pinch my arm! Is this for real? This is light years from the international standards that Koldau herself is claiming and calling for. Today, ethnomusicology is no longer defined by its subject, rather by its methodology and level of scholarly reflection: it is an interdisciplinary approach to all kinds of music in the world. Of primary interest to ethnomusicologists are music and musical practices in their social, historical, political, cultural, and many other settings. Focus could for example be on the relation between individual and group identity, issues of music and otherness, power relations and the right to define one's life and to perform one's music. Mostly, ethnomusicological projects are influenced by anthropology and thus involve fieldwork, but otherwise they tend to overlap with a wide range of other musicological disciplines, be it popular music studies, historical and theoretical studies, etc. Hence ethnomusicology could be seen as an inclusive category consisting of multiple approaches to a plurality of music and contexts, and not of a single theoretical and methodological matrix.

In my own research on the Greek-Orthodox musical tradition, historiography and ethnography are merged.[7] Tradition implies that the participants in the social group in question – in my study a group of monks – relate to their past. As a scholar, I need to take this past (however it is defined) into consideration too. The separation of music studies into diachronic and synchronic is pure theory and it collapses in practice. Even the most 'traditional' societies cannot be denied a place in history. Now, is my research musicology, ethnomusicology, historical ethnomusicology, or musical anthropology? Who cares, really?

What I call for is a musicology which is pluralistic, interdisciplinary and inclusive in terms of methodology and theoretical orientation that in fruitful ways may open up the subject matters in radical new ways and push boundaries for musical thinking and knowledge. Accordingly, I see the ossified distinctions between musicology and its so-called sub-disciplines as an unnecessary limitation to scholarly work.

If we look at musicology departments in Denmark, musicology in its total could be characterized by heterogeneity, methodological pluralism, and otherwise a very wide range of approaches to various kinds of music. And everybody does not necessarily (have to) agree on everything. To follow this logic, there is also room for Koldau's way of doing musicology. Koldau advocates for the classical education, which has been under challenge for some time by now. This need not be a problem, as I see it; classical virtues might easily find ways into the curricula if they are

---

6 'Musiketnologi beskæftiger sig med musik i andre [dvs. ikke vestlige] kulturer, men også med europæisk folkemusik' (my transl.); follow the link to Koldau's full analysis: http://professorvaelde.blogspot.dk/2012/04/faget-musikvidenskab-og-dets-srlige.html.

7 Tore Tvarnø Lind, *The Past Is Always Present: The Revival of the Byzantine Musical Tradition at Mount Athos* (Lanham: Scarecrow Press, 2012).

not already there. But there is a problem: Koldau's version of musicology (note: version and not vision) is normative: everybody must follow her head to ensure international standard. This is where Koldau's ideas of how to run a university seem to predate 1968, a bygone age when professors still had sovereign power.

NUANCED UNDERSTANDING

Media publicity is important. Many musicologists are frequently present in the media: on national radio broadcasts, in newspapers, on Internet debates, and on television. It remains important, I believe, that scholars challenge existing and dominating ideas about music and qualify debates and discussions with research based knowledge. Perhaps scholars in Denmark ought to be better to communicate their research to a wider public, and create a more nuanced, and a more positive understanding of what music research today is about and why it is important – whether that be in newspaper articles, participation in public debates, presentations in unorthodox contexts, or the production of new tutorial books.

I welcome critique of musicology: critique is tantamount to inspiring us to think music in new ways. Yet, critique must be based on a genuine interest in what musicology in Denmark actually consists of. The arrogance in Koldau's critique is almost entertaining – had it not been for the total lack of curiosity for the work of her colleagues in Denmark writ large. As Koldau's attack is devoid of genuine commitment to musicology as it unfolds (in many different ways) at Danish universities, and as she seems unwilling even to imagine the possibility of other ways of doing musicology than *her* way, I wonder: exactly who did Koldau expect to take her critique seriously?

'This Charming Invention Created by the King'
Christian IV and his invisible music

ARNE SPOHR

Even for a Renaissance monarch, King Christian IV had an exceptionally wide range of interests. He was one of Europe's most significant patrons of the arts, drawing renowned musicians, painters, and sculptors to his court. He was also highly interested in science, architecture, engineering, and trading, and invested in the infrastructure of his kingdom on a hitherto unprecedented scale. He founded new towns, trading companies and colonies, established manufactures, and mining in Norway, and pursued prestigious building projects, including representative buildings in Copenhagen and the castles of Rosenborg and Frederiksborg.[1] The remarkably wide range of his interests and activities stems from the range of skills he learned during his education at the court of his father, Frederick II.[2] His expertise was noted and admired by many of his contemporaries, for example by the German nobleman Heinrich Reuss who attended the king's coronation in 1596. Reuss reported that the king not only was a good musician, able to play various wind and string instruments, but also a good horseman, excelling in knightly games, 'a fully trained sailor, [also] excelling in fortification, in the art of painting, in short – in all distinguished arts'.[3]

His comprehensive education and training enabled Christian IV to supervise and control a variety of aspects, with regard to both courtly and state affairs. The Gottorf court official Gosche Wensin, who frequently visited the Danish court, noted in his diary: 'The king looks after everything, be it of small or high importance, knows everything, orders and supervises everything, even in regard to household management'.[4]

---

1   Jørgen Hein, *The Treasure Collection at Rosenborg Castle I. The Inventories of 1696 and 1718. Royal Heritage and Collecting in Denmark-Norway 1500–1900* (Copenhagen, 2009), 6.

2   See, for instance, Steffen Heiberg (ed.), *Christian IV and Europe. The 19th Art Exhibition of the Council of Europe, Denmark 1988* (Copenhagen, 1988), 262–67.

3   Original text: 'Sonst haben sie [= die königliche Majestät] uff vielen Instrumenten sich geübt als ein guter Trompeter, ein horniste, instrumentist uff der zincken, geigen, posaun, und was nur müglich einem grossen herrn zu lernen, auch ein guter reitter, in ritterspielen excellirt, ein auslernd schiffmann, in der fortification und malerkünsten und in summa in allen vornemen sachen haben i[hro] k[önigliche] mai[estät] zu der zeit excellirt'; author's transl., quot. Ole Kongsted, 'Christian IV. und seine europäische Musikerschaft', in Robert Bohn (ed.), *Europa in Scandinavia. Kulturelle und soziale Dialoge in der frühen Neuzeit* (Frankfurt a.M., 1994), 117.

4   Anders Andersen (ed.), *Jacob Fabricius den Yngres Optegnelser 1617–1644*, ([Tønder], 1964), 9: 'Rex ad omnia attendit [the King looks after everything]; ist nichts so gross oder klein, scit omnia [knows everything], bestellet und ordnet alles, etiam in oeconomicis [also in regard to household management]'; author's transl.

This seemingly archaic trait of his governmental style[5] is, for instance, evident in the planning and execution of the lavish festivities of the so called 'Great Wedding' of 1634, about which a contemporary eyewitness reports: 'otherwise His Majesty has written down and drawn up everything that was supposed to happen, small and great, with his own hand, and has personally given orders on everything that was supposed to be carried out'.[6]

Christian IV's wide ranging interests and knowledge in the arts, in technology, and in other fields were clearly not ends in themselves, but tools to create and maintain control and power. The arts not only served as a means of royal propaganda,[7] but also set the royal power 'apart from the nobility by means not only of overwhelming splendour but also by certain new cultural forms, which in Denmark became the cultural monopoly of the court, [for instance, by] Renaissance (Manierist) architecture, silver furniture, court ballets and music at an international level'.[8]

Like many monarchs of his time, Christian IV used his expertise in the arts to create by their aid, to quote Jörg Jochen Berns, 'a media-strategic system for the creation and maintenance of princely-courtly representation and pretension to power'.[9] Court ceremonial was a particularly important 'stage' for the display of these strategic tools that he had assembled and that he commanded in front of an 'audience' of both foreign visitors and local nobility. Since, 'according to early modern conceptions, every earthly ceremony is the realization of a heavenly ceremonial order that has descended to earth', and since 'every earthly ceremony has to be realized by means of all five senses',[10] music *had* to be represented in court ceremonial – mostly in connection with arts representing other senses, often creating a synesthetic experience.

Soon after his coronation in 1596, Christian IV established an impressive *Hofmusik*, comprising musicians of European fame, such as the English lutenist John Dowland (?1563–1626) and the English string players William Brade (?1560–1630) and Thomas Simpson (1582–?1628). The king used his *Hofmusik* as an acoustic 'instrument of power', both at home and when he was travelling abroad. But how and where was this outstanding 'instrument' actually 'set in scene' in ceremonial

5   On the term 'hausväterlicher Hof' (house-fatherly court) in early modern Europe, see Volker Bauer, *Die höfische Gesellschaft in Deutschland von der Mitte des 17. bis zum Ausgang des 18. Jahrhunderts. Versuch einer Typologie* (Tübingen, 1993).

6   Christian Cassius, *Relation von dem hochfürstlichen Beylager* (Hamburg, 1635): 'Sonsten haben Ihr Maytt. alles was fürgehen sollte / klein vnd groß mit selbst eigener Hand verzeichnet vnd auffgesetzet; in eigener Persohn zu allem was sollte fürgenommen werden / ordre außgetheilet'; author's transl., quot. Dieter Lohmeier, 'Das Kopenhagener Große Beilager 1634. Politischer Anspruch, Repräsentation und höfisches Fest', in Bohn (ed.), *Europa in Scandinavia*, 114.

7   Jørgen Hein, 'Collecting in Prague and Copenhagen', in Lubomír Konečný (ed.), *Rudolf II, Prague and the World* (Prague, 1998), 121.

8   Sebastian Olden-Jørgensen, 'State Ceremonial, Court Culture and Political Power in Early Modern Denmark, 1536–1746', *Scandinavian Journal of History*, 27 (2002), 70.

9   Jörg Jochen Berns, 'Instrumental Sound and Ruling Spaces of Resonance in the Early Modern Period: On the Acoustic Setting of the Princely *potestas* Claims within a Ceremonial Frame', in Helmar Schramm, Ludger Schwarte, and Jan Lazardzig (eds.), *Instruments in Art and Science: On the Architectonics of Cultural Boundaries in the 17th Century* (Berlin and New York, 2008), 479.

10   Ibid. 480.

situations, how was it used? 'What spatialities [were] opened by what sound instruments, or more precisely, what spatial types [were] made and served by what sound sources?'[11] Moreover, when and how was it used in connection with other 'media' such as visual arts, dining, and dancing? The spatial dimension of early modern court music, more specifically the use of both spaces and technology in performance situations, as well as the combination with other arts to create synesthetic effects in particular spaces, is a hitherto under-explored field of historical musicology. The Danish court music of Christian IV and the innovative ways of its spatial use in the context of court ceremonial can offer a particularly instructive case study in this field.

Regarding space, the uses of court music seem to fall between the two extremes of 'exposing' and 'hiding', of 'presence' and 'absence'. The physical presence of court musicians in ceremonial contexts is well known and is generally seen as the 'normal' case in their performance routine. Musicians performed in musicians' galleries or on the floor during banquets or balls. In special cases they were publicly displayed as precious 'objects', for instance at the coronation festivities of Christian IV when they acted as lavishly dressed allegorical figures and played silver wind instruments.[12] This has a parallel in the use of musicians in the sixteenth-century intermedi and early opera, where instrumentalists 'appeared on stage and in character', for instance in the intermedi performed in Florence in 1589.[13]

However, apart from the visual display of musicians there was another, perhaps even more spectacular, form of use: in certain situations the Danish king kept his court musicians from view so that their music appeared as an acoustic miracle to visitors. The invisible music of Christian IV has been known to scholars, mainly art historians, for some time;[14] it has quite recently been brought to the attention of a more general audience by the British writer Rose Tremain in her novel *Music and Silence*.[15] She very evocatively describes a group of freezing court instrumentalists, performing in an unheated wine cellar of Rosenborg castle for Christian IV, who has breakfast in the Winter Room above and listens to the invisible music reaching him by sound channels. Since the publication of the novel, new evidence for sound conduits connecting the wine cellar with the Winter Room has come to light, documented by the curator of the royal collections in Rosenborg, Jørgen Hein.[16] Hein has also discovered and made accessible hitherto unknown travel accounts that document the use of invisible music in buildings of Christian IV.[17] Both discoveries shed new light on where and how the invisible music was used at his court. It is my aim in this article to describe what is currently known about the places of

11 Ibid.
12 Augustus Erich, *Außführliche vnd warhaffte Beschreibung Des Durchlauchtigsten… Herrn Christians / des Vierdten …den 29. Augusti Anno 1596 glücklich geschehenen Königlichen Krönung* (Copenhagen, 1597), sig. Tʳ.
13 John Spitzer and Neal Zaslaw, *The Birth of the Orchestra: History of an Institution, 1650–1815* (Oxford and New York, 2004), 39.
14 See, for instance, Vilhelm Wanscher, *Rosenborgs Historie 1606–1934* (Copenhagen, 1930), 62.
15 Rose Tremain, *Music and Silence* (New York, 2001), 28–30.
16 Hein, *The Treasure Collection at Rosenborg Castle*, 44.
17 Ibid. 140–45.

invisible music at the court of Christian IV, to compare his invisible music and the contexts of its uses in Denmark to two parallel cases in northern Europe (Dresden and Stuttgart), and to discuss possible functions and meanings of this phenomenon and its technology.

According to the current state of research, invisible music could be heard in three different royal buildings in Denmark: in the garden house Sparepenge that was located in the Frederiksborg castle park, built between 1599 and 1601;[18] in Rosenborg Castle, built in several stages between 1606 and 1634;[19] and in the Golden Summerhouse, a small octagonal structure built in 1619, located on the north-western side of the castle islet, very close to Rosenborg castle.[20] Sparepenge and the Golden Summerhouse were eventually demolished in later times,[21] but many details regarding the construction and function of these two buildings can be ascertained from a number of travel accounts dating from the seventeenth century.[22]

Sparepenge was one of the first representative building projects that Christian IV carried out after his coronation in 1596. It was an Italianate summerhouse comprising two storeys, a vaulted cellar and a flat roof, built to house the first mixed collection of the Danish royal family.[23] This collection was essentially 'an armoury that combined dress weapons and technical novelties and objects of ethnographic interest'.[24] The inspiration for the design and purpose of Sparepenge very likely came from Dresden, which Christian IV had visited incognito in 1597.[25] On the city ramparts of the Jungfernbastei, the present-day Brühlsche Terrasse, a summerhouse (Belvedere) of similar shape as Sparepenge was begun in 1589[26] (see Ill. 1). Its architect was the Italian Giovanni Maria Nosseni (1544–1620), a multi-faceted artist and art organizer who had been first employed at the Saxon court in 1575 and had expertise as a 'sculptor, stone-carver, painter, designer of court festivities' and even as a historian and poet.[27] The breadth of his activities and interests resembles those of other Renaissance architects, such as Bernardo Buontalenti (?1531–1608), who served the Medici Court in Florence during most of his life, and who most likely represented a professional model for Nosseni.[28] Nosseni and Christian IV must have been in contact in or before 1596, since the Italian designed an invention for

18 Ibid. 32–34.
19 Ibid. 46; see also Jørgen Hein and Peter Kristiansen, *Rosenborg Castle. A Guide to the Danish Royal Collections* (Copenhagen, 2005), 5–6.
20 Hein, *The Treasure Collection at Rosenborg Castle*, 146, 148.
21 Sparepenge was eventually demolished in 1720, see ibid. 32.
22 Documented ibid. 140–45.
23 Ibid. 32.
24 Ibid. 34.
25 Ibid. 14.
26 Helen Watanabe-O'Kelly, *Court Culture in Dresden. From Renaissance to Baroque* (Basingstoke and New York, 2002), 65.
27 Ibid., 42. See also Walter Mackowsky, *Giovanni Maria Nosseni und die Renaissance in Sachsen* (Berlin, 1904), 106–8.
28 Barbara Marx, 'Giovanni Maria Nosseni als Vermittler italienischer Sammlungskonventionen und ästhetischen Normen am Dresdner Hof', in Sibylle Ebert-Schifferer, *Scambio culturale con il nemico religioso: Italia e Sassonia attorno al 1600* (Milan, 2007), 105.

Ill. 1. The Dresden Belvedere, after a painting by Friedrich Hagedorn in the Stadt-museum Dresden (Mackowsky, *Giovanni Maria Nosseni*, 78).

the running-at-the-ring at the king's coronation festivities,[29] and was also present during these festivities as a member of the entourage of Margrave Christian Wilhelm of Brandenburg, for whom he had designed this invention.[30]

It is very likely that Nosseni was the architect of Sparepenge. This is not only suggested by the similarity of its layout to the Dresden Belvedere as well as Nosseni's connection to the Danish court, but also by the fact that Nosseni produced art work for Sparepenge such as 'a doorframe of Saxon serpentine'[31] as well as Corinthian capitals.[32] It is therefore very likely that Nosseni was also responsible for installing sound conduits for invisible music in Sparepenge, since they were also installed in the Dresden summerhouse (see below).

In 1623, Prince Christian II of Anhalt-Bernburg (1599–1658) visited Rosenborg and Sparepenge on his travels to northern Germany and Denmark. Christian of Anhalt had participated in the Battle of the White Mountain in 1620 on the Prot-

---

29 Mara Wade, *Triumphus Nuptialis Danicus. German Court Culture and Denmark. The "Great Wedding" of 1634* (Wiesbaden, 1996), 45–46.

30 Mackowsky, *Giovanni Maria Nosseni*, 94. It seems significant that Christian IV used a 'mobile' invisible music in his pageant at the *Huldigung* festivities in Hamburg in 1603; he placed his court instrumentalists underneath his chariot and covered them under a silver cloth. On this chariot he posed as 'sun king'. See Arne Spohr, '*How chances it they travel?' Englische Musiker in Dänemark und Norddeutschland* (Wiesbaden, 2009), 259. It seems possible that Georg Engelhart Löhneysen, a court equerry and festival designer employed at the courts in Dresden and Wolfenbüttel, had learned this idea from Nosseni.

31 Hein, *The Treasure Collection at Rosenborg Castle*, 34. See also: Copenhagen, Rigsarkivet, Regnskaber 1559–1560. Bygningsregnskaber. 1596–1646 Bygningsregnskaber, Beholdningerne af marmor 1600.

32 Meir Stein, *Christian den Fjerdes billedverden* (Copenhagen, 1987), 83.

estant side, had been imprisoned by imperial troops, but had eventually been freed in 1621. He 'presumably acted as imperial informer during his visit to Denmark',[33] which would explain his very detailed accounts of Christian IV's buildings. His travel diaries[34] are important political and cultural documents of his time, recording a multitude of aspects, including art and music. His record of Sparepenge, for instance, allows us to reconstruct the organization of the building as well as that of the royal collection, which was on exhibit there:

> The Prince's visit falls into three parts. He starts in the armoury, which was arranged in several rooms and encompassed firearms and blank weapons as well as saddlery... After the armoury the Prince saw the dining room, which had ceiling paintings, a buffet boasting 120 cups that Christian IV had won in tilting at the ring and a model of a mine.[35]

Finally, Christian of Anhalt visited the musicians's room ('Musikantenstube'), about which he notes:

> I saw the place in the musicians's room where the musicians make a sound for the king when he is in his room above. The sound reaches him through lions' heads that are placed above, so that the musicians and the trumpeters can play music invisibly. Moreover, there is a little trap door under the king's table which allows, whenever the king opens it by his foot, the music underneath to be heard, so that a foreign visitor does not know where it comes from.[36]

Tubes in the walls and ceiling transmitted the sound of the court ensemble from the musicians's room to the banquet room situated above, where the king dined, and where his model of a mine and his cups were on display for guests. When someone visited the royal collection in Sparepenge, he not only experienced visual splendour, but also heard a miraculous sound coming from out of sight. Besides Christian of Anhalt's travel diary, there are more travel accounts dating from the 1630s to the 1660s describing technical provisions for invisible music. However, they do not refer to Sparepenge, but to Rosenborg castle and the neighbouring Golden Summerhouse. Charles Ogier, the author of one of these accounts, was a French diplomat who had been sent to Denmark as an envoy to the wedding of the Prince Elect and the Saxonian princess Magdalena Sibylla in 1634.[37] While the authors of the other travel accounts describe only the technical provisions for the invisible music, Ogier describes his aural impressions of it.

33 Hein, *The Treasure Collection at Rosenborg Castle*, 141.
34 Modern edition: Gottlieb Krause (ed.), *Tagebuch Christians des Jüngeren, Fürst zu Anhalt* (Leipzig, 1858).
35 Hein, *The Treasure Collection at Rosenborg Castle*, 34.
36 See Krause, *Tagebuch*, 101. German original: 'In der Musikantenstube den Ort gesehen, da die Musicanten dem König droben, durch Löwenköpfe die droben stehen, einen Ton geben, und unsichtbarer weise Musiciren können, wie auch die Trommeter. So hatt es auch unter des Königs Tisch ein Thürlein, welches, wann es der König mit dem Fuss eröffnet, kann man auch die Musica so drunten ist hören, und ein frembder nicht wissen wo sie her kompt'; author's transl.
37 See Wade, *Triumphus Nuptialis Danicus*, 157–278.

When Christian IV received Ogier in Rosenborg, he first led his guest 'to a small pavilion with windows on all sides, in which on one stone table there lay some sweetmeats, which the King offered him'.[38] Hein has identified this small pavilion as the Golden Summerhouse. After visiting the pavilion the king took Ogier, according to his report, 'to a square antechamber adorned by paintings, beneath which he was accustomed to placing his musicians'.[39] According to Ogier, the invisible music suddenly started at that very moment when the king and he were standing in the very centre of this room:

> All the musicians, both instrumentalists and singers, [began] to play music in which they harmonised with each other, which sudden delight we experienced with amazement, as the sounds reached our ears through various vents, as though they were sometimes closer, sometimes more distant. In the meantime the French ambassador with delight praised this charming invention created by the King, and we tried to communicate this [our amazement] to the King by our looks. When we had come outside and were sitting in the carriage in the actual gatehouse, we could still for a long time distinguish that subterranean and invisible, but not unpleasant music, which presumably was played at the behest of the King.[40]

It should be noted that the context of Ogier's visit to Rosenborg is entirely different from Christian of Anhalt's visit to Sparepenge. While the latter informally toured through the building, possibly led by a local court official, Ogier had the favour of being personally guided by the king, and experienced the invisible music as part of a ceremonial situation.

The actual location of the 'square antechamber' in which Ogier heard the invisible music has been disputed by scholars. H.C. Bering Liisberg located the music in the 'round summerhouse in Krumspringet to the south-west of the islet',[41] whereas Vilhelm Wanscher placed Ogier's experience of the invisible music in the so-called Winter Room on the ground floor of Rosenborg Castle.[42] Wanscher's theory is supported by newly found evidence: During recent restoration work of the castle cellar, three sound conduits were discovered that connect the Winter Room with the cellar room directly underneath, 'running from the vaulting in the castle cellars to the floor in the Winter Room',[43] where they emerge in three places, originally hidden by armchairs (see Ill. 2). A fourth sound conduit discovered in a cellar wall seems to have led to the Golden Summerhouse, which was technically possible due to its close proximity. Thus it was possible to hear the invisible music both in the Winter Room in Rosenborg and the Golden Summerhouse.

A travel account recently discovered by Hein supports this new evidence. The lawyer Heinrich Meyer, a member of Bremen City Council, visited both Rosenborg

38 English transl. from the Latin original, Hein, *The Treasure Collection at Rosenborg Castle*, 141.
39 Ibid. 141.
40 English transl., ibid.; transl. of the second sentence by author.
41 Ibid. 149.
42 Ibid. 149–50.
43 Ibid. 44.

Ill. 2. Sound conduit in Rosenborg Castle. Picture reproduced by kind permission of Jørgen Hein and Rosenborg Castle.

and Sparepenge in 1642. While he does not mention any provisions for invisible music in Sparepenge, this phenomenon clearly caught his attention in Rosenborg and the Golden Summerhouse, along with a number of works of art and technical devices. In the Winter Room, Meyer notices an oven capable of bearing very high heat, as well as a device through which the king could raise and lower the draw-bridge near the castle.[44] He also reports: 'By the table of His Majesty there was a small, covered hole, through which, by means of a channel, one could speak to someone at the door, even though people who are in this room cannot hear it'.[45] In the same room there was a very similar device for invisible music: 'In both corners there are two hollow armchairs, through which the music coming from the vaults downstairs sounds, whenever His Majesty wants to entertain in the chamber'.[46] Moreover, Meyer's travel account demonstrates that the Golden Summerhouse had the same device, transmitting music through sound channels from the cellar vaults of the castle. In this summerhouse the sound of the invisible music came out of an

44 Ibid. 142.
45 Ibid. English transl. of this quotation and the two following ones by the author. German original: 'Bey I. K. Mtt. Tisch war / ein klein Loch, drin per Canalem, so / Verdecket, man mit jemandt an der / thür reden könte / ob schon die mit im / Gemach sein, nichts davon vestehen'.
46 Ibid.: 'An beiden ecken seindt zwo durch= / gehölete Sessel drauff / drauss wan I. K. / Mtt. erlustigen wollen im Gemach / die Musica auss dem Gewölbe drunten erklin= /get'.

opening in the floor that was situated underneath a table'.[47] Meyer's statements are supported by a later travel account, Nils Rubinus's diary from 1662.[48]

The invisible music, however, seems to eventually have fallen out of use soon afterwards:

> After 1668 the travel accounts have no more to say about summerhouses containing music conduits. In 1681, the Wine Cellar was fitted out as State Archives and could no longer be used by the King's Musicians. The sound conduits thus lost their original function, and the Golden Summerhouse disappeared.[49]

Ogier mentions paintings in the 'square antechamber', which he saw while he was hearing the invisible music. Even though he mentions them en passant, without specifying their subjects, character and function, it is clear that paintings were, together with the invisible music, part of a larger, multi-media concept, a concept that resembles the arrangement found in Sparepenge. There are two paintings still extant, associated with the Danish court and having musical themes, dating from the 1620s. They have attracted a considerable interest of art historians and music historians.[50] However, these paintings have to this date hardly been evaluated in their original function, namely to 'visualize the hidden music',[51] that could be heard in the same room in which they were exhibited. One of them is the illusionist ceiling painting that today covers the ceiling of the southern gable room (also known as the Queen's Room) in Rosenborg Castle (see Ill. 3). As the art historian Meir Stein suggests, it may have been painted by the Danish artist Søren Kiær around 1620, although it has also been attributed to the German painter Francis Clein.[52] It shows musicians playing from a gallery in illusionistic perspective, a heavenly ensemble that might at the same time show real members of the Danish *Hofkapelle* active in the 1620s.[53] The other painting, signed by Reinhold Timm (Thim) and dated ca. 1623, shows four lavishly dressed court musicians (see Ill. 4), in the foreground a harpist, most likely Darby Scott (Skott), who had been recruited in Britain in 1621, and a viol player, possibly the Englishman Thomas Simpson who was employed at the Danish court between 1622 and 1625. There are two more musicians in the background, a lutenist, and a flautist. It seems likely that these four musicians formed a standing ensemble that specialized in repertoire from the British Isles.[54]

47 Ibid.: 'Uffgerichtet ist auch daselbsten / ein rundes Lusthaus übergüldet / untern Tisch ist ein durchgebrochen Loch, / daselbsten per canalem der Musichlen kan / hingeleitet werden, aussem Schloss, wie / wohl die Musici weith von dannen auch / nicht gesehen werden können'.

48 Ibid. 143.

49 Ibid. 150.

50 See, for instance, Meir Stein's seminal article on the ceiling painting: 'A Ceiling Painting at Rosenborg Palace and Its Prototype', in Joan Römelingh (ed.), *Art in Denmark 1600–1650* (Leids Kunsthistorisch Jaarboek, 1983, 2; Leiden, 1984), 127–36.

51 Hein, *The Treasure Collection of Rosenborg Castle*, 151.

52 Ibid.

53 Stein, 'A Ceiling Painting', 133. See also Spohr, *'How chances it they travel?'*, 209, 219–20.

54 Ole Kongsted, 'Christian IV and Music', in Steffen Heiberg (ed.), *Christian IV and Europe. The 19th Art Exhibition of the Council of Europe* (Copenhagen, 1988), 121–43. See also Spohr, *'How chances it they travel?'*, 173, 222–23; and Peter Holman, 'The Harp in Stuart England. New Light on William Lawes's Harp Consorts', *Early Music*, 15 (1987), 188–203.

Ill. 3. Francis Clein or Søren Kiær, 'Christian IV's Court Musicians' (detail of ceiling painting), Rosenborg Castle *c*.1620. Reproduced by kind permission of Jørgen Hein and Rosenborg Castle.

The history of the display and use of both paintings can be partially reconstructed. The ceiling painting 'was hung in the southern gable room in the ground floor … during Frederick's conversions of Rosenborg 1705–9 …, when the ceiling paintings from Christian IV's audience chamber … were moved to the Winter Room'.[55] Hein suspects that 'Clein's ceiling painting might originally have derived from [either] the Golden Summerhouse or the Winter Room'.[56] According to an inventory, in 1718 Timm's painting of the four musicians 'hung above the fireplace in the bottom room in the Summerhouse with the Four Knobs', another summerhouse situated in the park surrounding Rosenborg, where it had been previously placed either in 1669–70 or in 1707, to be combined with ceiling allegories by the Dutch painter Karel van Mander. It is tempting to suggest that it was originally part of the internal decoration of the Golden Summerhouse, since it

55 Hein, *The Treasure Collection at Rosenborg Castle*, 151.
56 Ibid.

Ill. 4. Reinhold Timm, 'Musicians from Christian IV's Court', *c*.1622, MMCCS Inv. No. OB 122; photo by Ole Woldbye, The Danish Music Museum (Musikhistorisk Museum & The Carl Claudius Collection).

cannot have hung in the Winter Room, where the panelled walls are set with Flemish landscapes. So it cannot be excluded that Clein's and Timm's pictures of musicians both derive from the Golden Summerhouse, Clein's from the ground floor, Timm's from the first floor.[57]

As the travel accounts demonstrate, the sound conduits for the provision of invisible music installed in Sparepenge, Rosenborg, and the Golden Summerhouse clearly caught the attention of visitors; together with other works of art and technological devices, they formed a prime attraction of these buildings. The accounts also suggest that the invisible music was part of a larger concept involving different senses, particularly the visual and aural, and were meant to create a synesthetic effect. In Rosenborg and the Golden Summerhouse, paintings of a 'heavenly ensemble' and four precious foreign musicians visually corresponded to a mysterious music whose source could not be located, thereby causing amazement and admiration. In Sparepenge, the invisible music was an acoustically present item of a royal *Kunstkammer*.

There are other contemporary examples of invisible music in the context of court culture illustrating how it was employed in connection with visual arts. It has been mentioned that the Dresden summerhouse designed by Nosseni was very likely a model for Sparepenge. According to the detailed description of the Dresden Belvedere by the Augsburg merchant, diplomat and art agent Philipp Hainhofer (1578–1647), the ground floor of the Belvedere was designed to house a *Kunstkammer*, displaying 'drinking vessels and dishes made from every kind of semi-precious stone', as well as a grotto and 'an organ made of green serpentine', while the walls 'were decorated with paintings of the most important deeds of the Saxon dukes'.[58] Next to its function as *Kunstkammer*, this room could also serve as a dining room. The chamber on the upper floor could also be used as a banquet room; it had a ceiling painting 'depicting the four elements, Day and Night, … the seven planets and the twelve signs of the Zodiac and the history of troy'. The room also 'contained twenty stone statues of the last five Holy Roman Emperors, the last five Electors and the ten Virtues'. Tubes led from the ground floor through the walls to behind each of the twenty statues, where, according to Hainhofer,

> there were holes designed for a special [invisible] music. Whenever there is a banquet in this upper hall, one places the musicians in the lower hall and closes it off, so that the sound pleasantly arises through the air holes. On top of the room, underneath the ceiling, there are also devices for invisible music, so that one can hear invisible music separately in 32 different places.[59]

---

57 Ibid. 152.
58 For this and the following two quotations, see Watanabe-O'Kelly, *Court Culture in Dresden*, 67–68.
59 German original of Hainhofer's text quoted after Oscar Doering (ed.), *Des Augsburger Patriciers Philipp Hainhofers Reisen nach Innsbruck und Dresden* (Wien, 1901), 217: 'Hinder iedem bild ist es hool, vnd dergestalt gerichtet, das man aine sondere music darhinter halten kan. Wann man in disem obern saal speiset, so stellet man die musicanten auch in vndern saal, schleusset zu, so

It is obvious that the aesthetic concept realized in the Dresden 'Belvedere' has strong similarities to those concepts found in the Danish buildings. Just as in Sparepenge, the musicians perform underneath the banquet room on the first floor, so that the invisible music becomes part of dining ceremonies. In the banquet room the invisible music resonates with ceiling paintings above with 'heavenly' themes, resembling the painting of the 'heavenly court ensemble' in either Rosenborg or the Golden Summerhouse. The multitude of pipes and air holes providing invisible music must have greatly added to the mysterious effect of acoustic blurriness and displacement as described by Ogier. However, it is a novelty in the Dresden concept that not only paintings, but also statues are involved in this audio-visual generation of illusion, and that in a particularly sophisticated way, since each statue offers an individual hearing experience. The *Kunstkammer* on the ground floor recalls the mixed collection in Sparepenge, even though a (possibly automatic) organ made of green serpentine takes the place of the invisible music produced by real musicians. This precious 'musical machine', itself a visible *Kunstkammer* object, presumably provided the music for downstairs dining and visitors of the *Kunstkammer*, recalling the automatic organs found in gardens of Italian Renaissance villas, the Villa d'Este in Tivoli being a prominent example.[60]

There is another example of a garden house north of the Alps that provided both music by an automatic organ *and* invisible music performed by a hidden court ensemble as acoustic attractions – the Neues Lusthaus in Stuttgart, built between 1583 and 1593 by the architect Georg Beer.[61] Here, a musicians' room was located above each of the two main doors leading into the main hall on the first floor, which was used for dances, allegorical representations and other festivities.[62] In each of the rooms was an organ, one of them automatic.[63] To the visitors and dancers, the invisible music performed by either the court ensemble or the organ seemed to emerge out of sculptures located on top of the doorframes, namely armed soldiers who thus seemingly played music on their weapons.[64]

Both the (automatic) organ and the invisible music as parts of a larger scale 'installation' of different art forms seem to have been derived from Renaissance garden villas in Northern Italy.[65] Thus neither Nosseni nor the Danish king were the true creators of this 'charming invention'; it seems very likely that the Italian artist had brought this idea from northern Italy where he had visited several palaces in the Florence area during his travel to Italy in 1588, such as the Villa Pratolino,

---

gehet die resonanz durch die lufftröhrer lieblich hinauf. Oben hero vnder der deckin ist es auch zu verborgner music gerichtet, so, das man von 32 orthen verborgne music, iede absonderlich, hören kan'; author's transl.

60 Walter Salmen, *Gartenmusik. Musik – Tanz – Konversation im Freien* (Hildesheim, Zürich, and New York, 2006), 121–25.

61 Ulrike Weber-Karge, *'Einem irdischen Paradeiß zu vergleichen'. Das Neue Lusthaus in Stuttgart* (Sigmaringen, 1989), 26–27.

62 Ibid. 46–47.

63 Ibid. 51.

64 Ibid. 47.

65 The present author is currently preparing a study on the cultural origins and theory of invisible music in Italy.

and where he had met with the local 'gardener and fountain engineer'.[66] It has been suggested that Nosseni 'modelled his plans [for the Dresden Belvedere] on the Forte di Belvedere in Florence which he had seen'.[67]

All spaces of invisible music hitherto discussed were located in garden houses. The Renaissance garden villa in Italy was a revival of a cultural practice of Roman antiquity and became a model for garden houses north of the Alps.[68] The Italian garden villa 'embodied artifice and control at several overlapping levels – siting, geometry, hydraulics, and scenography – often with close connections to contemporary theatrical practices'.[69] Garden houses represented an ideal world of aristocracy, microcosms of their own, containing the world and its richness in a nutshell. They were places of recreation, representation, and experimentation, places to demonstrate, exhibit, and develop instruments of power. They housed *Kunst-* and *Wunderkammern*, and galleries representing the ruler's ancestry, they were used for dining, for dancing, court festivities and spectacles.[70]

Significantly, Bernardo Buontalenti, the architect of the Belvedere in Florence, was also a stage designer, and was involved in the production of the Florentine Intermedi of 1589. The practice of hiding musicians backstage to create a particular effect was frequently practised in intermedi and early opera,[71] and it seems possible that the idea of the invisible music was originally conceived in the context of theatre before it was applied to other spaces, such as garden houses. For instance, in Claudio Monteverdi's *dramma per musica*, *L'Orfeo* (1607), there were five string players hidden backstage to create a special sound effect, as part of his concept of 'symbolic instrumentation'.[72] The same effect was used in Monteverdi's next opera, *Arianna* (1608), where the whole instrumental ensemble was hidden offstage.[73] In the first production of Antonio Cesti's opera, *Il pomo d'oro* (1668), musicians were hidden on stage behind statues, a setting that resembles the arrangement in the Dresden Belvedere.

Christian IV's 'charming invention' in the context of his garden houses illustrates the Danish king's knowledge of cultural and technical innovations of the South and the remarkable speed at which he brought these innovations to Denmark. Since the

---

66 'Gärtner und Wasserkünstler', see Monika Meiner-Schawe, 'Giovanni Maria Nosseni. Ein Hofkünstler in Sachsen', *Jahrbuch des Zentralinstituts für Kunstgeschichte*, 5/6 (1989/90), 289.

67 Watanabe-O'Kelly, *Court Culture in Dresden*, 65.

68 Steffen Heiberg, *Christian 4. Monarken, mennesket og myten* (Copenhagen, 1988), 71.

69 James M. Saslow, *The Medici Wedding of 1589: Florentine Festival as Theatrum Mundi* (New Haven and London, 1996), 135.

70 Weber-Karge, 'Einem irdischen Paradeiß zu vergleichen', 74.

71 For invisible music in the Florentine Intermedi, see, for instance, Daniel P. Walker (ed.), *Les fêtes du mariage de Ferdinand de Médicis et de Christine de Lorraine Florence 1589. I. Musique des Intermèdes de 'La Pellegrina'* (Paris, 1968), xxxviii; Massimo Ossi, 'Dalle machine ... la maraviglia: Bernardo Buontalenti's Il rapimento di Cefalo at the Medici Theater in 1600', in Mark A. Radice (ed.), *Opera in Context. Essays on Historical Staging from the Late Renaissance to the Time of Puccini* (Portland, 1998), 22; Nina Treadwell, 'Music of the Gods: Solo Song and *effetti meravigliosi* in the Interludes for La pellegrina', *Current Musicology*, 83 (2007), 61–63.

72 Spitzer and Zaslaw, *The Birth of the Orchestra*, 43.

73 Ibid. 44.

construction of the Dresden Belvedere was completed about 20 years after Spare-penge, Christian IV was among the first princes north of the Alps to have provisions for invisible music at his court. Christian IV must have quickly realized the propa-gandistic potential of the invisible music when he became acquainted with this idea and technology.[74] Which functions and meanings, then, did the invisible music have within his 'media-strategic system' (Berns) that he employed in his garden houses? I am going to discuss three aspects which are central to the aesthetics of invisible music.

1. THE INVISIBLE MUSIC, 'MUSIC OF THE SPHERES' AND 'HEAVENLY CHOIR'

The presence of both invisible music and paintings in the 'square antechamber', most likely the Winter Room in Rosenborg Castle, during Ogier's 1634 visit created a synesthetic, illusionistic effect. The ceiling painting of the 'heavenly *Hofkapelle*' that the French diplomat must have seen either in the Golden Summerhouse, right be-fore his entry into Rosenborg, or in the Winter Room itself, recalled the idea of the 'heavenly music' still present in early modern philosophical discourse. It was acousti-cally enforced by mysterious, bodiless music coming from out of sight. There were two complementary models of heavenly sound in seventeenth-century philosophy and theology – the Neoplatonic model of the 'music of the spheres' and the 'bibli-cal model of the heavenly choir as described in the vision of Isaiah'.[75] Both ideas could be adopted 'in earthly ceremonial sign systems',[76] drawing on the idea of a correspondence between macrocosm and microcosm:

> The Pythagorean theory of universal harmony states that the cosmos is a harmonious structure conforming to natural laws that can be experienced musically, that identi-cal laws operate in nature, in human hearing, and in music. According to Christian theologians, on the other hand, the heavenly music described by Isaiah is present in liturgical song and in the movement of the human pulse.[77]

Ogier's report subtly implies how the king's body and his 'earthly ceremonial' were linked, stressing the staged, choreographic character of the king's movement: the music began this very moment when both the king and Ogier himself had entered the centre of the room, presumably being surrounded by an audience of foreign visi-tors. This movement points at the king as the centre of this arrangement, showing himself as the cause of the mysterious music,[78] as well as the 'creator' of this 'charm-ing invention'. By the aid of his 'invention' the king staged himself symbolically as centre and cause of harmony in the microcosm and, accordingly, as the cause and the preserver of political order and peace. This reading becomes even more plausible

---

74 This is not to say there were no practical reasons behind his adaptation as well. For instance, the Winter Room was probably too small to house a large-scale court ensemble during a reception of foreign diplomats, thus the placement of the musicians in the cellar certainly saved space.
75 Berns, 'Instrumental Sound and Ruling Spaces', 480.
76 Ibid. 481.
77 Ibid.
78 Ibid. 488.

when the political context of the Great Wedding is taken into account: next to forging a dynastic link between Denmark and Saxony, the wedding and its spectacles

> served as a platform from which to launch and maintain the proposed role of the Danish king as the arbitrator of the European, that is, the German peace. The spectacles consolidated both domestic and international support for Christian IV as the creator and sustainer of peace among nations. Moreover, it served as a summit meeting for the powers of Europe at a critical moment in the Thirty Years' War, at a time when many hoped for – and came to expect – a cessation of strife.[79]

2. THE INVISIBLE MUSIC AS A MACHINE

Both art and technological aspects equally attracted the attention and admiration of visitors to Sparepenge and Rosenborg. Heinrich Meyer, for instance, mentions the secret 'house phone system', a 'special heat-saving stove of Norwegian stone'[80] and the technical provisions for invisible music in the same breath. This interest in technology reflects a Renaissance and Baroque fascination with machines, and it seems that the invisible music and its technical provisions were viewed within this categorical framework. The most obvious analogy between invisible music and machine is its seemingly automatic functioning, the cause of its impetus being hidden. It is significant in this context that, for instance, in the Stuttgart Lusthaus *either* an ensemble of real musicians *or* an automatic organ was used to create an acoustic illusion. Thus (automatic) organ and invisible music were closely related phenomena that served very similar purposes.[81]

The early modern concept of the machine reflects a transition period between pre-rational (magical) and rational thinking: even though the construction of a machine is founded on rational principles, and therefore rationally intelligible, it also became a symbol for transcendence, creating 'wonder and astonishment at the order of things'.[82] It is, therefore, not surprising that performances of machines were frequently staged in the seventeenth century, just as a play in a theatre.[83] The theatre, in turn, became a particularly prominent field for the use of machines. The collaboration between machine and art for the purpose of heightened illusion reached its climax in the stage machinery of late Renaissance and Baroque theatre.[84]

The invisible music as a virtual machine not only was a tool to generate illusion and create admiration, but also an instrument to execute control over sound. Since

79 Wade, *Triumphus Nuptialis Danicus*, 16.
80 Hein, *The Treasure Collection at Rosenborg Castle*, 44.
81 'The organ, one could say, is not an instrument but a partly automated machine because it integrates many and potentially all musical instruments, thus making them superfluous – it is a universal and universalizing sound machine, and it tends towards automation', Berns, 'Instrumental Sound and Ruling Spaces', 501.
82 Jan Lazardzig, 'The Machine as Spectacle: Function and Admiration in Seventeenth-Century Perspectives on Machines', in Schramm, Schwarte, and Lazardzig (eds.), *Instruments in Art and Science*, 153. For the Renaissance concept of *meraviglia* in the context of literature, see, for instance, Baxter Hathaway, *Marvels and Commonplaces. Renaissance Literary Criticism* (New York, 1968).
83 Lazardzig, 'The Machine as Spectacle', 153–54.
84 Ibid. 153, 162–64. For a particularly instructive case study on Bernardo Buontalenti's stage machinery, see Ossi, *'Dalle machine … la maraviglia'*, 15–35.

Ill. 5. Athanasius Kircher, *Musurgia universalis* (Rome, 1650). Image courtesy of the Herzog August Bibliothek Wolfenbüttel.

the king was, in early modern understanding, 'the origin and center of ceremonial',[85] he had to have means to regulate the sound that was at his disposal. As Christian of Anhalt's account of Sparepenge illustrates, the king could 'turn on and off' the music by a trap door. As part of a multi-media arrangement, the invisible *Hofkapelle* became even more an object at the king's disposal than in its visible, bodily present form. With the physical source of sound hidden, music was represented in idealized, artificial visual objects, such as paintings and sculptures. In this arrangement, the musicians lost their 'real bodies', to be replaced by artefacts created by court painters and sculptors at the king's order, to serve his propagandistic goals even more effectively.

It fits to its purpose of control that the system of sound conduits and tubes could also be used in the opposite direction, to 'speak to someone at the door, even though people who are in this room cannot hear it', and surely also to spy on court officials and other subjects. It is several decades later that we find this acoustic technology of sound transmission as an instrument of sound control described in Athanasius Kircher's works *Musurgia universalis* of 1650 and his *Phonurgia nova* of 1673 (see Ills. 5 and 6), showing how much Christian IV was ahead of his time. Kircher demonstrates 'how princely power could be secured acoustically – by subjecting the people to a barrage of sound, as well as by means of listening systems'.[86]

85 Berns, 'Instrumental Sound and Ruling Spaces', 496.
86 Ibid. 489.

Ill. 6. Athanasius Kircher, *Phonurgia nova* (Kempten, 1673). Image courtesy of the Herzog August Bibliothek Wolfenbüttel.

3. THE INVISIBLE *Hofkapelle* AS AN ACOUSTIC *Wunderkammer*

According to Christian of Anhalt's report, invisible music could be heard during a visit of Sparepenge and the royal collection on exhibit there. Whenever an ensemble of court musicians performed in Sparepenge, it became part of this collection, as an invisible, but audibly present *Wunderkammer* item. This way of presentation points at the construction of the Danish *Hofkapelle* itself, which can be viewed as a royal collection, as a musical *Wunderkammer* purposefully assembled by the Danish king.[87] The Danish king's systematic construction of his *Hofkapelle* as a microcosm of European musical traditions and his use of invisible music as a *Wunderkammer* object strongly resonate with the theme of collecting.[88] By collecting rare and exotic works of art, natural objects, and scientific instruments, princes and scholars attempted to give a summary overview on the universe.[89] There was a variety of

87 Susan Lewis Hammond sees another analogy to the *Wunderkammer* idea in Christian IV's building projects in Copenhagen: 'The city itself was "collected" together almost instantaneously from the best, most necessary, internationally acknowledged requisites for a capital: the castle, the tall spires, the city hall, the ship works. There was a strangely anthologized nature to the new city; its creation testifies to the same acquisitory juxtapositions one finds, in displaced form, in the anthology of musical objects'; Susan Lewis Hammond, 'Collecting *Italia* Abroad: Anthologies of Italian Madrigals in the Print World of Northern Europe', Ph.D. diss. (Princeton, 2001), 201.

88 For the following, see also Spohr, *'How chances it they travel?'*, 200–7.

89 Arthur Mac-Gregor, 'Die besonderen Eigenschaften der Kunstkammer', in Andreas Grote (ed.), *Macrocosmos in Microcosmo. Die Welt in der Stube. Zur Geschichte des Sammelns 1450 bis 1800* (Opladen, 1994), 61.

concepts and motives behind this fashion of collecting and the establishment of prestigious *Kunst-* and *Wunderkammern*, reaching from intellectual curiosity to the representation of wealth and princely power.[90]

There are, in fact, various analogies between Christian IV's employment policy and the principles of collecting that can be observed in *Wunderkammern*. The extent to which the Danish king himself controlled the employment policy of his *Hofkapelle* illustrates the political importance of his court music. The king often personally chose his musicians, examined their skills and determined their appointment.[91] It is evident that Europe-wide networks of agents, similar to princely collectors of art or books, enabled the king's success in recruiting musicians.[92] Historians frequently explain his commitment simply through his personal interest in music, but it can only be fully understood in the context of politics and court ceremonial. The king used his *Hofkapelle* as one of his most prestigious instruments of political power.

The king's recruitment policy followed distinctive patterns, by recruiting specialists for certain instruments and favouring musicians from a variety of foreign countries. Moreover, he initiated a 'study abroad programme' for native Danish musicians that princes in Protestant Germany soon imitated. He sent young Danish talents such as the instrumentalists and composers Mogens Pedersøn and Hans Nielsen to Venice to study with Giovanni Gabrieli.[93] As a result of this policy, Christian IV had, only a few years after his coronation, a *Hofkapelle* that was not only equal to the largest European *Hofkapellen* in terms of quality and quantity, but also incorporated an immense variety of European musical traditions. There is hardly another *Hofkapelle* at that time that had such a diverse profile, comprised of musicians from western, eastern, central and southern Europe as well as native Danish musicians.[94]

One of the most striking parallels to the idea of the *Wunderkammer* is the exclusive character of the court music, since the Danish king appointed a number of musicians with extraordinary skills who received higher salaries than ordinary musicians.[95] Another analogy can be seen in the exemplary character of the recruitment, since the king was keen on drawing the best available musicians for particular instru-

---

90 For the political aspect of collecting, see, for instance, Thomas DaCosta Kaufmann, *The Mastery of Nature. Aspects of Art, Science and Humanism in the Renaissance* (Princeton, 1993), 174–94.

91 See, for instance, Angul Hammerich, *Musiken ved Christian den Fjerdes Hof. Et Bidrag til Dansk Musikhistorie* (Copenhagen, 1892), 132, 187.

92 For instance, the merchant John Stokes acted as the king's cultural agent in England. See also Spohr, *'How chances it they travel'*, 130–32.

93 See, for instance, Heinrich W. Schwab, 'Italianità in Danimarca. Zur Rezeption des Madrigals am Hofe Christians IV.', in Bohn (ed.), *Europa in Scandinavia*, 127–53. See also Bjarke Moe, 'Italian Music at the Danish Court during the Reign of Christian IV. Presenting a picture of cultural transformation', *Danish Yearbook of Musicology*, 38 (2010/11), 15–32.

94 For musicians from Eastern Europe, see Ole Kongsted, 'Polnisch-dänische Musikbeziehungen im späten 16. und frühen 17. Jahrhundert', in *Musica Baltica. Danzig und die Musikkultur Europas* (Danzig, 2000), 94–112; and Hammerich, *Musiken*, 20–21. For musicians from the British Isles, see Spohr, *'How chances it they travel?'*, 176–225. For musicians from the Netherlands and Bohemia, see ibid. 203–4.

95 Ibid. 212–14.

ments or particular voice ranges to his court. There is also an aspect of exoticism in the *Hofkapelle* that is reminiscent of the exotic objects of *Wunderkammern*: the Danish king recruited musicians in distant and remote countries, such as the harpists mentioned before; he was probably the first and the only prince in continental Europe around 1600 who employed a musician from Ireland (the harpist 'Carolus Oralii')[96] and who owned an Irish wire-strung harp. During the 1620s, the Irish harpist Darby Scott seems to have been a particular musical attraction at the court. Both Christian of Anhalt and Gosche Wensin record that they heard him play and particularly mention his instrument for its exotic qualities.[97]

According to Christian of Anhalt, it was the custom at the Danish court that the instrumentalists – there were about 40 at that time – played in small ensembles rather than a large orchestra, so that every day of the week a different ensemble could be heard – similar to the organization of *Hofkapellen* at other European courts at the time, such as the English court music.[98] This way it was possible to show off the virtuosi with their special qualities and also to demonstrate the variety of the different performance traditions and instrumental and vocal colours available within the Danish *Hofkapelle*, which had, due to its cosmopolitan nature, become for some time a 'laboratory' for musical exchange and experimentation and a centre of musical innovation in northern Europe.[99]

As Reinhold Timm's painting suggests, not only large instrumental and vocal ensembles (as described in Ogier's report) were featured as invisible music, but also (and, perhaps, more frequently) individual ensembles, such as the mixed ensemble of flute, bass viol, lute, and Irish harp depicted by Timm. The exotic sound of this court ensemble must have greatly added to effects of aural displacement and mystification. Exotic sound qualities of particular ensembles as well as their respective repertoires have to be considered to more fully understand the manierist concept[100] of the sound installations in Christian IV's garden houses.

In turn, it seems possible to suggest that the invisible music as a manierist form of sound presentation corresponded with aesthetic currents in the musical repertoire

---

96 His name might have been Charles O'Reilly, see Peter Holman, *Four and Twenty Fiddlers. The Violin at the English Court* (Oxford, 2nd edn 1995), 161.

97 Krause (ed.), *Tagebuch Christians des Jüngeren*, 98: 'Nach dem Abendessen hat Georg Rasch auf der Lauten und ein Irländer auf einer sonderbarlichen Irländischen lieblichen harffe gespielet'; 'Bericht des Gottorfer Gesandten Gosche Wensin', 1622: 'Endtlich seỹn J.K.M. zuo waßer widerumb nach derho garthen undt kunnichl. lusthauße gefharen, daselbst taffell gehalten, undt nhiemandts mher, dhan deroselben Canzler Crỹstian Frieße, der hoffmarschalck, undt meỹne pershon darzuo erfordert worden. aber ganz liebblich erstmaln auf eỹher Irlandischen harffen midt meßingst seỹden bezogen, dan durch Willhelmb Brahe undt seỹner schöne gesampten music, und herrlich durch achte Vhiolen instrumentalisch alleỹn villmalß musiciren laßen.'; Schleswig, Landesarchiv Schleswig-Holstein, Abt. 7, Nr. 74.

98 Krause, *Tagebuch Christians des Jüngeren*, 98. For the organization of the English court music, see Holman, *Four and Twenty Fiddlers*, 173.

99 Spohr, 'How chances it they travel?', 176–225, 353.

100 For the use of the term manierism in art history and literary history, see Wolfgang Braungart, 'Manier, Manierismus', in Harald Fricke (ed.), *Reallexikon der deutschen Literaturwissenschaft* (Berlin and New York, 2000), vol. 2, 530–35.

composed and performed at the Danish court. In this context, not only the afore-mentioned mixed ensemble centred around an Irish harp can be viewed as manierist, but also the daring formal experiments that William Brade, an English string player and composer active at the Danish court during three periods (1594–96, 1599–1606, 1620–22), pursued in his pavans for string ensemble.[101] The complex interaction between sound, performance, musical style and form, spatial presentation of music, and arrangements of acoustic, visual and other media in late Renaissance court culture certainly deserves further study. Locating court music within the larger context of illusionist and manierist aesthetics and their use of media, can significantly add to our further understanding of the musical culture at the court of Christian IV and that of other European courts in the late sixteenth and early seventeenth centuries.

SUMMARY

Court ceremonial in early modern Europe functioned, in Jörg Jochen Berns's words, as 'a media-strategic system for the creation and maintenance of princely-courtly representation and pretension to power.' Music was an essential part of this system, since it legitimized the ceremonial by linking it to the Pythagorean idea of the 'harmony of the spheres'. This idea, still present in early modern discourse, was evoked through music in connection with other media, such as visual arts, and in specific spatial situations.

This article explores a particularly spectacular form of musical display that was practised at several European courts during the late Renaissance and has so far largely escaped the attention of musicologists. The Danish King Christian IV (1577/1588–1648), who employed musicians of European fame in his *Hofmusik*, not only publicly staged them as precious objects, but also kept them from view so that their performance, through the 'charming invention' (in the words of a contemporary visitor) of sound conduits, appeared as an acoustic miracle to visitors. Provisions for invisible music could also be found at the courts of Stuttgart and Dresden.

The article presents an outline of what is currently known about the settings of invisible music at the court of Christian IV, discussing both recently discovered sound conduits in Rosenborg Castle and hitherto unnoticed seventeenth-century travel accounts. Moreover, it evaluates possible cultural sources, such as installations in garden villas in northern Italy as well as theatrical practices in the Florentine *Intermedi*, placing invisible music in the context of other currents in mannerist aesthetics, such as *Kunst-* and *Wunderkammern* and musical machines. It also discusses Christian IV's use of his 'charming invention' as a political instrument. The king used this acoustic device not only as a cultural capital that set him apart from the local nobility and neighboring princes in northern Germany, but also as a tool that allowed him to symbolically stage himself as cause and center of earthly harmony and, accordingly, of political order and peace in the destructive times of the Thirty Years War.

101 William Brade's pavans for string ensemble, are, in fact, hybrid forms between pavan, galliard, allemande, and the multi-sectional Italianate canzona, which he developed into a kind of miniature suite, comprised of contrasting sections like a kaleidoscope; see Spohr, *'How chances it they travel'*, 328.

When Angels Dance for Kings
The beginning of Scandinavian music theatre

KRISTIN RYGG

On the night of 7 October 1634 a *ballet* was performed at the royal palace of Copenhagen. It was not a ballet in the modern sense of the term; it was a *ballet de cour*, music theatre with elaborate scenery and stage machinery, a large amount of music and singing, and extensive dancing. It was sponsored by the Danish Prince Frederik as part of the magnificent wedding celebrations (known as the *Triumphus nuptialis*) for his brother, Prince-Elect Christian V and his bride, the Saxon princess Magdalena Sibylla. It was the very first performance of music theatre in Scandinavia,[1] and Heinrich Schütz, who was in charge of the musical side of the entire wedding celebrations, probably composed music for the show.[2]

When the Danish king Christian IV and two of his sons, the prince-elect and bridegroom Christian, and Frederik, the sponsor of the *ballet*, chose to stage a *ballet de cour* as one of the main entertainments of the wedding festivities, they were following traditions already flourishing at leading European courts. The purpose of this article is twofold: firstly, to reach an understanding of what they wanted to achieve by staging a ballet. Did they simply wish to copy the grand music theatre performances of leading European courts because the shows themselves were insignia of power and monarchical grandeur? Or did they see them as more flexible tools of communication through which they could also convey messages other than the pure display of power? And if the latter, what did they wish to convey? Secondly, and this is clearly related to the first purpose, the article seeks to explore how this onset of Scandinavian music theatre related to leading traditions of courtly music theatre in Northern Europe. In the course of this process I will also discuss the interpretations of the ballet offered by Mara Wade in her study of the *Triumphus nuptialis* of 1634.

MUSIC THEATRE AND COURTLY AMATEURS

A remarkable feature of the late Renaissance and early Baroque era is the emergence of various forms of courtly theatre in which music plays an essential role.[3] The

---

1 Performances of various kinds which to some extent included music were at this stage part of European theatre traditions. The case here, however, is theatre where music and dance constitute the essence of the genre, and is therefore referred to as music theatre.

2 Schütz had left his post at the Dresden court for the occasion and stayed in Denmark for a longer period. On Schütz' contributions to the wedding festivities and his further involvement with the Danish royal family see Mara R. Wade, *Triumphus nuptialis danicus. German Court Culture and Denmark. The "Great Wedding" of 1634* (Wiesbaden: Harrassowitz, 1996), 221–46.

3 For a brief introduction to these forms, see Kristin Rygg, *Masqued Mysteries Unmasked: Pythago-*

creation of opera is normally understood as the most important – and lasting – result of these developments, but two other forms were at least equally prominent in their own day, namely the French *ballet de cour* and the English court masque.[4] They share some basic characteristics. They were performed in the great halls of the royal palaces, and the audience consisted above all of royal families, nobility, ambassadors and other prominent guests from abroad. Members of the royal family and noble courtiers are the main actors in the shows; together with selected court singers and musicians they dance the roles of the mythic-allegorical cast stemming from Greek and Roman antiquity.[5] Speaking parts were taken by professional actors or amateurs who were neither noble nor royal. The imagery deployed in the dialogue and the scenography somehow implicate the monarch as semi-divine with power to command even the divine beings represented. Music and dancing are essential to both genres. Costumes, scenic designs and stage machinery made for the performances were extravagant and extremely costly. The French *ballets* and the English masques enjoyed great fame in their time, and they were sufficiently influential to make monarchs and artists of other courts and countries create entertainments which were clearly inspired by them.

While they have a lot in common, there are differences between the two genres. A theatrical form with dancing at its core, referred to as *ballet*, started to develop in the 1570s at the French court. The first show of this kind which becomes famous is *Ballet Comique de la Reine* in 1581.[6] It tells the story of the sorceress Circé who captures men and turns them into beasts, but is finally conquered. Several spectacular dancing scenes take place as part of the action, and a final *grand ballet*, a spectacular, choreographed dance with the whole cast participating, ends the performance. Because the show tells a coherent story with a happy ending, it is described as 'comique'.[7] Many *ballets* were performed in France during the century following the beginnings of the tradition, but for decades they formed a rather heterogeneous genre. Often they had the form of a *ballet à entrées*, where a unifying story is lacking and several groups of actors merely perform various tableaux including singing and dancing. Only from 1610 onwards was the more narrative form of *ballet comique* used

---

reanism and *Early Modern North European Music Theatre*, Dr.art. thesis (Trondheim: Norwegian University of Science and Technology, Department of Musicology, 1997).

4 In the following I shall refer only to the English court masque as it develops under the reigns of James I and his son, Charles I, in other words from 1604 onwards. Entertainments from the earlier reign of Elizabeth are not taken into account.

5 A series of minor *ballets* are exceptions from this main trend. In these smaller entertainments the cast can consist of various groups of persons, animals, etc. See for example Margaret M. McGowan, *L'art du ballet de cour en France: 1581–1643* (Paris: Editions du Centre national de la recherche scientifique, 1963); Henry Prunières, *Le ballet de cour en France avant Benserade et Lully, suivi du Ballet de la délivrance de Renaud: Seize planches hors texte* (Paris: H. Laurens, 1914).

6 Balthazar de Beaujoyeulx et al., *Balet comique de la Royne: faict aux nopces de monsieur le duc de Joyeuse & madamoyselle de Vaudemont sa soeur. Par Baltasar de Beaujoyeulx, valet de chambre du Roy, & de la Royne sa mere* (Paris: Adrian Le Roy, Robert Ballard, & Mamert Patisson, 1582).

7 'Comique' did therefore not imply that it was a comical show. The opposite was 'tragique', which implied that the end would be tragic for the protagonist.

again on a few occasions, but the genre *ballet de cour* remained quite heterogeneous until the era of Louis XIV, that is after the great wedding in Copenhagen.[8]

In England quite varied forms of courtly entertainments were referred to as 'mask(e)s' during the sixteenth century, but shortly after James I and Anna became king and queen of England in 1604, a more unified court masque genre was established.[9] Two artists in particular were at the core of shaping this genre, the poet Ben Jonson and the architect Inigo Jones, and they would collaborate with the king's dancing masters, composers and other musicians in creating the shows. The masques differed significantly from the *ballets* in at least two respects; they included 'revels', and from around 1608 they also included 'antimasques'. An antimasque was a comic or grotesque section preceding the masque proper, preparing for the story of the masque by functioning as a kind of foil. Professional actors would play the rôles of the antimasque. The royals and the nobles, referred to as masquers, did not take speaking parts; their performance consisted in dancing their *rôles*. Court singers, musicians and choreographers would take *rôles* both in the antimasque and the masque proper.[10] Within the masque proper was the section called the 'revels'. Here the masquers invited members from the audience to dance and soon all spectators would be able to join in. This social dancing could go on for quite a long time before the masquers returned to the stage area to resume their roles and finish the play.

In the decades leading up to the Great Wedding the court masque stands out as a much more unified genre than the *ballet de cour*. It is worth noting that, due to the similarities of the two genres, the terms are sometimes used interchangeably, depending on who the writer was and even to whom he was writing.[11]

MUSIC THEATRE AS STATECRAFT

That this kind of theatre has to do at least in part with the display of power is generally accepted among scholars. But the seminal studies of the English masque by Stephen Orgel are the first to explore its political implications on a larger scale.

8   For information about the history of the *ballet de cour* see for example McGowan, *L'art du ballet de cour*; Kristin Rygg, *Masqued Mysteries Unmasked: Early Modern Music Theater and Its Pythagorean Subtext* (Hillsdale, N.Y.: Pendragon Press, 2000).

9   Sara Smart, 'The Württemberg Court and the Introduction of Ballet in the Empire', in J.R. Mulryne et al. (eds.), *Europa triumphans: Court and Civic Festivals in Early Modern Europe* (Aldershot: Ashgate, 2004), ii. 35–45. Courtly entertainments often called mask(e)s also took place during the sixteenth century. For information about these early forms, see esp. Enid Welsford, *The Court Masque; A Study in the Relationship between Poetry & the Revels* (New York: Russell & Russell, 1962).

10   For more extensive descriptions of the masque genre, see for example Rygg, *Masqued Mysteries* (2000); Martin Butler, *The Stuart Court Masque and Political Culture* (Cambridge: Cambridge University Press, 2008). The most extensive study of music in the English masque is Peter Walls, *Music in the English Courtly Masque, 1604–1640* (Oxford: Clarendon Press; 1996). Excellent discussions of musical aspects of the masques are also provided in Peter Holman, *Four and Twenty Fiddlers: the Violin at the English Court, 1540–1690* (Oxford: Clarendon Press, 1993).

11   See for example Sara Smart commenting on this mixing of terms in Smart, 'The Württemberg Court', 35–45.

He argues that the exploitation of the masque by the monarch is an extreme case of topdown strategy to enforce his own political power. The many aspects of the masques connected with philosophy and mythology are seen as constituents of a metaphorical, multimedial language serving the greater political allegory. The basic form consisting of three sections – the antimasque, the masque proper, and the revels as part of the latter – supports three illusions which are, according to Orgel, essential to the intended effect of the masque. 1) There is a contrast between the comic antimasque, representing the world of normal, flawed human beings, and the masque proper with its realm of divine beings, portrayed mainly by royalty and no-bility. 2) The king is always given a role which makes him appear as semi-divine and as the commander of the divine beings of the masque, with the aim of persuading both the English nobility and powerful foreign guests of the king's divine right and ability to reign. 3) Through the revels the whole audience is included in the world of the masque proper and thus apotheosized into the divine realm of the king, his family and their closest associates, thereby experiencing an identification with the ruler and by extension with his politics.

According to this reading, this kind of theatre is primarily concerned with political discourse, or statecraft, and the masque stands out as the ultimate politicized poetics of absolutism. The *rôles* of the creative artists behind the masques are then subsumed under the greater goal; Orgel at one stage refers to the Jonsonian masque as 'an extension of the royal mind'.[12] This Orgelian understanding of the masque has been seminal for decades, and it has also inspired scholars working with similar types of court theatre in other countries.[13] The persistent influence from Orgel is also witnessed in Peter Walls' major study on the music of the masques, in which he basically integrates music into Orgel's analysis and interprets the role of music within this framework.[14] It should be added, though, that over the last decades prominent scholars such as Kevin Sharpe, Clare McManus and Martin Butler have explored very different and broader political aspects of the masques.[15] Likewise Georgina Cowart has put forward a new reading of the various political *rôles* played by the French *ballets de cour* during the times of Louis XIV, but the contributions of these studies will not be discussed in the present article.[16]

---

12 See for example Stephen Orgel, *The Illusion of Power: Political Theater in the English Renaissance* (Berkeley: University of California Press, 1975), 43 and 52; and Stephen Orgel, *The Jonsonian Masque* (New York: Columbia University Press, 1981), 36–37, 63, and 76.

13 Mulryne et al. (eds.), *Europa triumphans* is a splendid example of how the Orgelian understanding still underlies much recent scholarship in this field.

14 Walls, *Music in the English Courtly Masque*; see particularly vii, 7, 8, and 12.

15 Butler, *The Stuart Court Masque*; Clare McManus, *Women on the Renaissance Stage: Anna of Denmark and Female Masquing in the Stuart Court (1590–1619)* (Manchester: Manchester University Press, 2002); Kevin Sharpe, *Criticism and Compliment: the Politics of Literature in the England of Charles I* (Cambridge: Cambridge University Press, 1987).

16 Georgia Cowart, *The Triumph of Pleasure: Louis XIV & the Politics of Spectacle* (Chicago: University of Chicago Press, 2008).

The Copenhagen *Ballet*

Masked dances performed as courtly entertainments had occasionally taken place in Denmark before the Great Wedding, but nothing like a coherent theatre piece consisting of singing and dancing had ever been performed.[17] In spite of the fame Prince Frederik's *ballet* enjoyed in its own day, it does not hold a prominent position within Scandinavian music history. This is understandable: the music is lost, as are sketches showing scenery and costumes. There are only a few main sources giving us information about this *ballet*. The earliest is a booklet containing the actual texts of the solo songs and the choirs, and interpolated explanatory sections describing the action. This text was probably printed before the performance; the front page says that the *ballet* 'will be performed'. As was the case with similar texts printed in for example France and England it must have been intended as an explanation of the show for the audience, and of course as an artefact to commemorate a splendid occasion. This booklet is signed by Alexander Kückelsom (see Ill. 1).[18] He was probably of French origin and had come to the Academy of Sorø as a teacher and dancing master, but at this stage he was tutor to the royal children.[19] It is highly unlikely that he was the author of the poetic songs, but it is of course possible that he wrote the descriptions of the action which are printed in between the song texts, and it seems probable that he was the choreographer of the dances. Wade has shown that one of the songs for the *ballet*, 'Klagliedt dess Orphei vber seine Euridice', is extremely similar to a song composed by Schütz to the poem 'Galathee' by Martin Opitz (1597–1639),[20] but this fact gives no proof of a possible involvement by Opitz in writing for the *ballet*. The question of authorship is not essential to the discussions of the present article, however, and will not be pursued. But since the booklet was signed by Kückelsom, it will be referred to as the *Kückelsom Text* in the following.

There was also a description of the *ballet* which was part of the full published account of the wedding festivities. This account was first published in 1635 and issued in several editions, and will be referred to as the *Festival Account* in the following.[21] Both the *Kückelsom Text* and the *Festival Account* are in German. An account of all

---

17 The lack of earlier entertainments which can be seen as music theatre was tested to as early as in Torben Krogh, *Hofballetten under Christian IV og Frederik III. En teaterhistorisk studie* (København: Povl Branner, 1939), 1–14. See also Wade, *Triumphus nuptialis*, 17–56 for information on courtly entertainments during the reign of Christian IV.

18 Anonymous, *Kurzer Einhalt und Bedeutung des Ballets, So der Hochwürdigster/Durchleuchtiger/und Hochgeborner Fürst und Herr Friderich/Erwelt und Postulierter Ertz und Bischof zu Bremen und Wehrden/Coadjutor zu Halberstatt/Erbe zu Norwegen/Herzog zu Schleswigh/Holstein/Graff zu Oldenborg und Delmenhorst/mein Gnediger Fürst und Herr/geliebt es Gott/bey bevorstehendem Prinzlichem Beylager/nebens andern repræsentieren wirdt* (Copenhagen: n.n., 1634).

19 Wade, *Triumphus nuptialis*, 68–69.

20 Martin Opitz, *Martini Opitii Weltliche poëmata, Der ander Theil* (Amsterdam: n.n., 1645), 324–29. Quoted from Wade, *Triumphus nuptialis*, 82–83.

21 Since details concerning the different publications are not important for the discussion in this article, readers are referred to Wade's extensive presentation of sources for further informaton; Wade, *Triumphus nuptialis*.

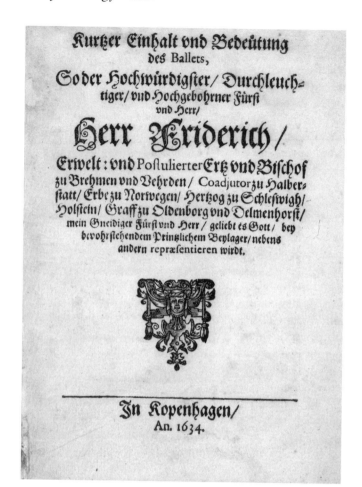

Ill. 1. Alexander Kückelsom, *Kurtzer Einhalt vnd Bedeutung des Ballets* (Copenhagen, 1634).

the nuptial festivities written in Danish was published in 1648, indicating a continued interest in the Great Wedding.[22] In addition, there is a brief commentary on the entertainment written by Charles Ogier, secretary to the French ambassador, in his diary from his journey to Denmark to take part in the wedding celebrations.[23]

Some aspects of the *ballet* and its music have been discussed in a few publications about music at the time of Christian IV.[24] Other than that, little attention has been given to this early Scandinavian music theatre till Mara Wade published her major

22 *Regiæ nuptiæ, eller Kort Beskriffuelse om huis sig vdi Stormectige oc Høybaarne Førstis oc Herris Christian den V. Danmarckis oc Norgis etc. Udvalde Printz, oc Høyb. Førstinde oc Frøicken Magdalenæ Sybillæ Fød Hertuginde aff Saxen, deris Brøllups Fest er tildraget* (Copenhagen: Jørgen Holst, 1637).

23 The diary is in Latin but translated into Danish and published as Charles Ogier, *Det store Bilager i Kjøbenhavn 1634* (Copenhagen: August Bang, 1969).

24 Angul Hammerich, *Musiken ved Christian den Fjerdes Hof: et Bidrag til dansk Musikhistorie* (Copenhagen: Wilhelm Hansen, 1892); Krogh, *Hofballetten*; Anne Ørbæk Jensen and Ole Kongsted (eds.),

study *Triumphus nuptialis danicus*. In addition to including a well of relevant sources she offers challenging interpretations of this and other shows from the nuptial celebrations and other courtly festivals.

The primary sources for Prince Frederik's *ballet* are not easily accessible and are hard to read. Modern publications containing accounts of the performance do not give sufficient information for the discussion that follows; a fairly detailed résumé is therefore given below.[25] It is divided into paragraphs to make the structure clearer. The paragraphs giving the content of songs are highlighted in grey, those without are summaries of the action-describing sections between the songs.

Résumé of the Copenhagen *ballet*

The introduction explains how Neptune through divine help has cleansed his oceans of monsters.[26] His ever watchful eye is securing peaceful and happy government for the fish in the oceans, the animals in the woods and all his subjects. All peace-loving people and the gods in particular rejoice. They are now gathering at his court to accept his bounteousness. And heaven and earth, the elements, animals, hills and trees are rejoicing over this happy gathering and even going there to join the banquet themselves.

A heavenly choir sings a 'Sonnet or invitation to dance and happiness', and there is dancing. This is a poetic description of night falling and the moon and the stars leading a dance. Pan starts playing his pipes, and everybody dances to his music as the wine is poured.

Pan and his satyrs dance with 'various satyric positions', while Invidia (Envy) makes a threatening appearance. Mars sounds an alarm, and Pan hides, frightened, in a cabin where Hercules has left his beloved Deianeira and gone hunting. Pan is instantly infatuated and tries to make love to her, only to be caught in the act by the returning Hercules. He takes Pan's tail from him to shame him forever and drives him back into the forest. All honour-loving people present are happy about this.

A 6-verse song and dance of the Muses praises the banishment of Pan. The nymphs and the shepherdesses are happy because they need no longer fear his

Heinrich Schütz und die Musik in Dänemark zur Zeit Christian IV. Bericht über die wissenschaftliche Konferenz in Kopenhagen 10.-14. November 1985 (Copenhagen: Engstrøm & Sødring, 1989).

25 The ballet is described in a few modern publications. See for instance the appendix to Ogier, *Det store Bilager*, 133–36; and Wade, *Triumphus nuptialis*, 61–68.

26 Whereas Greek and Roman mythologies on a whole share the same group of main deities, their names are different in the two traditions. Poseidon is the Greek name for the god of the seas; Neptune the Roman. Hermes is the Greek name of the messenger god bringing divine information to the human world, Mercury the Roman; (Pallas) Athena is Greek, Minerva her Roman equivalent, etc. The documents concerning the 1634 wedding festivities mix names from both the Greek and the Roman tradition, and they also include different names for one god(dess), like Phoebus or Apollo, Pallas or Athena.

unwelcome advances. As the music sounds, a mountain on which the nine Muses are seated glides into the room. They descend and dance with complicated and graceful movements. Tired by their dancing, they retire to their mountain, which leaves the room while of one of the verses is being repeated.

The virtuous ladies of the woods have reminded Orpheus of the loss of his own beloved Eurydice, and sitting on a hill he sings a lament, also playing on his violin.

Orpheus' lament over Eurydice consists of 11 strophes. He grieves over the power of death which has killed his beloved so suddenly. His singing makes the birds and the woods sing, too, but to no avail; his light – Eurydice – is gone. Through Pluto's tyranny he has lost his happiness, and he will teach the natural world surrounding him to echo his lament.

As Orpheus sings his song of his grief over Eurydice, trees and hills follow him, dancing, as do animals both wild and tame. Invidia, however, cannot bear to see the consolation this brings to Orpheus. She calls on the Bacchantes. Making music with their thyrsus-wands and cymbals, in an ecstatic fury they tear to pieces Orpheus and the animals following him. The gods present are shocked and let four 'Génios' gather up the remains of Orpheus. Then three Pantaloons gather up the dismembered animals and thus cleanse the hall. As the gods now realize that Orpheus' unshakable love for his spouse is the reason for the hatred they have seen in action, they decree that out of Orpheus' ashes a new world and a new love shall arise. As Orpheus loved Eurydice, the first-born son of the Neptune will always love his Pallas Athena.

Mercury sings a song consisting of ten consoling verses. 'What is this sadness that has taken hold of the audience? Orpheus is not dead, he is alive!' His deeds will be sung till the last day comes. Although you cannot see him in his usual forests, hills, mountains, valleys and fields, he is not dead! What was mortal in him is dead, but his love, so chaste and pure, will not perish as long as this world lasts and the gods are in Heaven. Through Orpheus a new world will emerge in which the false, carnal love of Venus has no place. The true love of Orpheus will bless thousands of wedded couples, and Neptune's great son and his people shall experience this love. This love will also be experienced by Pallas, who cannot otherwise enjoy any other love. Cupid must leave, for his love is inadequate. He will be chased away by Atlas, who is going to bring the new world which harbours the new love.

The choir sings a sonnet of praise. The gods are hailed for having given a new and chaste love, and praise of Orpheus' virtue and art will be heard in the lands of Tigris and Parnassus. To prevent love and truthfulness and art from dying out, a new world has arisen from Orpheus' ashes, in which a chaste love lives that pleases God.

The grand ballet enters together with a highly accomplished Cavalier who, in spite of the fact that he had been serving Diana faithfully, is ensnared by the goddess Voluptas. Enslaved by lust he has remained with her as if asleep, under the guardian-ship of a dragon. But Fama has called upon the Virtues and, with the help of Pallas who has subdued the dragon, rescued him from the lure of sensual lust. Pallas, together with the freed Cavalier, goes to make sacrifices to the gods.

> Sonnet of thanksgiving for the sacrifice made by the Virtues and the redeemed Hero sung by a full choir: 'Praise be to the Highest, for the hero has been freed from all vices'. Let the triumphant song sound throughout nature even up to the heavenly castle!

Atlas arrives with the new world out of which the new Cupid promised by the gods comes forth.[27] He shoots his arrows into the hearts of the young Neptune and Pallas.[28] Because the light from Phoebus (an epithet for Apollo, particularly used when he appears as the god of Light/god of the Sun; my remark) now for a while has started shining through the rays of Pallas, without whom there would now be no light over our hemisphere, Apollo has left his heavenly abode and come to earth for a short while – also out of compassion for the wounded hearts to comfort them and rejuvenate their true love.[29] He seeks the company of the noblest gods, such as Jove, Hymen, Bacchus, and Morpheus, so that they all can celebrate the wedding.

> Phoebus' 15-verse wedding invitation to the gods praises the beauty and splen-dour of the new princess and urges the gods to take part in the celebrations, saying that everybody will want to praise the bride and the groom with hands, feet and exclamations of joy.

The performance ends with the *grand ballet*, in which at one point the dancers form the letters of the names of the bride and groom.

This is what the *Kückelsom Text* relates and to which the *Festival Account* basically agrees. Some details vary, but mostly these have no significance for the present arti-cle. In two instances, however, there are interesting differences. Where the *Kückelsom Text* says that four 'Génios' gather up the remains of Orpheus, the *Festival Account* says that four angels do this. Furthermore, it also states that an altar was provid-ed for the sacrifice performed by Pallas and the Cavalier, and that the role of the

---

27 An additional piece of information is given in a different document, a letter that the king wrote to Mogens Pax which makes it clear that the latter's son, Christopher Pax, danced the role of the 'new Amor', the second Cupid. See Wade, *Triumphus nuptialis*, 81.

28 As the prince-elect had the same name as his father, he is now talked about as 'the young Nep-tune', whereas his father was referred to as 'Neptune' in the introduction.

29 Here there is a play with the usage of two names for the same god – both Apollo and Phoebus – thereby suggesting that the brides' shining light is comparable to that of Apollo/Phoebes, and that her light has made Apollo visit this earthly abode for a short while.

Cavalier was danced extremely well by one of Christian IV's sons, Ulrik Christian, and that Mercury was sung by the castrato Chelli from Venice; his performance was clearly judged to be impressive. We are also told that the *ballet* lasted two hours.

Neither the *Kückelsom Text* nor the *Festival Account* makes it clear whether there was any spoken dialogue in the *ballet* performance. The introductory lines could very well have been spoken by a presenter, as was sometimes the case in the English masque. Some of the lines between the various songs and other musical pieces could also easily have served as a basis for spoken explanations, too. But perhaps the booklet produced for the show, and most likely distributed among the audience before the performance, was felt to give sufficient information together with the verses for the action to be understood.

WADE'S INTERPRETATION OF THE *BALLET*

There are good reasons for exploring possible influences of the English court masque on Prince Frederik's *ballet*: Jacobean masqueing was for many years largely centred on Queen Anna and her ladies, and she was the sister of Christian IV and the aunt of Prince Frederik. There were also a few musicians from England staying at the Copenhagen court for shorter or longer periods, and the converse,[30] and Inigo Jones, the main masque designer throughout the Stuart era, was in Copenhagen in 1603 and then had some contact with Christian IV on the king's visit to England in 1606.[31] Wade attaches great importance to these connections and especially to the 1606 visit to the English court by Christian IV, and to the visit by his brother Ulrik just after James' accession to the throne in 1604/5, and she finds significant influence from the masque on Frederik's *ballet*, particularly on two counts: the scenes with Pan and Orpheus are typical antimasques; and the social dancing following the *ballet* performance is seen as being the same as the revels of the court masque, where the noble masquers invited the audience to dance before they returned to the fictive, divine world of the masque proper and resumed their roles. These analyses create the foundation for Wade's further interpretation. Here she applies Orgel's basic reading of the masque to the *ballet*. According to him, the revels function as a means of making the audience identify with the world of the masque proper, that is with the royal family and the inner court circles. And this world shines the more beautifully because it is juxtaposed to the common world of the antimasque. In Wade's understanding the social dancing taking place after the *grand ballet* would then create a similar identification between the audience and the royal/noble masquers.[32]

---

30 Niels Krabbe, *Træk af musiklivet i Danmark på Christian IV's tid* (Copenhagen: Engstrøm & Sødring musikforlag, 1988), 40–42, 74–84. John Bergsagel, 'Danish Musicians in England 1611–1614: Newly Discovered Instrumental Music', *Dansk Årbog for Musikforskning*, 7 (1973–76), 9–20.

31 John Harris and Gordon Higgot, *Inigo Jones: Complete Architectural Drawings* (London: A. Zwemmer, 1989), 13–14; Wade, *Triumphus nuptialis*, 47–50 and 55–56.

32 Wade, *Triumphus nuptialis*, 73–80. I remain unconvinced by Wade's claim that Ulrik sponsored a masque and took part in its performance when he was visiting, mainly because sufficient information to support it is lacking.

There are several problems with this argument. Both Christian IV and his brother Ulrik visited the English court well before the first antimasque was created, and thus never saw one, and as a corollary the contact between Inigo Jones and the Danish king took place before the invention of antimasques, too. There is also a report suggesting that Christian had been extremely drunk at the masque performance which he attended.[33] If this is true, he would hardly have remembered the show well enough to inspire the creation of a similar performance, and if he actually was sufficiently impressed with the masque he attended to wish to have similar shows in his own court, why wait for almost thirty years to do so? His brother died in 1624, ten years before the mounting of the Copenhagen *ballet*, and it seems equally unlikely that he should have left descriptions of court masques that suddenly were taken as a basis for the *ballet* mounted ten years after his death. That a significant influence should have travelled through these two brothers to the 1634 show in Denmark therefore seems implausible for several reasons. But then there are no antimasques in Frederik's *ballet* either! On the contrary, the threatening, comic or grotesque elements run through the whole ballet as a scarlet thread. Such elements, however, are not at all alien to the French *ballets*, but there they are not singled out in isolated sections like antimasques.

There are two main points in Orgel's analysis of the significance of the revels. One is that the masque proper has been purged of everything inferior through the creation of the antimasque, and the masque proper has thus taken on a semi-divine character. The other is that because the revels are included specifically in the masque proper, the audience is drawn into the ficticious, divine world of the masquers precisely because they take part in the performance and are thus included in its world. The continuation of the play after the revels is therefore crucial to the function of this dancing. And this is not what happens in the Copenhagen *ballet* at all; there the audience dance after the show has ended, which was a perfectly normal procedure at a court feast. So there is no apotheosis of the audience into a royal, semi-divine world other than the elevation they may have felt on being invited to the feast, which is standard for any courtly entertainment. Further, Frederik's *ballet* has no strong focus on the king. He is briefly mentioned in the introductory lines, but other than that he is not implicated in the story at all.

All in all, it seems that Wade's Orgelian interpretation does not really fit the show which actually took place.[34]

---

33 See Butler, *Stuart Court Masque*, 126–27, and 400 n. 3, for a useful discussion on the sources regarding this occasion.

34 I would like to add, however, that Wade also offers a reading of this *ballet* as part of the larger wedding festivities. In this connection she sees the show as a representation of the element *earth*, but exploring the implications of such a larger framework in the present article would be impossible. See Wade, *Triumphus nuptialis*, 148–53.

A NEW INTERPRETATION

The most immediate meanings of the allegories of the *ballet* are obvious and thoroughly in tune with the tradition of Renaissance courtly spectacle. It does not take much imagination to recognize that the great Neptune represents Christian IV himself, who was after all king of one of the world's largest sea powers at the time. Hence 'the young Neptune' is the Prince-Elect and bridegroom, Christian V, and Pallas Athena can be none other than his bride, Princess Magdalena Sibylla.

The ascent to true love.

The main theme of the *ballet*, highly appropriate for a royal wedding festival, seems to be love.[35] First we are introduced to the vulgar, egotistic love of Pan who is capable of rape to satisfy his own lust. This love is conquered by the heroic Hercules and his love for Deianeira. The well-read among the audience would know that she was his third wife, and that Hercules had killed the river god Achelous to be with her. He had also saved her life, and clearly his love was of a much purer and more elevated kind than that of Pan.[36] But alas, in the long run he did not manage to stay faithful to her. Therefore his love could not serve as an allegory for ideal love either, and he disappears from the stage. Only the faithful love arising from Orpheus' ashes was sufficiently pure and noble to serve as an image for a love appropriate for the royal couple.

The fight between good and evil

Mingled with this ascent to true love is the strife between good and evil. Monsters have been cleared away by the powerful and peace-creating Neptune before the start of the show. Nevertheless Invidia continues to cause problems throughout. Naughty Pan is conquered by brave Hercules. Good Orpheus and his followers are slain by the Bacchantes frenzied through Invidia's vindictiveness, but Orpheus rises to new life through the help of benevolent beings, and the enslaving Voluptas with her servants are banished through the powers of the Virtues and Pallas Athena. Not surprisingly the Good always wins. And finally the new world arising from Orpheus' ashes of course signifies the future realm of the king- and queen-to-be, ruled over by purified love, where the divine powers of the queen are those of Athena, capable of forcing the evil powers of Voluptas to surrender.

Some puzzling features

This is of course a standard courtly allegory appropriate for a wedding celebration. There are, however, aspects of the story which are truly strange. At the time of the Great Wedding the myth of Orpheus and Eurydice was one of the most famous stories from antiquity and had already been used in three of the first operas ever made, *Euridice* by Peri and Rinuccini in 1600; Caccini's opera with the same name, also

---

35 The obvious love theme is also commented upon by Wade, *Triumphus nuptialis*, 147.
36 Ovid, *Heroides*, ix; Ovid, *Metamorphoses*, ix. 101–238.

with Rinuccino's libretto; and *L'Orfeo* by Monteverdi and Striggio in 1607. Orpheus with his superhuman musical powers lost his beloved wife Eurydice when she was bitten by a snake. Through his magical singing and playing he managed to pacify the guardian of the gates to Hades and thus descended to this realm of the dead hoping to bring his wife back to life. Here he sang with such a beauty that even the cheeks of the Furies were wet with tears, and Hades, the god of the underworld allowed him to bring Eurydice back to the human world. There was one condition, however: he must not turn around and look at her before they were both in the land of the living again. Overcome with fear that she was not following, he could not help himself and looked back. Eurydice therefore died a second time, and Orpheus was torn to pieces by bacchantes (or Thracian women).

Although there are many sources for this story, with many differing details, there are none that mention Orpheus being burnt and something new rising from his ashes![37] No other reworking of the story contains anything like that either. Also Mercury's claim that Orpheus is not dead, but alive, is rather strange.

There is also one allegorical figure that does not belong to the most common allegorical-mythological cast, Fama. However, she is included in Cesare Ripa's famous *Iconologia* from 1603,[38] but she makes a rather strange appearance in the *ballet*, since her natural task would not be to call the Virtues.

Further, the cast of the *ballet* consists entirely of mythological or allegorical figures, with three exceptions, namely the angels or 'Génios' gathering up Orpheus' remains, the Pantaloons gathering up those of the animals, and the Cavalier appearing towards the end of the show. His appearance introduces a new element which seems unnecessary for the main story; at this point the new world with the new love has already arrived. Admittedly he is connected with the presentation of Princess Magdalena Sibylla as Athena, but one would have thought that the introduction of the princess could have been obtained by other means earlier in the show, even in a more unified way, if that was what was wanted. So what exactly is he doing there? Moreover, considering that this is a *ballet de cour* the appearance of angels on the stage is extraordinary; they do not belong in this tradition at all. Nor are altars where sacrifices take place part of the French *ballet de cour* tradition. One could, of course, explain away these oddities by suggesting that the makers of the *ballet* were not sufficiently acquainted with the genre or the mythology and therefore got both content and form a little mixed up and then made up things as they went along. However, that does not seem very likely. The lavish wedding festivities alone abound with mythologically based elements and speak of a very thorough knowledge of the field on the part of the creating agents, as do so many of Christian IV's self-representations throughout his reign. That leaves us with the possibility that these oddities were there for a reason.

---

37 Jenny March, *Cassel Dictionary of Classical Mythology* (London: Cassel, 2002), 290–92.
38 Cesare Ripa, *Iconologia, overo Descrittione di diverse imagini cauate dall'anticita, & di propria inuentione* (Roma: Lepido Faey, 1603).

Secrets and cultural tropes

In his *Music as Cultural Practice*, Lawrence Kramer speaks not only of the interpretation of music, but of all interpretational acts, and he makes three points that are of particular relevance in our connection. Firstly, he says that

> We enable the interpretation of a text by depreciating what is overtly legible and regarding the text as potentially secretive, or at least as a provocation to understanding that we may not know how to answer. The text, in this frame of reference, does not give itself to understanding; it must be made to yield to understanding. A hermeneutic window must be opened through which the discourse of understanding can pass.[39]

Secondly, he discusses various types of such hermeneutic windows, and says that 'structural tropes' are 'ultimately the most powerful of hermeneutic windows'. And structural tropes 'cut across traditional distinctions between form and content [and can] evolve from any aspect of communicative change'. Further he points to how a network of structural tropes instigates processes of expressive activities where the object of interpretation becomes open to understanding. Thirdly, he stresses how we are likely to encounter and recognize such tropes precisely when the object of interpretation seems to be 'explicitly problematical', when we face 'breaking points' like for instance 'a surplus of pattern' or 'an excessive connection'.[40]

Alchemical tropes

This view of interpretational processes seems particularly appropriate in the case of the present ballet. The burning of Orpheus' dead body and a new world arising from his ashes is precisely such a breaking point, because it adds to a very well-known story a pattern which does not belong there at all. It also constitutes a cultural trope because it gives very specific hints at a different story which has a strong standing in a given culture: the alchemical tradition. Western alchemy can be traced back to at least 300 B.C. Superficially it is about seeking to make gold out of base metals, but at a deeper level it is a quest involving an ascent to higher spiritual levels together with the pursuit of chemical and medical knowledge. Alchemy has always been understood as an occult tradition and surrounded with great secrecy. This was still so at the time of the Great Wedding, but there was also a more general interest in alchemy, and many works connected with the alchemical tradition were published during the late Renaissance and early Baroque.[41]

The image of something rising out of the ashes is essential to alchemical thinking. The ash is first and foremost the incorruptible substance which is left after the

---

39 Lawrence Kramer, *Music as Cultural Practice, 1800–1900* (Berkeley: University of California Press, 1990), 6.
40 Ibid. 12.
41 For example, Lyndy Abraham, *A Dictionary of Alchemical Imagery* (Cambridge: Cambridge University Press, 1998), esp. xix–xxi; Ioan P. Couliano, *Eros and Magic in the Renaissance*, transl. Margaret Cook (Chicago: University of Chicago Press, 1987); and Stanton J. Linden, *The Alchemy Reader: From Hermes Trismegistus to Isaac Newton* (Cambridge: Cambridge University Press), esp. 149–247, all give good information about alchemical texts from this period.

Philosopher's Stone has been subjected to the purgatorial fire, and it is the substance out of which the Purified Stone, the Phoenix, rises.[42] Lynn Abraham describes the idea of the Philosopher's Stone as

> the Arcanum of all arcane, possessing the power to perfect imperfection in all things, able to transmute base metals into pure gold and transform the earthly man into an illumined philosopher. It is the figure of light veiled in dark matter, that divine love essence which combines divine wisdom and creative power.[43]

So the ash, then, is an even more purified version of these powers, and the Phoenix arising from it symbolizes the final stage of all alchemical transmutation, when the gold is made, the final resurrection.[44] One of the other characteristics of ash in alchemical understanding is that it can no longer be set on fire, therefore it is free of passion.

Interestingly, there is one more cultural trope arising from Orpheus' ashes. Alchemy was essential to the Rosicrucian movement of the early seventeenth century, and one of the three fundamental Rosicrucian texts is *Chymische Hochzeit Christiani Rosencreütz anno 1459* (1616), written by Johann Valentin Andreae (see Ill. 2). In this long, Hermetic romance the body of the beheaded Philosophical Bird is burnt to ashes out of which the bodies of the king and queen in the story will be resurrected.[45]

A possible connection with Rosicrucianism also links up to other elements in the *ballet* story. In *The Chymical Wedding* Cupid serves as a special case. Christian Rosenkreutz is pricked with a dart by Cupid after he has accidentally seen the naked Venus, and this is clearly a necessary step in his process of initiation. In another tract which was generally seen as Rosicrucian, Robert Fludd's *Truth's Golden Harrow*, Cupid is used as a symbol for 'the love essence released by the Stone or Elixir'.[46] Also the strange appearance of angels is interesting in a Rosicrucian light. Angels do not hold a prominent position in alchemy or hermeticism in general, but they most certainly do in Rosicrucianism. Frances Yates repeatedly discusses the importance of angels in the various Rosicrucian tracts, and one of their tasks is to illuminate man's intellectual activities.[47] And finally, one of the three already mentioned fundamental Rosicrucian texts is the *Fama fraternitatis* – in which cherubim appear.[48]

Alchemical imagery, textual or pictorial, is rarely explicit. Rather it speaks in metaphors and has the character of information being revealed in veiled form. It also speaks through mirrors, as it were, although the pictures emerging in the mirrors are never exact renderings of what is mirrored. With this in mind a story on a deeper

---

42 Abraham, *A Dictionary of Alchemical Imagery*, 12–13.
43 Ibid. 145.
44 Ibid. 152.
45 Johann V. Andreae, *Chymische Hochzeit Christiani Rosencreütz anno 1459 Arcana publicata vilescunt: & gratiam prophanata amittunt. Ergo: ne Margaritas obiice porcis, seu Afino substernerosas* (Strassburg: Zetzner, 1616). See for instance the English translation by Foxcroft in Paul Marshall Allen (ed.), *A Christian Rosenkreutz Anthology* (Blauvelt, N.Y.: Rudolf Steiner Publications, 1981), 67–162.
46 Abraham, *A Dictionary of Alchemical Imagery*, 51.
47 Frances A. Yates, *The Rosicrucian Enlightenment* (New York: Barnes & Noble, 1996), 223.
48 Ibid. 127.

Ill. 2. Johann v. Andreae, *Chymische Hochzeit: Christiani Rosencreütz* (Strassbourg, 1616).

level seems to emerge from the *ballet*. The king and queen arising from the ashes in Christian Rosenkreutz' wedding are admittedly themselves metaphors and not earthly royalty. However, the connection with the newly wedded king- and queen-to-be seems too obvious to be ignored, and the indication is that the royal couple are aspiring to the spiritual wisdom of alchemy or perhaps more specifically Rosicrucianism. This would also explain another strange feature of the *Kückelsom Text*. It claims that love purged of passion is the only love that Magdalena Sibylla can tolerate. Seen in an alchemical light this passage could signal that she is preoccupied with the path to enlightenment; not that she is incapable of feeling passion, even for her husband, which is a somewhat strange suggestion in a text for a wedding celebration.[49]

49 Although it should be added that in Elizabethan tradition the coldness of a virgin was a rather desirable feature.

In this new light the roles of the two Cupids are more understandable. In Mercury's song Cupid is chased away because his love is no longer sufficient. When the new Cupid enters as part of the new world brought in by Atlas, he reminds us strongly of the Cupid we encounter in Robert Fludd's *Truth's Golden Harrow*. About this pure love essence Fludd says: 'This Elixir is the true temple of wisdom, the impregnable castell of Cupid that powerful god of love' and in the *Chymical Wedding* Christian Rosenkreutz is pricked by Cupid as a necessary part of the initiation he is going through.[50] When the *Kückelsom Text* says that the new Cupid is shooting his arrows at Christian and Magdalena Sibylla, this may not only be a playful hint at their hopefully new-found love, but also, possibly, an indication that they are linked to a tradition of initiation. And when Fama calls the Virtues to help rescue the Cavalier, Fama can be more than the goddess of fame, she can also represent one of the leading Rosicrucian tracts.

Indeed, the very role of Mercury takes on a new character seen in this light. He is of course one of the stock figures in any mythological cast. But he is also *the* central God in alchemy. He is present at every stage of the alchemical process, and he carries the divine love essence which kills falsehood and allows truth to arise. When Mercury in the *ballet* sings about Orpheus not being dead, but alive, he speaks as the god of purification, the god who knows about transmutation from fleshly mortality to immortality. When he speaks of the new world and the new love arising, he is undoubtedly referring to the quest for spiritual development which is essential both to alchemy as such and to the Rosicrucian movement.

This reflects back on other aspects of the *ballet* as well, and the field of ancient mystery traditions opens up. It is obvious that for a theatre performance which has love and its development to higher stages running through it as a scarlet thread, it makes sense to take Pan who revels in sensual lusts as a point of departure. But why choose Hercules to represent the next stage of love? Not that it seems a bad choice, but with the whole field of mythology to choose from, there may be a specific reason behind the choice of Hercules. And by implication, why specifically choose his third wife, Deianeira, to be included? Could this be yet another reference to ancient mysteries where the neophyte had to go through various trials, two of which have left traces in ordinary language since we speak of 'going through fire and water'? To win Deianeira, we remember, Hercules actually had had to kill the river god. This must surely count as conquering water. And then Orpheus, in this very special *ballet*, also goes through the most gruesome ordeals thinkable and is finally purified – through fire, and this is what finally brings new life, and the mysterious proclamation that he is not dead after all.

This line of interpretation also helps explain the presence of the Cavalier. Why is he inserted into a theatre performance as the single human being playing a major role with a mythological and allegorical cast surrounding him? At first he is enslaved by the lustful life in Voluptas' world, but then he is freed through the influence of the Virtues and of Athena. This again corresponds with ancient mysteries and their

---

50 Quot. from Abraham, *A Dictionary of Alchemical Imagery*, 51.

Renaissance revival, where precisely virtue and the qualities of Athena – who reigns over the sciences and music – are needed to aid the human soul in its ascension to a purified, higher spiritual consciousness. Through the presence of the Cavalier it is made clear that the spiritual quest presented through the *ballet* is valid not only for the mythological cast, but for ordinary human beings.[51]

Seen in this light the angels and the altar become more understandable. We shall probably never know who actually wrote the *Kückelsom Text*, or whether this author had originally written 'Génios' or 'angels', or, perhaps, whether the author of the *Festival Account* might have misunderstood what he was seeing and taken génios to be angels, or whether the writer found the possible difference insignificant. Perhaps that does not matter. What is important, is that in the scene where Orpheus' torn limbs are collected, this is done by benevolent higher beings with the capacity to bring about a metamorphosis where new life on a higher level arises. This process implies an encounter with the sacred, which is made visible through the presence of the altar. There are also text fragments like 'till the last day dawns' and 'the heavenly castle', references to a divinity higher than the mythological ones, and generally a hymn-like quality in several of the songs which also contributes to a sense that the play fundamentally is about spiritual development and religious experience.

It may be of further interest to note that the inclusion of an altar and the performance of a sacrifice in courtly theatre is not unique to this show. Sara Smart mentions that the same is also present in a Stuttgart *ballet* in 1617 written by Weckerlin, and she suggests an influence from masques written for the wedding of the English princess Elizabeth and Frederick V, Elector Palatine of Rhine, by Beaumont.[52] However, this is far from the only instance of such an occurrence. The insertion of elements indicating that a religious ceremony is being performed is a prominent feature of the Early Stuart masquing era.[53] This is perhaps the strongest indication that there has been significant and specific influence of the English masque tradition on the first Danish *ballet*. How this influence might have travelled is hard to know. Publication of English masque texts made many of them accessible on a scale very unusual for courtly entertainments. Most important were the two publications of Ben Jonson's masques, the first arriving in 1616 and the second containing his later masques in 1631.[54] But perhaps equally important is the web of contacts between intellectuals, artists, musicians, authors and courtiers. The paths of information and inspiration in such a web are often untraceable; it is often only through their results that some of the exchanges which have taken place can be sensed.

The music which sounded in the first Scandinavian music theatre performance is still silent. But the choice of Orpheus as one of the main protagonists, as the one who goes through a metamorphosis to new life and divine love, is hardly a

---

51 See Rygg, *Masqued Mysteries* (2000), 53–74 and 180–214, for a thorough discussion of such initiation based upon ancient mystery traditions.
52 Smart, 'The Württemberg Court', 40–42.
53 Rygg, *Masqued Mysteries* (2000).
54 For publication details, see for example Ben Jonson, *The Complete Masques*, ed. Stephen Orgel (New Haven: Yale University Press, 1969).

coincidence. Although the transformation taking place depends partly on the help of higher beings, the fact cannot be ignored that it is Orpheus, the ultimate master of music, who has become ready to undergo metamorphosis. This may also indicate part of the meaning of the spectacles presented through the ballet: a reign where the pursuit of music and the arts may lead to the development of a higher consciousness is proclaimed. And it could be said that there were three kings watching the angelic dance which is preparing for the ascent to the highest love: the reigning king; his eldest son, the bridegroom, who had already acted in the capacity of king on several occasions and was supposed to become king, but who died before his father; and then Frederik, the sponsor of the *ballet* who actually turned out to become the future king.

Conclusion

In one sense this *ballet* is a celebration typical of leading Renaissance courts, and as far as form is concerned, it is undoubtedly a version of the French *ballet de cour*. Apparently unrelated scenes actually form a coherent narrative and thus the entire show as such is more typical of the *ballet comique* than the *ballet à entrées* tradition. But the performance can be assumed to be more than a celebration of royal power. It signals that a new era is to be expected in which rulership is based on spiritual ideals related to alchemy and probably even Rosicrucianism. The question therefore arises to what degree this represented the ideas of the royal Danish family – or some of its members – at that time. Only further research can answer that question.

Summary

The first music theatre performance in Scandinavia, the so called *ballet* given at the royal wedding in Copenhagen in 1634, is explored in this article. The first main question is what the royal family and the various artists working for them wanted to achieve by staging this *ballet*. The second main question is how this onset of Scandinavian music theatre was related to leading traditions of courtly music theatre in other North European courts, primarily those in England and France. In this connection Mara Wade's interpretations of the Copenhagen *ballet* in her study *Triumphus nuptialis* are discussed.

The article shows that as far as form is concerned, the Copenhagen performance is clearly structured like a French *ballet de cour*. However, the actual contents demonstrates that the potentiality of the performance as political propaganda is hardly exploited, whereas signs linked to occult trends like alchemy and Rosicrucianism are manifold, indicating that these trends were essential to at least parts of the royal family itself. In this respect the first music theatre performance in Scandinavia also shows surprising influence from the English court masque.

Kurt Weill's *Deadly Sins* in Copenhagen
A thistle in the Danish kitchen garden of 1936

Niels Krabbe[1]

Ill. 1. Scene image from the first performance of *Die sieben Todsünden* at the Royal Theatre in Copenhagen, 1936 (Photo: Holger Damgaards Teaterfotos, The Royal Library, Copenhagen).

Bertolt Brecht and Kurt Weill's *Die sieben Todsünden* (The Seven Deadly Sins, in Danish *De syv Dødssynder*)[2] is an exile-work. It was composed while its authors were living as expatriates in Paris and the few performances that took place during Weill's lifetime were all presented *outside* Germany: in 1933, in Paris; re-staged (in an English translation) a month later in London;[3] and in 1936, in Copenhagen, while

1   The article, including the quotations from Danish literature and newspapers, is translated by Dan A. Marmorstein.
2   Throughout the article the title in German and Danish, including the abbreviated form *Dødssyn-derne*, will be used interchangeably.
3   Behind the performances in Paris and London stood the famous dance troupe, *Les Ballets 1933*, which was primarily cultivating the avant-garde repertoire. For the London production, the libretto was translated into English, and the work's title was changed from its original religiously charged title to the more neutral *Anna-Anna*. Apart from this, the two productions were identical.

Brecht was living in exile in Svendborg. The Royal Theatre's production in Copenhagen was accordingly the last presentation before the work was taken up again in 1958, in New York City, having been prepared by George Balanchine. Not until 1960 did the work have its first German performance, in Frankfurt, in the somewhat adapted version that Lotte Lenya had carried out a few years earlier (more discussion about this matter is presented in App. 2).[4] From this time on, the piece was included on the roster of immortal works by Brecht and Weill and today it appears to be, musically speaking, what might be the best of Weill's works from his 'German' period.

Only very infrequently (or not at all) is the staging at the Royal Theatre in Copenhagen mentioned in the international Weill-literature, primarily because the show was taken off the bill after only two performances. On the other hand, the persistent assertion claiming that the work's sorry plight can be attributed to demands voiced by the German ambassador in Denmark is marketed everywhere. In what follows, there is attempt to set this myth in a broader perspective. Similarly, the whole scenario surrounding the theatre's staging of this highly controversial work will be further elucidated. Full documentation of what it was, in the final analysis, that caused the theatre to suspend any further performances after the first two evenings can hardly be presented here, but a number of factors of a (theatre-)political nature and other related factors can contribute to the work's and Weill's reception-history in Denmark.

THE PIECE

In point of fact, the collaboration between Brecht and Weill lasted only a little more than six years; after *Die sieben Todsünden,* created in 1933, it was all over.[5] Already a few years earlier, the two creative artists had started to drift apart for political and personal reasons; that this new work could have come forth at all can presumably be chalked up to the very extraordinary and stressful circumstances in which the two collaborators found themselves at this time. It must be added that only Weill was fully committed to the work; he actually considered it one of his most important works to date. Brecht, on the other hand, was not particularly engaged with the project. He hurried to Paris, where he stayed a couple of weeks in connection with the preparations for the production, which he prosaically characterized in this levelheaded way: 'das Ballett ging ganz hübsch, war allerdings nicht so bedeutend'.[6]

---

4 Large portions of Anna I's part were transposed down a perfect fourth to better accommodate Lenya's deep voice (a similar transposition was effected in Jenny's part in *Aufstieg und Fall der Stadt Mahagonny*).

5 The work's genesis and reception in 1933 are described in detail in the Weill-literature. Here, among the numerous accounts available, the reader is referred to Joanna Lee and Kim Kowalke (eds.), *Die 7 Todsünden. The 7 Deadly Sins. A Sourcebook* (New York: Kurt Weill Foundation for Music, 1997), containing a plentiful supply of documentary material; David Drew, *Kurt Weill. A Handbook* (Berkeley, 1987), 222–48; Kim H. Kowalke, 'Seven Degrees of Separation; Music, Text, Image, and Gesture in *The Seven deadly Sins*', *The South Atlantic Quarterly*, 104/1 (Winter 2005), 7–62.

6 Postcard from Brecht to Helene Weigel, dated 10 June, 1933. Published in Bertolt Brecht, *Werke. Große kommentierte Berliner und Frankfurter Ausgabe der Werke Brechts in 30 Bänden* (Frankfurt a.M, 1998), vol. 28, 361.

It was not until 1959 that the libretto was printed, now bearing the title, *Die sieben Todsünden der Kleinbürger.*[7]

The work was originally built up around an idea conceived by Brecht with the ambiguous working title, *Ware Liebe*. The very realization of the idea was brought about through the agency of the English financier, poet and art patron, Edward James, who wanted to commission a work by Weill where his then wife, the Austrian dancer-choreographer, actress and painter, Tilly Losch, would have a prominent role. It was very likely Weill himself who wanted to create a work that would transgress the limits of the traditional ballet genre and he suggested that a text by none other than Jean Cocteau be solicited. However, the collaboration with Cocteau did not come to fruition. Instead, the task was placed on the shoulders of Weill's tried and true collaborator from the successes of the Berlin era, Bertolt Brecht, who – albeit half-heartedly – was being handed the chance to deploy his idea about Christian doctrine's Deadly Sins,[8] embedded in a modern fable about the heart and brain and about the terms of the individual's existence within the capitalist system.

For Weill, it was a chaotic time: he had fled from Germany; he was dealing with marital troubles with Lotte Lenya (who, at this time, was living with the tenor, Otto Pasetti) and he was having problems in his collaboration with stage designer Caspar Neher (who initially found the text for *Die Sieben Todsünden* to be too trivial but subsequently agreed to design the scenography).[9] Added to this were the business problems with his publisher, Universal Edition, as well as the already tense relationship with Brecht after *Mahagonny*. Nonetheless, Weill managed to create a work which he himself, as mentioned, regarded to be the best he had ever turned out – a work which, in stylistic terms, brings the preceding years' *song* style to a close and ushers in a new epoch in Weill's output. Finally, it marks, as mentioned above, the conclusion of the collaboration between the two artists, Brecht and Weill; moreover, this piece is unique in the overall context of the collaboration in the sense that this time around, it is *Weill* in front – and not Brecht. The piece was mounted in 1933 – both in Paris and London – with the patron's wife, Tilly Losch, in one of the main roles (the dancing Anna) and the composer's wife, Lotte Lenya, in the other (the singing Anna). In both cities, the work received a lukewarm reception – not altogether dismissive, but neither with any pronounced enthusiasm. One of the stumbling blocks was, at the time, and is, still now, the work's genre affiliation: in the many reviews, both from 1933 and later from the production in Copenhagen in 1936, we meet genre designations like cantata; short opera; ballet-chanté; ballet-pantomime; pantomime; a story acted, danced and sung; and so on. The audience was thus having a difficult time attuning its expectations in the proper direction and the traditional ballet audi-

---

7   Brecht, *Werke*, vol. 4, 495–98.

8   In the Christian tradition, *the deadly sins* hark back to the First John Letter 5:16–17 where a distinction is made between (venial) sins *not* leading to death, which can be forgiven, and (mortal) 'sins leading to death'. From the early Middle Ages and onward, the Seven Deadly Sins (aka Capital Vices or Cardinal Sins) include *pride, greed, lust, envy, gluttony, wrath*, and *sloth*.

9   See Lys Symonette and Kim H. Kowalke (eds.), *Speak Low (When you speak low). The Letters of Kurt Weill and Lotte Lenya* (London, 1996), 80.

ence, in particular, felt disoriented – in the best instances, or, in the worst instances, felt shocked by what was being presented.

WEILL AND BRECHT IN COPENHAGEN IN THE 1930S

Not surprisingly, it was *Dreigroschenoper* (The Threepenny Opera) – Weill and Brecht's legendary breakthrough work from 1928 – that introduced Kurt Weill's music to the Danish public. This occurred with the performance of the piece at The New Theater (Det Ny Teater) in 1930. After this, a string of theatrical works that were the result of the fruitful collaboration between Brecht and Weill during the years just before and just after 1930: *Der Jasager* (He who Says Yes), *Der Lindberghflug* (The Flight across the Ocean), *Aufstieg und Fall der Stadt Mahagonny* (Rise and Fall of the City of Mahagonny) and finally, in 1936, *Die sieben Todsünden* (The Seven Deadly Sins). Accordingly, we can establish that, with the exception of *Berliner Requiem*, all of Weill's major works that accompanied texts by Brecht were performed in Copenhagen only a few years after they were composed.[10] This early breakthrough for Weill's music in Denmark is thrown dramatically into relief when we consider that the first time anybody in England could actually hear a work by Weill was in June 1933 when, as previously mentioned, *Die sieben Todsünden* opened under the title *Anna–Anna*.[11] On the other hand, The Royal Theatre had not introduced either Brecht or Weill prior to the performance of *De syv Dødssynder* in 1936. As far as Brecht is concerned, another seventeen years would pass before another one of his works appeared on the national stage's programme.[12] When it comes to Weill, another twenty-seven years would elapse.[13]

10 To this could be added two further works involving the use of texts by Brecht, *Happy End* and *Mann ist Mann* (Man Equals Man), though it must be pointed out that Brecht's contribution to the former includes only the songs (the libretto itself was actually written by his assistant, Elisabeth Hauptmann), while the musical score accompanying the latter appears to be lost. For an overview of the reception of Weill's work in Denmark, the reader is referred to Michael Fjeldsøe, *Den fortrængte Modernisme* (Copenhagen, 1999), 75–78. A more detailed exposition of the Danish performances of *Mahagonny* can be found in Niels Krabbe, 'Mahagonny hos Brecht og Weill', *Musik & Forskning*, 16 (1991), 69–144, esp. 126 ff., as well as in Michael Fjeldsøe, 'Syngende skuespillere eller agerende operasangere. Om den rette sangstil i operaen "Mahagonny"', in Anne Ørbæk Jensen et al. (eds.), *Musikvidenskabelige kompositioner. Festskrift til Niels Krabbe* (Copenhagen, 2006), 605–24, reprinted in a revised version as 'Aufstieg und Fall der Stadt Mahagonny in Copenhagen, 1933/34: An Early Debate about Performing Style', *Kurt Weill Newsletter*, 25/1 (2007), 4–8.

11 The libretto was translated in 1958 into English by W.H. Auden and Chester Kallman with the full title 'The Seven Deadly Sins of the Petty Bourgeoisie'.

12 *Mutter Courage og hendes børn* (Mutter Courage und ihre Kinder / Mother Courage and Her Children), performed in 1953. As a matter of fact, *Jeanne d'Arc fra Slagtehallerne* (Die heilige Johanna der Schlachthöfe / Saint Joan of the Stockyards) was actually approved for being staged at The Royal Theatre in the middle of the 1930s, even though it appears that nothing ever came of any plans to mount the work. In his *Brecht, A Biography* (London, 1983), 176, Ronald Haymann claims, erroneously, that *Trommeln in der Nacht* (Drums in the Night) had already been performed at The Royal Theatre sometime prior to Brecht's arrival in Denmark; the performance took place at a small theatre in Copenhagen in 1930.

13 *Mahagonny*, performed in 1964 (see Krabbe, 'Mahagonny hos Brecht og Weill', 133–34).

Brecht's own works were actually very much part of the agenda in Copenhagen during these years. In 1935, RT (Revolutionært Teater, Revolutionary Theatre, i.e. Copenhagen's Worker's Theatre), spearheaded by Ruth Berlau, presented *Moderen* (The Mother) at Borups Højskole (Borup's College) and two years later, Berlau staged *Fru Carrars geværer* (Señora Carrar's Rifles) for the same ensemble. In both productions, Dagmar Andreasen appeared in the lead role and both productions were arranged as touring theatrical productions that were performed on make-shift factory-hall stages.[14] The hot topic of conversation in the time around *De syv Dødssynder*, however, was the premiere only a week earlier of *Rundhoder og Spids-hoder* (Round Heads and Pointed Heads) in the Riddersal Theatre in Copenhagen, in Per Knutzon's staging.

Several of these plays had been created while Brecht, from the summer of 1933 until the spring of 1939, was living at Skovbostrand near Svendborg.[15] As we can see, Brecht moved to Denmark almost immediately after the performance of *Die sieben Todsünden* in Paris. Although Brecht, during these years, refrained from getting involved either personally in the Danish cultural life or as a writer in the Danish press, he was obviously both well known and notorious in wide intellectual circles for both his communist and his anti-Nazi convictions. The fact that the greatest portion of his output generated in precisely these years is targeted directly at the Nazis might have been a contributing cause to the formation of the myth surrounding the fate of *Die sieben Todsünden* at the Royal Theatre. However, it must be mentioned that Weill's ballet plays a very minor role in Brecht's life story when it comes to the playwright's sojourn in Denmark. As we shall see, if we put aside the – ostensibly erroneous – information in Harald Engberg's report, cited in the following paragraph, there are evidently no sources offering any proof that Brecht was involved, to any considerable extent, in setting up the production at the Royal Theatre.[16] Similarly, it does not appear that Brecht himself had anything to say about the show. Whereas he had witnessed the rehearsals and the premiere of *Rundhoder og Spidshoder* the week before, there is nothing to suggest that Brecht was in Copenhagen in connection with *Dødssynderne*. By and large, Brecht had adopted a very distanced relation to

14 In a letter from Brecht to Hella Wuolijoki, written in 1940 or 1941, it appears that it actually was Ruth Berlau who originally came up with the idea of having *Die sieben Todsünden / De syv Dødssynder* produced at The Royal Theatre. See John Willett (ed.), *Bertolt Brecht Letters* (New York, 1990), letter no. 419. As is made evident by source material at The West Dean Estate, this can hardly be the case (see a discussion about these source materials in Appendix 1).

15 In addition to *Die Gewehre der Frau Carrar* (Señora Carrar's Rifles / Fru Carrars Geværer) and *Die Rundköpfe und die Spitzköpfe* (Round Heads and Pointed Heads / Rundhoder og Spidshoder), *Drei Groschen Roman* (The Threepenny Novel / Laser og pjalter), *Furcht und Elend des Dritten Reiches* (Fear and Misery of the Third Reich / Det tredje Riges Frygt og Elendighed), the *Svend-borg Poems* (Svendborger Gedichte), and *Leben des Galilei* (Life of Galileo / Galileis Liv) were also written in whole or in part during Brecht's stay in Denmark.

16 In Birgit Nielsen and Erwin Winter (eds.), *Bertolt Brecht i Danmark* (Brecht-Zentrum der DDR and Svendborg Kommune, 1984), not a single word about *De syv Dødssynder* appears notwithstanding that the book, in the form of a journal, presents a detailed overview of the most important events in these years.

Denmark and Danish intellectual life in these years; he was on the run and Denmark was a tolerable stopover on the expedition leading further. Famous is his laconic and somewhat condescending observation about the country:

> The worst thing about these much too small islands is that there is not really anything missing; everything is here, but in terribly small proportions. Here, nothing exists that you can measure it by, because the yardstick itself is too short. A hill that is situated in Jutland, which is called *Himmelbjerget* (Heaven's Mountain), is 200 metres high.[17]

Even though Brecht's stay in Denmark during this period is so very well documented, it would not be at all correct to say that Weill was here, as is claimed every now and then. Harald Engberg goes so far as to describe how Otto Gelsted (who had translated Brecht's text into Danish) drove by car, along with a number of the players, to Karen Michaëlis's house on the island of Thurø and that here, they worked 'hard, together, with the Brecht-Weill pair, around a grand piano, in order to grab hold of the right style in the performances'.[18] Upon examination of Weill's passport, however, it appears unmistakably that the composer never entered Denmark.[19] Furthermore, at this time, Weill and Lenya had been living in New York since September 1935; they could hardly have had any clue about what was going on in Copenhagen. It might be the case that what we have here is a conflation with Brecht's second important composer, Hanns Eisler, who *did* make visits to Brecht in Svendborg several times.[20]

The performance in Copenhagen in November 1936

Through much of November 1936, almost all the Copenhagen newspapers ran shorter or longer articles about *Dødssynderne*. The extensive press coverage falls into three main categories: advance notices about this strange work, in what was hitherto a largely unknown genre, which the Royal Theatre was about to present; the mixed reviews of the premiere performance; and the subsequent debate circling around *Dødssynderne* as a textbook case of the theatre's alleged neglect of its obligations as a national institution and an example of the pervasive brutalization in society.

The copious amount of advance notices of the work that appeared on the days from the 9 until the 12 of November, featuring an extensive quantity of illustrative material from the rehearsals, is connected in part with the work's unusual genre designation already mentioned (variously: 'ballet', 'ballet pantomime', 'ballet with song and speech' and 'pantomime opera') and also with what was the apparently somewhat mismatched collocation with another piece being performed on the evening's bill, August Enna's opera *Den lille Pige med Svovlstikkerne* (The Little Match Girl),

17 Nielsen and Winter, *Bertolt Brecht i Danmark*, 23.
18 Harald Engberg, *Brecht på Fyn* (Odense, 1966), vol. 2, 61.
19 Ascertained upon the author's personal inspection of Kurt Weill's passport at The Kurt Weill Foundation for Music in New York.
20 As a curious anecdote, it ought to be mentioned that around ten years ago, the composer, Bernhard Christensen, claimed – in a conversation with the author – to have greeted Kurt Weill on the street in Copenhagen, adding, for that matter, that he was not particularly fond of Weill's music.

Ill. 2. Illona Wieselmann and
Margot Lander as Anna 1 and
Anna 2 at the performance in
Copenhagen in November 1936
(Photo: Holger Damgaards Teater-
fotos, The Royal Library, Copen-
hagen).

from 1897 ('"The Little Match Girl" will not fail to give rise to the effect of an old
pastel rendering, while *"Die sieben Todsünden"* will just as certainly call to mind a
surrealistic picture of 1936.').[21] On top of this, there was a summary of the plot
and a clarification of the work's theme as the conflict between reason and emotion
('heart' and 'brain') – all of this marked by a certain curiosity and a certain joyful
anticipation.[22] One of the daily notices (appearing in the newspaper, *Børsen*, 10
Nov.) reports, however, that during the rehearsals, a certain sense of dissatisfaction
was smouldering beneath the surface among some of the involved performers, in
the form of different kinds of protests – directed especially against some of the
signboards with objectionable content. With an admixture of anticipation and aver-
sion, attention is called to the fact that this happens to be the second premiere of a
piece by the exiled German writer within a few weeks' time (the first, as has been

21 *Aftenbladet*, 12 Nov. 1936.
22 'Frib.' in *Ekstrabladet*, 9 Nov. 1936, draws an interesting parallel between the respective motifs in
Dødssynderne and Svend Borberg's play, *Cirkus Juris*, which was performed at the theatre in Febru-
ary 1935 – a parallel that not only encompasses the shared theme of mankind's dual nature but also
both pieces' fable-like character unfolding inside an unreal world. The influential theatre critic,
Frederik Schyberg, characterized *Cirkus Juris* with words that just as aptly could have been applied two years later to *De syv Dødsynder*: '… it does have, within Danish theatre's solid block of
traditionalism, its interest and its significance as an experiment in dissolution'; *Berlingske Tidende*,
9 Febr. 1935. Already on 16 Oct. 1936, *Socialdemokraten* had published a full article by Otto Gelsted
about Bertolt Brecht, in connection with the impending production of *Dødssynderne*.

mentioned, being *Rundhoder og Spidshoder*). As something altogether untypical for these kinds of advance notices, the coverage focuses on Svend Johansen's elegant decorations with the stationary backdrop of skyscrapers in front of which changing set pieces mark out the individual scenes. Taken together, these scenographic decorations can safely be said not only to constitute one of the high points in Svend Johansen's own output but also one of the culminating achievements in theatrical history of that time. The style embodied in these decorations – much like the style of the whole production – was influenced, to some extent, by Kjeld Abell's ballet from 1934, *Enken i Spejlet* (The Widow in the Mirror), with music by Bernhard Christensen – an observation that is also mentioned in one of the reviews. As far as the work's essential idea and content, some writers struck up an expectant and wondering attitude:

> From what can be judged [i.e. upon consideration of the list of the Seven Deadly Sins], it appears that there will be quite a few acerbic and dark premonitions being articulated in this ballet pantomime (*Politiken*, 6 November 1936); Anna is an American danseuse who has to move her way through the sins before she can attain success (*Børsen*, 6 November 1936).

The premiere took place on 12 November, 1936, staged in the form of ballet master Harald Lander's direction and choreography and performed under the musical direction of Johan Hye-Knudsen – and, as has been mentioned, sharing the bill with August Enna's nearly 40-year old Hans Christian Andersen opera, *Den lille Pige med Svovlstikkerne*. Appearing in the role of the singing Anna was the young actress, Illona Wieselmann (already known to the theatre public for her interpretation of Esther in Henri Nathansen's *Indenfor Murene* (Within the Walls) but not reputed to be a particularly strong singer), while Margot Lander performed the dancing Anna's part. As has been mentioned, the scenographer Svend Johansen was responsible for the decorations. The reviews that appeared in the dailies after the premiere were indeed very mixed but the one-sided picture of a unanimous rejection of the piece, which has been proliferated in the judgment of posterity, is simply not correct; as a matter of fact, the criticism covers the full spectrum, ranging from total deprecation to wholehearted approval and enthusiasm. A modest sampling of the many and in-depth reviews that appeared after the premiere will illustrate this:

> ... very picturesque and often absolutely beautiful music in a jazz-sounding attire, as well as ... splendid execution. ... It appeared that the ballet caught the interest of the whole crowd of spectators. (*Børsen*, 13 November)

> As far as the text is concerned, 'De syv Dødssynder' has nothing to do with art but a lot to do with communist propaganda. Leaving Kurt Weill's music aside, the pantomime is a masked propaganda stunt without any spirit or wit. (*Nationaltidende*, 13 November)

> The satire sometimes seems to be strained and artificial. The librettist moves his way into peculiar serpentine paths, but he has superb helpers, first and foremost in the

composer and next in the theatre's formidable apparatus, directed by Harald Lander.
... modern stylization that trumps anything that has ever been seen before. ... as far
as the manipulation of the projector goes, The Royal Theatre is soon going to be the
leading venue among Europe's stages. ... This is a *tour de force*, an experiment, which
will be called 'dangerous' by some and will be called a magnificent explosion by others.
(*Politiken*, 13 November)

The choir was stationed down in the orchestra pit – and the next outburst may well be
that the Royal Theatre Orchestra's musicians will be moved up underneath the chande-
lier and that the actors will be walking on their hands. (*Socialdemokraten*, 13 November)

As was the case with 'Katerina' [Shostakovich's *Katerina Ismailova*], The Royal Theatre
is once again making a contribution that is remarkable, whatever one's objections to
'Dødssynderne' as a work of art might be. (Otto Mortensen in *Arbejderbladet*, 13 November)

The most vehemently bombastic tirade was spewed forth by an anonymous reviewer
in the *Berlingske Aftenavis*. Under the headline 'Ballet Fiasco at The Royal [Theatre]',
we can read these few excerpts:

Only a ROYAL of, if you prefer, a NATIONAL THEATRE possesses the naïveté necessary for presenting this kind of lampoon for its regular patrons, who generally reside
in villas and generally eat their fill. ... When the curtain fell, the response on the part
of the public can be described as follows: a grand total of one solitary person clapping;
a grand total of one lone whistler; and the rest – sleeping peacefully! ... A performance that serves up old-fashioned Danish culture as the main course and symbolism
for the mentally retarded as dessert does not belong on Kongens Nytorv![23] (*Berlingske
Aftenavis*, 13 November)

The Royal Theatre's own choice of genre designation (*pantomime*) induced *Berlingske Tidende*'s reviewer to offer a few penetrating and critical reflections on the future
of modern ballet, taking a point of departure in the daring experiment with precisely
this staging, which is juxtaposed, in the review, with Kjeld Abell's *Enken i Spejlet*.
After having ascertained this connection between the two productions, the reviewer
(writing under the signature, 'S') continues:

The genre is an attempt at making a renewal of ballet as a branch of art; what is interesting, though, is that modern ballet-goers, who have heretofore reacted so fiercely,
for example, to all the narrative aspects in the Bournonville ballets are now being
faced with modern ballets – where everything is narrative. ... The next step is going
to be that ballet will nullify itself as a branch of art ... We are balancing on the fringe
of this branch of art. But in 'De syv Dødssynder', as in 'Enken i Spejlet', the balance is
maintained. After all, is appears that *theatre* has emerged from the experiments: a very
extraordinary and intransigent yet living modern theatre. ... There is really a renewal
that dwells in a ballet like 'De syv Dødssynder'; – that Harald Lander has so daringly
applied himself to the way of working deserves a great deal of recognition and the
results he has achieved deserve its just rewards with a genuinely sympathetic backing
from the interested public. (*Berlingske Tidende*, 13 November)

23 Location of The Royal Theatre in Copenhagen then and today.

Viewpoints like these – albeit with a much less nuanced form of expression – subsequently gained resonance in the international ballet literature. The relatively brief mention of Harald Lander's *Dødssynderne* that appears in Cyril W. Beaumont's ballet lexicon from 1955 is positioned as an extension of a discussion about the expressionistic style in the two ballets mentioned above:

> Although this expressionist style was opposed to the tradition of academic ballet, as a ballet, it offered no unusual contrast, theatrically considered, to the older Bournonville ballet-drama; it was the nature of the theme and not its form that evoked discussion.[24]

The daily newspapers' reception does not appear to corroborate this assumption.

In a special section, *Nationaltidende* printed an in-depth discussion about the music, written by the university's professor in musicology, Erik Abrahamsen. Here, we can read:

> This time around, Kurt Weill is really just – Kurt Weill again. It is the tone from the other pieces [*The Threepenny Opera* and *Mahagonny*], now moved over into new surroundings, without advance, without energy. ... and what is more, Weill himself falls every now and then into one of the very worst mortal sins: tediousness ... A few of Anna's songs will probably be plugged as *Schlagers* and will presumably be sold in numerous copies in shops dispensing sheet music and record stores. But before a month has passed, people will get sick and tired of them. (*Nationaltidende*, 13 November)

In his prophecy about the work's future reception, the professor was wrong here! Such a thing *can* happen. By contract, Axel Kjærulf's comments, printed in *Politiken*, were more nuanced:

> As long as Weill complies with the scenic tableaus, his work is admirable, young, new and fresh. But one can hardly be as enthusiastic about the idea of letting one of the Annas, the representative of reason, sing everything that is happening in a kind of recitative style. It is – musically speaking – low-grade and insufferable jazz affectation, which has gradually degenerated into a commonplace and insipid jargon. (*Politiken*, 13 November)

Meanwhile, *Ekstrabladet*'s Christen Fribert expressed his unmitigated enthusiasm:

> But what would it be altogether without Kurt Weill's music? With such mysterious skill, you see, has this gifted composer understood how to paint time in music! Seemingly, so very atonal and jazz-tinged but nonetheless so sincerely melodic and saturated with timbres and sounds. (*Ekstrabladet*, 13 November)

---

24 Cyril W. Beaumont, *Ballets Past and Present: Being a Third Supplement to the Complete Book of Ballets* (London, 1955), 75. Ballet scholar Knud Arne Jürgensen has most amicably pointed out that Beaumont's formulation is, in all likelihood, a simplified condensation of a passage on p. 126 in Allan Fridericia's *Harald Lander og hans Balletter* (Copenhagen, 1951); Lander and Beaumont were friends and were connected to each other, professionally.

Ill. 3. The sisters' family, to whom they send back the money they earn during their tour so that they can build a small house in Louisiana (Photo: Holger Damgaards Teaterfotos, The Royal Library, Copenhagen).

Ill. 4. Street scene from the 7th tableau, with Illona Wieselmann and Margot Lander as, respectively, Anna 1 and Anna 2 in the foreground and an unknown number of Annas in the rear (Photo: Holger Damgaards Teaterfotos, The Royal Library, Copenhagen).

In summary, it can be ascertained that the premiere certainly aroused a considerable degree of interest in the Copenhagen press and that opinions, as has been made evident, were sharply divided: predictable dismissals of Brecht as a communist, a lack of understanding for what the piece signifies and also contemptuous deprecation of Weill's music as a carbon copy of the *song* style from *The Threepenny Opera* and *Mahagonny* stand side by side with acknowledgements of the theatre's courage to tread new pathways, praise of Svend Johansen's scenic decorations and Lander's staging, as well as a sense of openness about the exceptional quality of expression in Weill's music. Thus it appeared that the stage was set for a run that would extend for a number of performances that could offer a wider public the opportunity to judge for themselves.

As fate would have it, things did not pan out in this way. The second performance, presented on the day after the premiere – and, like the premiere, before a sold-out house[25] – unfolded without any problems, even though some of the newspapers emphasized that the audience did appear to be responding rather apathetically to the performance. However, after this second performance, the show was taken off the bill without any advance warning and the production was not resumed again – and all this despite the great deal of preparation that had been put into the production and the long sequence of rehearsals preceding the opening night. The post-war era's explanation for all this, which is recapitulated in one account after the other is that

25 According to The Royal Theatre's *Journal* for Friday, 13 Nov. 1936.

the theatre manager was supposedly subjected to some kind of pressure from either the Danish royal house or from the German ambassador in Denmark, with reference to the ballet's anti-Nazi content. This hypothesis will be elaborated further and rendered thematic in the following section.

ANDREAS MØLLER, THE NAZIS, THE FATE OF THE PERFORMANCE

The story that it was an intervention from the German quarter that stopped the production of *De syv Dødssynder* after only two performances has laconically been expressed many places in the literature. However, there is no place that this part of the saga has been convincingly documented or further qualified. The main source of the 'story' is supposedly Harald Lander's memoirs from 1951.[26] Here, Lander mentions the ballet as being one of his very best works and calls it, on the one hand, an 'artistic peak' in his collaboration with Svend Johansen and, on the other hand, 'a resounding fiasco'. About the alleged German intervention, Landers has this to say:

> From the German embassy, an unofficial protest against the ballet was directed to the [Danish] Foreign Ministry. Unfortunately, I have never managed to have the form in which this transpired explained to me. After the war was over, I made an inquiry 'on the highest rung of the ladder', but even though people could remember very well that there had been 'something', it was utterly impossible to find anything more out about this 'something'. Maybe people just weren't all that interested, either, in pulling up the roots of this matter.[27]

The same rumours are also vented in the first major biography about Lander, which was written by Allan Fridericia and was published the same year as were Lander's memoirs – both books appearing at a time, furthermore, when the public outcry about Lander's personal exploits was at its most volatile point.[28] After having offered an account of the press's smear campaign against the ballet, which was fuelled by the work's alleged 'communistic' leanings, Fridericia adds this brief comment:

> Rumours have been circulating that the German legation made a request to the foreign ministry to have the ballet closed down. Closed down it was, in any event.[29]

In this connection, Fridericia stresses that resistance to the production was grounded in 'the communistic Brecht and the Jewish Kurt Weill – not [in] the artistic style that the work had come to acquire, even though it broke away from classical ballet in many ways'.[30] In point of fact, the latter circumstance – i.e. the ballet's expressionistic style and its plot-characterized content – ought to have felt less foreign to a Danish ballet public, according to Fridericia, than it would have felt to ballet-

---

26 Harald Lander, *Thi kendes for ret –? Erindringer* (Copenhagen, 1951), 58.

27 Ibid. 59.

28 It was in this connection that Lander was compelled to relinquish his position as ballet master after having served for nineteen years at The Royal Theatre.

29 Allan Fridericia, *Harald Lander og hans Balletter* (Copenhagen, 1951), 125.

30 Ibid.

goers in so many other places in the world, as a direct consequence of Denmark's Bournonville-tradition, which – albeit in an very different way – placed an emphasis on the mimic element.

The most recent Lander biography, which appeared in 2005, is somewhat more circumspect. In a caption to a photograph of the performance in 1936, it says, laconically: 'The Royal Theatre got scared of its own audacity. Or was it the Germans that intervened?'[31] Later on, in the biography's main text, Aschengreen writes that it was the theatre manager who had confirmed the Germans' intervention but that he also forbade Harald Lander from pursuing the matter further. In a footnote, Aschengreen offers an account of his own vain attempts, through examining documents at various archives, to either confirm or deny the story about the German interference.[32] Neither did my own investigations made at The Danish National Archives, where I was able to examine the theatre manager's personal files in the summer of 2007, unveil any kind of documentation pertinent to these circumstances.[33]

The story that the Danish king might also have been implicated apparently stems from Ruth Berlau who, in her memoirs, claims that the king (King Christian X) left his loge inside the theatre in a fit of protest against the performance, uttering the words: 'No, this is not what the illustrious Danish Royal Ballet was intended for'.[34] About this, it can only be remarked that not even one of the many reviews makes any mention that the Danish king was present at the premiere, let alone that he would have stood up and stormed out from the show. When we consider how much attention is concentrated whenever there happens to be royalty in the house at The Royal Theatre, it seems unthinkable that such an event could have transpired without the press catching sight of it.

Both explanations about the affair – German intervention and royal indignation – have been reproduced in virtually all the Danish and foreign accounts of the piece's fate in Copenhagen in 1936.[35] However, there is nothing in either the sources or in

31 Erik Aschengreen, *Mester. Historien om Harald Lander* (Copenhagen, 2005), 75; an English transl. has been published as *Harald Lander. His Life and Ballets* (Alton, 2009).

32 Aschengreen, *Mester*, 454.

33 The only document in theatre manager Andreas Møller's official archives that has to do with *De syv Dødssynder* is one item of correspondence, dating from the summer of 1937, with Skandinavisk Film- og Teaterforlag (Scandinavian Film- and Theatre-Publishers) touching upon Brecht's request to be paid a commission based on the box-office receipts (Rigsarkivet, *Det kgl. Teater. Teaterchef Andreas Møller. 1931-1938. Embedsarkiv. Kasse 1143*). Nor has the closed section of Andreas Møller's archives, to which I was granted right of access after having made a formal request, proved to contain any relevant material. Erik Aschengreen has amicably informed that neither his review of the full gamut of Lander's archive at The Royal Library nor other investigations that he conducted at a number of other archives before his book was published in 2005 yielded any results that could shed any light on this question.

34 Hans Bunge (ed.), *Brechts Lai-Tu. Erindringer af Ruth Berlau* (Copenhagen, 1985), 87.

35 Among the countless examples, I can mention the few accounts appearing in Ronald Haymann, *Brecht, A Biography* (London, 1983), 198; Bertolt Brecht, *Ausgewählte Werke in sechs Bänden. Jubiläumsausgabe zum 100. Geburtstag* (Frankfurt a.M., 1997), vol. 1, 678; Marianne Kesting, *Bertolt Brecht in Selbstzeugnissen und Bilddokumenten* (Rowolt Monographien, 37; 1970); Drew, *Kurt Weill. A Handbook*, 247.

the day's newspapers that serves to give credence to either story. More correctly, the affair has its roots in two entirely different circumstances: the one being altogether tangible, namely Illona Wieselmann's calling in sick after the second performance, where she appeared with 'feverish heat burning on her cheeks';[36] and the other being more diffuse as a kind of self-censorship emanating from theatre director Andreas Møller in the wake of the general criticism levelled at parts of the theatre's repertoire in November 1936.[37]

The criticism came from several different quarters. From the press's corner, the *Nationaltidende* led the charge. Full-page wide headlines like 'The Royal National Scene – an Experimental Bolshevik Theatre', 'Opinions are not tolerated on Kongens Nytorv unless the opinions agree with the salon-communistic propaganda line' and 'The red front on Kongens Nytorv is teetering' make their point in a very clear way.[38] On top of this, additional reinforcements from the ecclesiastical brigade turned up the following week in the form of an assault on the theatre launched by archdeacon Fog-Petersen at a clerical meeting in Odense that was covered exhaustively in the press. The tone in the archdeacon's attack calls to mind certain aspects of the cultural debate in today's Denmark.[39] Listen to what it says in *Nationaltidende*'s summary of an excerpt of the speech:

> And a few days after [the performance of *Katerina Ismailova*], a pantomime is per-formed, which has been written by a German communist who is making use of his right to seek asylum here in Denmark in order to agitate on behalf of communism: an agitation that is tinged by dubiousness and cunning. This is an attack on and a ridicul-ing of the church and of Christianity on our national stage and it is being paid for by Danish taxpayers. ... Luther did not shrink from battle and we must not do so, either.[40]

The latter assault brought about a brief reply in the form of an open letter from the theatre manager and the conflict heaved back and forth in this fashion for the rest of November, after which it appears to have subsided, although we can see that on 16 December, *Ekstrabladet* makes one last low-voiced attempt at resuscitating the hub-bub with an open letter set in large type, penned by Gudmund Roger-Henrichsen, which appears under the headline 'SEASON'S GREETINGS TO THE THEATRE

---

36 Press release, which simultaneously informs that the part cannot be performed by an understudy, reproduced in most of the Copenhagen newspapers on 17 Nov. 1936. Furthermore, *Ekstrabladet* announces on the following day that the production will be presented again in the new year, seeing as 'the theatre is said to have been assailed with requests to program the work from both season ticketholders and non-subscribers'.

37 The theatre manager's and the theatre's balancing act in relation to Nazi Germany have been described in detail in Hans Bay-Petersen, *En selskabelig invitation. Det Kongelige Teaters gæstespil i Nazi-Tyskland i 1930'erne* (Copenhagen, 2003).

38 *Nationaltidende*, 15, 22, and 29 Nov. 1936.

39 Elsewhere, mention is made of Brecht in this fashion: 'a communistic homeowner like Mr Brecht, who has taken asylum here in our country' and Svend Johansen is mentioned in this way: 'Svend Johansen, a Bolshevik, who frequents both Restaurant Nimb and the villas of the millionaires'; *Nationaltidende*, 15 Nov. 1936.

40 *Nationaltidende*, 26 Nov. 1936.

MANAGER. Let "De syv Dødssynder" come up again!' After this, it seems that the peace of Christmas time descended on Kongens Nytorv.

In the theatre magazine, *Forum*, theatre manager Andreas Møller summarized the whole dilemma around the national scene in more general terms – again, in such a way that calls today's current culture debate to mind:

> If The Royal Theatre produces a piece by Nordahl Grieg, then it is orthodoxly communistic; if we put on the old play 'Everybody', then the angriest reaction is enthroned. When we have a month filled with new things, then we are neglecting our obligation to the established legacy that has been handed down from generation to generation. And when we, for one time's sake, focus particularly on the classical or even the 'standard repertoire', then we are utterly deficient in showing any interest for what is new in our day. The Royal Theatre's repertoire has to be viewed in a more long-term perspective.[41]

Because the debate about *Dødssynderne* was raised in such a way that it came to encompass The Royal Theatre as a whole, this was due especially to the fact that just a few weeks earlier, a similar debate was taking place about the theatre's staging of Shostakovich's opera, *Katerina Ismailova* (with the original title, *Lady Macbeth fra Mtensk-Distriktet* (Lady Macbeth of the Mtsensk District)). With resounding success, the opera had premiered in Leningrad and Moscow only two years before, with numerous performances. Before being presented in Copenhagen, it had also been mounted in Stockholm – albeit without arousing much enthusiasm. In Copenhagen, however, the opera made quite a splash with the public even though certain critics bridled over its fundamentally 'politically correct' (i.e. communistic) stance. What is paradoxical about the latter critique is, of course, that the production on Kongens Nytorv was presented less than nine months after the famous article in *Pravda* (presumably written on behalf of The Supreme Soviet and maybe even by Stalin himself) that stigmatized Shostakovich, in no uncertain terms, as a foe of the system and, in any event, warned him against moving any further along the trail he previously had been treading.[42]

After the second performance of *Katerina Ismailova* at The Royal Theatre, the cigar-maker, Paul Wulff, and his wife wrote an open letter to the theatre manager where, in turns of speech that would come to evoke reminiscences, later on, of the Rindalism from the 1960s, Wulff protested that young people, in particular, could be endangered when they were presented with something like this on Denmark's national stage. It was especially the 'raw' sexual scenes to which the cigar-maker took exception. This resulted in a protracted newspaper debate around the topic – much like the debate about Weill's piece a few weeks later – where the lines were drawn in a very emphatic way. Also a number of rather amusing items concerning the matter turned up.[43]

41 *Forum*, Nov. 1936, quot. Bay-Petersen, *En selskabelig invitation*, 8.
42 The article with the headline 'Chaos instead of music' could be read in *Pravda*, 28 Jan. 1936.
43 For example, on 13 Oct. 1936, *Ekstrabladet* printed a cartoon of an affluent married couple who are leaving the Royal Theatre after a performance of the opera – *he* with a huge cigar in his mouth, *she* with an expensive fur coat. The caption reads: 'Art critics at Kongens Nytorv. / She: The cigar-maker is correct. That was an awful scene. / He: Yes, but she was a good little cigar, anyway!'

The debate that was carried on in the newspapers gave rise to rumours about demonstrations going on in front of the theatre but it also entailed that a number of subsequent performances were sold out – something which was unheard of before the debate! As we have noted, the debate about *Katerina Ismailova* came to bear an influence – albeit indirectly – on the calamitous fate that befell Weill's *Dødssynder*. In contrast to Weill's work, however, Shostakovich's opera was allowed to continue in the repertoire where, after fifteen performances, it was taken off the bill the following season.

CONCLUSION

The present reception-historical examination of the two performances of *Die sieben Todsünden* in Copenhagen in 1936 constitutes an attempt to map out, as far as the sources render it possible to do so, the circumstances behind the performances and the cultural and political climate surrounding The Royal Theatre that fashion the backdrop. Although the aim here has not been to debunk entirely the oft-repeated assertion that the production's ill-starred fate can be linked up with pressure from the German quarter, a question mark behind the validity of this hypothesis is introduced. Phenomena like 'public opinion', smear campaigns in the daily press and self-criticism in conjunction with an oddly incidental sick-leave sought by and granted to one of the key players in the show appear instead to have been the factors behind the cancellation of the show's run – more than any intervention from the German or from the Danish royal house; no such intervention, in any event, has been documented in any one of the contemporary sources. Such a conclusion might have some relevance to bear – provided that it is correct – because, in that event, it refutes virtually all previous accounts of this little corner of the Weill-reception in Denmark. We could move further and start to talk about narrow-mindedness and provincialism in the face of the foreign and the unknown – but this would fall outside the compass of the present exposition.

SUMMARY

Kurt Weill's *The Seven Deadly Sins* to a text by Bertolt Brecht from 1933 marks the end of the stormy collaboration during the six previous years between the two artists. The work was only performed a few times during Weill's lifetime, and among these the performance at The Royal Theatre in Copenhagen in November 1936 was the one that was given most public attention. Both before and after the performance, the Copenhagen press focused intensively on the work, partly because of its political contents, partly because it was not possible to pigeonhole the work in any of the well known musical and dramatic genres. To this should be added the myth that German interference was the reason why the work was only given two performances in Copenhagen. The article is based on sources in The Royal Theatre and The State Archives in Copenhagen, supplemented with contemporary newspapers.

APPENDIX 1: SOURCES

In the following, a brief overview of the source material is presented for purposes of casting light on the circumstances surrounding the present reception case.

There is a plentiful supply of press material that is quoted herein from The Royal Theatre's scrapbook covering the period 1 May, 1936 – 23 January, 1937. At that time, the theatre's scrapbook was maintained so conscientiously that there are hardly any daily newspaper notices or reviews that were not pasted into its pages. When it comes to the censorship's declaration, we face a somewhat odd kind of situation. Ordinarily, in connection with any piece submitted to The Royal Theatre for consideration, there is a handwritten evaluation ('censur') with an assessment of the piece in question as well as an indication of whether or not it has been accepted for being included in the theatre's repertoire. In the evaluation for *Dødssynderne,* which was apparently drawn up after the premiere, we read this laconic entry: 'Accepted and played. No evaluation'.[44]

The *stage manager's register* contains scrupulously entered specifications of the set pieces' disposition in each of the seven tableaus (in the 7th scene, even a 'set-piece from *Elverhøj*'(Elves' Hill) was employed!) and the register also contains photographs of the stationary skyscraper-set piece as well as details from the 2nd, 3rd, 4th, and 5th scene-tableaus.

The journal, which could be said to be the theatre's diary, with entries made for each and every rehearsal and each and every performance, indicates that the performance was sold out on both 12 and 13 November. Furthermore, the complete casting is specified and there is a special mention about the second performance that Enna's opera was received with applause that increased in intensity 'when the public noticed the composer in the stalls'. Nothing at all is noted about the reception of *Dødssynderne*. Finally, the journal also documents that Illona Wieselmann called in sick from Saturday, 14 November and was reported fit for standing on stage again on Wednesday, 18 November, as has been mentioned above.

The *stage management register* lists the complete cast, both for the two performances in 1936 and for the twenty-five performances presented in the 1969/70 season.

Finally, the *theatre's photographic archives* contain a good many photographs of people and decorations.

There are also parts of the performance material from 1936 that have been preserved, consisting of the full score and a few of the individual parts (fl.2, cl.2, cor.2, tr.2);[45] what we have is a professionally made copy with the marginal note, 'Transcribed from the original score on 4–12 January, 1936' (Afskrevet efter Orginalpartituret 4–12 Jan 1936). The Danish text, in Otto Gelsted's translation, has been inscribed with blue-coloured crayon and there is no German text appearing on the pages of the score. What is not indicated is: who it was that executed the copies; who it was that procured the original score; and what became of the rest of the parts.[46]

44 The Royal Theatre, [Evaluation] *1935-36, No. 81 1935/36.*
45 The Royal Theatre's Music Archives, *998: De syv Dødssynder. Partitur.*
46 The original performance material is registered by Drew, *Kurt Weill. A Handbook,* 245 ('Full Score').

The text exists in two versions which, first of all, deviate from one another with respect to the stage manager's comments and also deviate to some extent from the full score in the division of the scenes: as a mimeographed *ballet libretto* (15 pages) bearing the title 'Ballet in seven tableaus with prologue and epilogue' and as a type-written *manuscript* (26 pages) consisting of seven tableaus and a finale:

1st scene: 'Park with bench'
2nd scene: 'Night café with ceiling lamp and scene'
3rd scene: 'Film studio'
4th scene: 'The diva's room. Balance, dining table'
5th scene: 'Street scene. Sidewalk café'
6th scene: 'Street scene. Newsstand. Poster pillar'
7th scene: 'Street scene. Many Annas'
Finale: 'Lousiana. The house in the background. The river. Moonlight'
'Notice boards on the stage. The family'

Unfortunately, what is presumably a very important portion of the source material has not been made available in connection with the present study. This involves a number of letters between Weill, Edward James, Skandinavisk Teaterforlag (Scandinavian Theatre Publishers) and other parties related to the performance in Copenhagen, all of which are presently in possession of The West Dean Estate in England, which was owned from 1912 by Edward James, who originally approached Weill and Brecht in 1933, in Paris, and asked the two collaborators to create *Die sieben Todsünden*. A request to review this material submitted by the author to The West Dean Estate has not yet received a response and there is no information about their documents on the Internet. The Kurt Weill Foundation for Music in New York, which previously enjoyed access to these documents, has kindly informed that this body of correspondence touches upon the permission to mount the performance, upon efforts to get Weill to send the score to Copenhagen so that it could be copied out, upon certain controversies arising as a result of Brecht's attempts to obstruct the show (albeit at a time when it was already removed from the programme) and so on and so forth, but that nothing is revealed here concerning the reasons why the show was discontinued after the second performance.[47]

---

47 According to an e-mail sent to the author from Dr Dave Stein, former archivist at the Kurt Weill Foundation for Music in New York. Later, extracts from the correspondence have been published in *Kurt Weill Newsletter*, 29/1 (Spring 2011), 7.

Appendix 2: Vocal register

Upon Kurt Weill's death in 1950, Lotte Lenya took upon her shoulders the life mission of widening people's familiarity with her late husband's music, both in Europe and in the United States. On account of her energy, her artistic calibre and her role as Weill's life mate and collaborator, with all its ups and downs, in the course of all the years after 1926, her interpretation actually took on an almost canonical, school-generating status. It was not until after Lenya's death in 1981 that younger Weill singers dared to come forth with other bids on a Weill-interpretation.

However, what was conjoined with Lenya's admirable efforts dedicated to the spreading of Weill's music and the establishment of a special 'Weill style' was a specific problem that came to make a marked impact on the Weill-reception in the decades after 1950: the music had to be adapted to Lenya's voice and interpretive capabilities, and not the other way around. In order to illuminate this, we will cite three examples:

The famous 'Seeräuberjenny' (Pirate Jenny) song in *Dreigroschenoper* from Brecht's hand was intended for the innocent Polly. For a fleeting moment, in a dream, she experiences – like a play within the play – a sense of unbounded power that fortifies her with the possibility of chopping off the heads of all of her exploiters and joining up with the pirates who have arrived in the harbour. In Polly's mouth, this song appears in all its mortal danger before the spectators sitting in the theatre (read: the bourgeoisie). But when Lenya, after some years had elapsed, could no longer sing and play the role of the very young Polly – but still wanted to hold onto this bravura showstopper – the song was excised from Polly's part and transferred to the low-dive and cast-off madam Jenny, who was now being played by Lenya. While when sung in Polly's mouth, the piece is an ingeniously dramatic and political *memento* in the opera, it becomes altogether trivial in Jenny's mouth – and is reduced to nothing more than a 'number'.[48]

The second example has to do with the opera, *Aufstieg und Fall der Stadt Mahagonny*. Also here, Lenya acquired, and very early on, a kind of 'monopoly' on the role of the main female protagonist, Jenny. Due to the fact that, as the years rolled by, Lenya's voice could not tackle the high notes with finesse, certain hits like 'Denn wie man sich bettet' (As You Make Your Bed) and 'Alabama-Song' had to be transposed down, respectively, a perfect fourth and a perfect fifth: such a change obviously has an impact on the timbral picture. It knocks everything out of joint and makes matters utterly intolerable when Jenny's part is transposed down an octave in her duet with the tenor, with the result that a voice that was originally an upper part appears as the lower voice.[49]

---

48 On a good many CD-recordings of *Dreigroschenoper*, the song is presented twice: that is, it is sung first by Polly and later by Jenny – and thus the de-politicization has been carried off in a thorough way!

49 This problem has been illuminated further in Krabbe, 'Mahagonny hos Brecht og Weill', esp. 108–10.

Something analogous can be spotted in the third example, *Die sieben Todsünden*. Also here, Lenya's part had to be transposed down a perfect fourth in relation to how it is notated in Weill's original score (this involves parts 1, 3, 6, 8, and 9) thus dislocating the sound picture as well as the work's overall tonal disposition.[50]

This state of affairs is also reflected in the Danish source material for the performances of *Dødssynderne* at The Royal Theatre in, respectively, 1936 and 1969. The score from 1936, which is a copy of the original score, as has been mentioned, is not transposed. The material from 1969, on the other hand, which was used for the twenty-five performances on Kongens Nytorv during the 1969/70 season and also on the subsequent tour of the show, reproduces the aforementioned songs in the deeper transposed version.[51]

---

50 Lenya's transposed rendition is the basis in all the recordings of the work featuring her as the songstress, as well as in the piano score published by Edition Schott in 1960 (pl. no. 5078) which, complying with her request, reproduces the transposed version. Not until the edition from 1972 was the work restored to its original register and today, there is hardly anybody who would entertain the notion of performing *Die sieben Todsünden* in the transposed version.

51 From a perusal of the extant performance material from the tour, it comes to light that an adapted version of the original score for reduced ensemble was used, a version that was worked out by E. Lindorf-Larsen. The following instruments from the original version were omitted: fl.2, fg., tb. and banjo. In a pencilled-in note entered in the score, the arranger states: '*To whom it may concern*: I have not regarded it as my task to create a "new" instrumentation but rather the contrary: to retain, as far as it is possible to do so, the acoustic picture emanating from the original score. What this means to say, then, is that this [arrangement] is more of an adaptation of the original score than a genuine instrumentation'; The Royal Theatre's Music Archive.

Reports

Research Projects

POPULAR MUSIC AND MUSLIM YOUTH. STUDIES OF THE USE OF MUSIC AMONG YOUNG IMMIGRANTS IN DENMARK

Interesting new approaches are emerging as immigrant Muslim youth gain visibility and 'airtime' as cultural agents and consumers in a positive sense. It is the aim of this Ph.D. project (2011–2014, Section of Musicology, Department of Arts and Cultural Studies, University of Copenhagen) to apply tools of popular music research on selected groups of young Danes (age 13–20) who see themselves as Muslim. The goal is to identify and discuss significant characteristics of their everyday use of music, bearing in mind the dangers of reifying minority groups for such studies.

The project's central method is the anthropological small-scale study of people in their particular time and space, primarily by means of personal interviews and observation. This is backed up by webometric methods and virtual field work, since personal use of music and personal digital presence are getting increasingly inseparable qua mobile devices and Web 2.0. Technology potentially enables everybody to make their individual musical choices a public (even global) statement. 'Use of music' is thus to be understood in the broadest sense. Consequently, this project draws upon and elaborates on the theoretical idea of music as a 'technology of the self' (Tia DeNora, *Music in Everyday Life* (Cambridge, 2000)).

Religion and ethnicity are undoubtedly important factors in this context. But it is my hypothesis that they are far from simple or predictable determinants when it comes to the everyday musical choices made by individuals: the conflicts, the external forces, and (self-)censorship, which (I argue) affect music consumption in all cultures, are always having particular backgrounds and causes, whether that be gender, age, sexuality, socioeconomic factors, etc. It is worth considering, for example, whether some 'obvious' examples of conflicts between Muslim doctrines and music are in fact manifestations of mere generation clashes or other mundane power struggles involving music.

Johannes Frandsen Skjelbo

RESEARCHING MUSIC CENSORSHIP (RMC)

Researching Music Censorship is a researcher's network which started in 2009. The following year, the initiative was awarded a three-year grant from NordForsk and since its formal start in October 2010 the network has consisted of around 50 researchers and Ph.D. students from Norway, Sweden, Finland, and Denmark of which about 40 are full members. Added to this is an international group of associated scholars, who are leading in the field of censorship, human rights, and freedom of expression. The aim of RMC is to promote and encourage the scholarly study of music censorship, and to research the role of music in relation to human rights and artistic freedom of expression in its broadest sense.

The network operates in several formats. The Nordic members meet in workshops or larger meetings twice every year and are joined by shifting members of the extended network and invited speakers. The full group with international partners will meet in a final international conference in Copenhagen in June 2013. Concurrently the network also prioritizes activities, which add to the training of the research students connected to the network. Four separate Ph.D. seminars are offered and the students forming the core of the Ph.D. group also attend the shared meetings and workshops.

The main activities so far have been: 1) a workshop and Ph.D. seminar with international partners with the theme 'Contested Spaces: War, Torture, Violence, Suppression and Power' (Copenhagen, May 2011) with the keynote speakers Bruce Johnson and Martin Cloonan; 2) a Nordic meeting and Ph.D. seminar entitled 'The Politics of Difference; Gender and Race', held in Lund, September 2011, and on this occasion the keynote speakers were Julie Brown and Tari Leppänen; 3) a small thematic meeting on 'Women and Censorship in Islamic/ Muslim Music Cultures' (Copenhagen, October 2011) to which Mahsa and Marjan Vahdat, and Annette Belaoui were invited speakers; 4) a small thematic meeting on 'Censorship, Theory and Ethics' was held in Copenhagen, March 2012, with Martin Stokes as keynote speaker; 5) the second workshop with international partners as well as the third Ph.D. seminar was held in Oslo, April 2012; the theme of this workshop was 'Censorship and Self Censorship, Theory and Ethics' and invited keynote speakers were Karin van Nieuwkerk and John Hutnyk.

Other activities have included planning meetings with the international associates Steven Feld and Susan McClary and with NGOs such as Freemuse (Ole Reitov and Marie Korpe), Skarp (Swedish Popular Composers Union) and Kirkelig Kulturverksted (Erik Hillestad). These contacts have mostly been made by the coordinating committee consisting of Helmi Järvilouma-Mäkelä, Jan Sverre Knudsen, Jonas Otterbeck, and Annemette Kirkegaard. The larger planned activities include a Nordic meeting in Helsinki in October 2012 and an international conference in Copenhagen in June 2013.

RMC is based at University of Copenhagen, Department of Arts and Cultural Studies, headed by associate professor Annemette Kirkegaard, Denmark. The results and debates of the network will be made accessible to the public through a plan of dissemination in either digital or printed form. It is the goal to produce an anthology of texts, articles, and/or key-notes papers from the activities during the three-year period of the NordForsk grant; in addition, at least one digital volume in a periodical is planned. For further information and agendas for the meetings and workshops see the webpage www.rmc.ku.dk.

Annemette Kirkegaard

Conferences

Musics Cultures Identities – 19TH CONGRESS OF THE INTERNATIONAL MUSICOLOGICAL SOCIETY (IMS), ROME, JULY 2012

The congresses of the International Musicological Society (IMS) have been held since 1930, the first ten congresses with an intervening period of three years (and a ten-year disruption caused by World War Two), and since 1967 they has taken place every fifth year.[1]

In 2012 the congress was held in Italy for the second time – the first being 1987 in Bologna – namely in Rome on 1–7 July 2012, titled *Musics Cultures Identities*. The venue for the congress was the Auditorium Parco della Musica, situated in the northern part of the city, and consisting of a number of (very) large auditoriums and halls with more than enough space for the many different meetings and presentations, and all equipped with effective air-conditioning, absolutely imperative in the heat wave-ish summer. The walking distance

---

1   See reports from the 16th–18th congresses in *Danish Yearbook of Musicology*, 25 (1997), 79–80; ibid., 30 (2002), 96–99; and ibid., 35 (2007), 75–76.

between some of the rooms, though, was so big that it in effect rendered a 'zigzag' between sessions impossible.

Following the opening ceremony on Sunday afternoon the more than lengthy programme stretched from Monday morning to Saturday afternoon, the only 'departure' being Wednesday that consisted of three morning 'Special Round Tables' held at three different Roman universities, and a single – but expanded – 'Special Study Session' held in the afternoon at the Campo Santo Teutonico (Römisches Institut der Görres-Gesellschaft) in the Vatican City. For those who took this (half) day off a number of guided tours were arranged. In addition to the academic activities a spread of concerts, presentations, and tours to musical and non-musical institutions and sites were offered throughout the week.

More than 600 papers (*c.* 115 sessions) were presented at round tables (12 sessions), study sessions (21), and free paper sessions (59) on the one hand, and on the other in the context of the growing number of IMS Study Groups of which the following conducted sessions at the congress: Tablatures in Western Music, Music and Cultural Studies, Musical Iconography in European Art, RIIA Rapporti Italo Ibero Americani (Il teatro musicale), Digital Musicology, Shostakovich and His Epoch, Stravinsky between East and West, and Cantus Planus (yet another IMS Study Group, on Organology, was constituted on the so-called post conference on 8 July). Some of these sessions were actually closed meetings, and this also went for some of the activities related to the IMS Associated Projects, that is RILM, RISM, RIPM, and RIdIM, the two first mentioned also participating in one joint session on 'The transmission of musical knowledge in the internet age' with DIAMM (Digital Archive of Medieval Music), CESR (Centre d'Études Supérieures de la Renaissance), and Grove Music online.

To give an overview of a programme of this dimension is of course impossible. But given the important word 'international' in the title of the IMS one could ask if this congress – as opposed to nearly all other musicological gatherings that always are limited and confined in one way or the other – maintains its broadness in regard to geography and nationalities (as well as thematics)? Browsing through the titles of the many sessions it surely is evident that a significant number of papers were given on topics related to other continents than the European that, of course, is always well represented. Thus the most significant in this respect were five sessions on topics related to (East) Asian music, and nine sessions focusing on the music of Latin America, while topics related to Africa only took up one session.

Within the European context the growing interest in and subsequent research into the music cultures of Central Europe and the Balkans was reflected in five sessions. One of these, 'Central European identities in the 15th century', addressed the fact that while older literature on the subject viewed Central European culture as being of peripheral significance compared to the main European centres, more recent research has demonstrated that Central Europe should be regarded as a distinct region of Latin Europe. For instance, Michael Bernhard (Bayerische Akademie der Wissenschaften, Munich) in his paper, 'Music theory in the 15th century: Centres and interrelations', based on no less than 200 theoretical texts from the 15th century, pointed out significant similarities and differences between Italian and Central European treatises, among other things that elementary textbooks and books on chant theory from Central Europe outnumber the ones found in Italy, while the opposite goes for the more comprehensive presentations of music theory.

Another significant 'geographical' centre of attention was the Iberian Peninsula, while the overall thematic top scorer was – not surprisingly when taking the congress venue into consideration – Italian opera counting nearly ten sessions. As always in the IMS context jazz and popular music studies were grossly under-represented, this time reflected in only one session devoted to 'Popular music', while Medieval and Renaissance studies were well represented, in 2012 counting five sessions.

Another aspect of the 'international' denominator is the fact that IMS continues to uphold the old idea of five official languages – English, French, German, Italian, and Spanish – in writing and speech within the societal framework. Hence, nearly ten percent of the papers were not presented in English, and in some cases the discussion at a session were conducted in Italian, for instance. Viewed from one angle this courtesy towards communities that are not predominantly connected to the Anglo-American highway is sympathetic, and hopefully it occasions a higher attendance from these language groups than perhaps otherwise would be the case, but at the congress it seemed as if some of the sessions that were conducted in, say Spanish, predominantly attracted the 'home audience' of the speakers; so viewed from another angle perhaps an all-Anglophone congress actually would prompt a bigger audience to the 'marginal' topics and geographies, and isn't that what the whole idea of academic gatherings of this sort is all about?

The interest in the IMS in the Scandinavian countries has for many years been steadily declining, and only a few Scandinavian colleagues participated in the congress. Nevertheless, Karin Strinnholm Lagergren (Linneaus University, Växjö), in her paper 'Gregorian Chant and "Gregorian Chant" in popular music. A question of our own identity and search for meaning', focused on the use and inspiration of so-called Gregorian chant in western popular music culture, asking why it has come to invade something so alien from its original context. The presentation was given in the abovementioned Cantus Planus session and the reaction – especially my own inclusive – to the paper was that after decades and myriads of papers dealing with the contexts and technicalities of plainchant *per se* at last someone addresses the question of its widespread use and popularity in modern popular music. The programme displayed one singular session on a Nordic/Baltic theme, 'The scope of a Nordic composer's identity: National cultures and exotism', and the singular paper presented by a Danish musicologist was the author's 'A correspondence of 20th-century musicologists: The private archive of Knud Jeppesen at the Royal Library, Copenhagen', presented at a session on 'Historiography'.

Given the fact that no official IMS archive indeed exists and that Jeppesen acted as president of the IMS during 1949–52 and the editor of *Acta Musicologica* 1931–53 – for which reason his private archive contains a lot of correspondence related to the IMS in one way or the other – the Jeppesen collection in all probability can contribute to shed light on a number of 'chapters' in the history of the organization. One of the most interesting and intriguing events in this connection was the third congress of the IMS that took place in Barcelona in 1936. Although dealt with to some extend in the published literature, by Pamela Potter among others, a session titled 'Nationalism and international ideals in music and musicology: Barcelona, April 1936' was dedicated to this subject. Whether these efforts – with or without the inclusion of the Jeppesen files – eventually will result in a publication only time will tell, but it certainly would be in place, and in accordance with so many other historiographic projects of our time, if the history of the IMS, or at least parts thereof, could be published, involving all the materials and evidence – old as well as new – that by now have surfaced.

A publication of this kind inevitably would be forced to take into consideration the justification and legitimacy of the IMS, viewed in retrospect as well as ongoing and prospective. To my knowledge IMS is still the only musicological organization that on a worldwide scale encompasses the academic study of music almost without delimitations, which indeed makes it a rare bird: and a talk of rare birds easily becomes a talk concerning the risk of extirpation. The following years will show the survivability of this unique society, the congresses of which constitute a display window of great potential and truly contains *tutti frutti* literally speaking. At least until 2017 the species at any rate seems to be protected.

At the ordinary general assembly of the IMS conducted on Thursday afternoon, it was decided that the 20th congress of the IMS will take place in Tokyo, Japan, in 2017. The circumstances leading to this decision, though, were nevertheless scandalous. As has been the custom for many years the potential hosts of the next congress, in this case Melbourne (Australia), Tokyo (Japan), and Stavanger (Norway), presented a short invitation each – a speech supplemented with music and power point presentation – that was followed by a voting of the IMS-members present at the assembly. Due to the number of inviting cities the voting had to be performed repeatedly resulting in a total chaos that was both pathetic and unworthy of a general assembly. After the decisive ballot, Stavanger came out as the winning city, but after yet another, very dubious ballot, Tokyo was announced victor. The procedure was a much discouraging closing of the assembly that previously had voted for a number of changes of the statutes, among other things that the approval of the place of the next congress henceforth is determined not by the general assembly but by the Directory of the IMS; perhaps a small consolation upon the larceny Stavanger had suffered.

Two partly related things remain to be said: although the mandatory book containing information, the programme, and the abstracts of the congress was impressive (and valued at 50 euros) and the congress venue was nearly perfect, the congress fee of no less than 260–90 euros seemed undue. Coffee was served at a cup-to-cup-basis from behind a counter, so although the fee included 'free' coffee and although there were several counters at the Auditorium Parco della Musica, everybody had to queue again and again and again for tiny mouthfuls of the fuel congresses run on. More coffee, lower fee, next time, please!

Thomas Holme Hansen

SEVENTH INTERNATIONAL CONFERENCE ON MUSIC SINCE 1900 & LANCASTER UNIVERSITY MUSIC ANALYSIS CONFERENCE, LANCASTER, JULY 2011

For the latest instalment in the successful series of British biennial conferences on music since 1900, this time held at Lancaster University, 28–31 July 2011, the organizers had decided to join forces with the Lancaster University Music Analysis Conference and thus integrate the two events. As conference chairman Edward Venn put it in the programme book: 'I hope that the joint conference facilitates a productive intermingling and cross-fertilisation of ideas that would otherwise be much harder to achieve in separate events'. The result was almost one hundred and fifty papers on offer in seven more or less integrated parallel sessions and each with five simultaneous presentations. Most were given by British scholars or delegates from other English speaking territories. While picking one's way through this cornucopia of possibilities, at least this delegate was only marginally aware of the additions to the usual conference profile. As before, the main focus was on twentieth-century art music and culture. However, this in itself diversified core was encircled by a plethora of contributions that brought almost any imaginable kind of music and research question or approach into play, naturally with musico-analytical interests to the fore this time.

Four plenary sessions provided delegates with some common ground during their individual session shopping: the first of two panel sessions had members of the RMA Music and Philosophy Study Group present and debate various aspects of the notion of temporality in relation to the analysis of contemporary music under the heading 'Marking Time: On Contemporary Music and Historical Analysis'. As is often the case with panels based on input from individual research projects, all interesting in their own right, the lack of a specific key question addressed by all to facilitate dialogues resulted in the sum being less than its parts. The same was true of the second panel-based plenary session on metaphor where quite different conceptual understandings of this widely applied term did nonetheless demonstrate many current uses and the quite diverse insights they might generate. The first of two individual keynote lectures was given by Canadian music theorist Henry Klumpenhouwer, originator of an analytical methodology centred on Klumpenhouwer networks (K-net practice) used for the 'uncovering' of structural characteristics in so-called atonal music. This explicitly method-technical discourse was complemented by the concluding keynote lecture by American ethnomusicologist Philip Bohlman, whose attempt to couple his recent preoccupation with aporia as a contextual theme with an analytical cross-cultural exploration of how the aporetic is located within music, had an almost poetic quality. Whatever combination of analytically oriented paper presentations each delegate may have accrued besides these plenary sessions, at this conference it was difficult not to be struck by the wealth of often seemingly contradictory analytical approaches and strategies that are explored and applied in our incessant attempts to make sense of music. Not to mention the resulting ontological ramifications on the very concept or rather concepts of music.

To vary the programme and let the music speak, no less than four musical entertainments were included. Two lunchtime events with scholarly overtones, a concert by William Hughes dedicated to his own transcriptions of Bill Evans recordings and a lecture recital by Nicholas Ross on golden proportion in piano works by Debussy, were appropriately housed in the Jack Hylton Room, named for the legendary British dance band leader and impresario, a local musical hero. In the first of two evening concerts, pianist Martin Roscoe offered a varied recital programme ranging from Haydn to Rawsthorne, not forgetting to contribute to the anniversary celebration of Liszt, who stole the ears (at least of this listener) with the wonderfully brazen pop qualities of *Bénédiction de Dieu dans la solitude*. But the musical highlight was created by the RedArch Duo in a concert of exclusively contemporary British works. The combination of live electronics by Paul Archbold with the almost otherworldly obo playing by Roger Redgate on custom-built instruments made for an intense musical experience that put the intellectual exploration of musical worlds, the main purpose of the conference, into perspective.

As usual the conference was well organized and well run, not least thanks to a large team of efficient student helpers and technical assistants, so essential to today's laptop attached and multi-media juggling presenters. And no doubt the relaxed and almost intimate atmosphere of the conference did in no small measure stem from the new, beautiful LICA building (Lancaster Institute for the Contemporary Arts) functioning as the welcoming heart of the whole event.

Steen Kaargaard Nielsen

CARL NIELSEN: INHERITANCE AND LEGACY, COPENHAGEN, NOVEMBER 2011

The Royal Library was the venue for an international conference, 'Carl Nielsen: Inheritance and Legacy', 3–5 November 2011. The idea was to consider Carl Nielsen's position within European music history and to see what he inherited as well as how other composers carried on and how his legacy was shaped in public reception. The conference was organized as a co-operation by the Royal Library and the Section for Musicology at the University of Copenhagen, as well as the Royal Danish Academy of Music whose students gave a Nielsen recital in the Queen's Hall of the Library at the end of the conference. Another recital was given in the Foyer on Friday afternoon by MUKO, a choir consisting of the university's music students.

One unusual feature of the conference was the presence of postgraduate students as both part of the audience and contributors to the programme. Three students gave papers, of which one used his paper also as a final examination. The combination of up-coming scholars and experienced researchers from Denmark and abroad gave a very inspiring atmosphere and great expectations towards a new generation of Nielsen scholarship. There were contributors from the US, United Kingdom, Canada, Germany, and Denmark. During three days, nineteen speakers were presented. As a special guest, the Danish composer Hans Abrahamsen was invited to speak about his adaptations of Nielsen compositions.

The contributions featured some trends in recent scholarship. One was Nielsen as a national composer (Glenda Goss) and the reception of Nielsen's music within national(-ist) music cultures (Michael Fjeldsøe and Jens Boeg; Paolo Muntoni). Another was an interest in analysing Nielsen within concepts of late nineteenth- and early twentieth-century music theory (Jan Crummenerl; Robert Rival; Svend Hvidtfelt Nielsen). Other papers were considering how Nielsen fits European cultures of modern art and music (Daniel Grimley; Colin Roth; Raymond Knapp); his position within the history of genres (David Fanning; Patrick McCreless; Anne-Marie Reynolds); or were adding to the awareness of available sources (Thomas Holme Hansen; John Fellow).

In an on-going debate on how to integrate university teaching and international scholarship the concept of this conference might be inspiring. The university has included papers on full-scale conferences as a way of passing exams for MA-students, and a musicology class on Nielsen as well as a class on analysing Nielsen were preparing students to participate in the conference as audience and to join discussions between the presentations. Key organizers were Niels Krabbe and Michael Fjeldsøe. The papers are available in *Carl Nielsen Studies* 5 (2012).

Michael Fjeldsøe

16TH NORDIC MUSICOLOGICAL CONGRESS, STOCKHOLM, AUGUST 2012

The 16th Nordic Musicological Congress took place 7–11 August 2012 in Stockholm. The congress was hosted by the Department of Musicology and Performance Studies at Stockholm University and was located in the Frescati Campus, four metro stations, or 45 minutes of steady walking, north of the city centre of Stockholm. Jakob Derkert was in charge of the arrangement, and the planning of the Congress had been based on discussions and suggestions in a Nordic Reference Group consisting of representatives from the Musicological Societies of Denmark, Finland, Norway, and Sweden.

The Nordic congresses have been a regular, mostly quadrennial, event since 1948, circulating between the Nordic countries, and gathering both music researchers active in the Nordic countries, and researchers with an interest in aspects of Nordic music and musical life or in specific activities of Nordic music research.

One of the challenges for the arrangers of the congresses since at least the 1970s has been to maintain a balance between on the one hand discussing current agendas and emerging problems for musicological research, unifying or dividing as they may have been, and on the other hand to reflect what researchers actually do within musicology in the Nordic countries or dealing with matters of Nordic music. The question of having one (or more) overarching theme(s) has been discussed regularly. The latter of the two aspects have typically been dealt with through 'free papers' organized in a number of parallel sessions (two, three, up to five, at earlier conferences). The Stockholm Congress found it's balance between these considerations by having keynote papers in plenary sessions opening the program of each of the conference days and each representing aspects of the important current challenges to (Nordic) musicology. Pirkko Moisala (University of Helsinki) discussed political and ethical implications of music research, 'pure' academic research in music vs. 'impure', applied research, with examples from her own research within both applied ethnomusicology and historical musicology. Niels Krabbe (The Royal Library, Copenhagen) gave a survey of the state of the art of philological musicological edition in the Nordic Countries and discussed the role of scholarly editions of music in past and present. A main issue was the dilemma of going on publishing large series of bound folios as opposed to developing digital means of communicating the results of philological research in musicology. Sverker Jullander (Luleå University of Technology), in his keynote paper, showed a variety of examples of and issues attached to the concept of 'artistic research'. In each of the three mentioned keynote sessions a panel of discussants raised questions and issues of debate, and especially the issue of artistic research called for a large number of viewpoints and statements from members of the audience. The fourth keynote paper went beyond the Nordic perspectives. Paul Théberge (Carleton University, Ottawa) lectured on and showed examples of current trends of technological 'mediatization' of music.

The remaining part of the conference was organized as a combination of panels on different topics (Women in modern Scandinavian music life, Opera as cultural practice within the Nordic countries during 'the long 19th century', Wagner reception in different contexts, Heideggerian thought in music and music education) and some 70 free papers with a very wide range of subject matter and methodology, organized in four parallel sessions, and amply showing the diversity of research in the Nordic countries.

In attending a conference of this type it is a condition that nobody attends everything, and that you have to be selective, according to your own agendas, interests and curiosities. So did this reporter, and the most general reflection on what happened at the conference was a recurring scepticism as far as the free paper format is concerned and the, not very new, thought that other formats might be more fruitful for developing of ideas. Other types of sessions of a more collaborative character has been tried only once (Ljungskile, 1979), and it is possible that there is no better way to organize a conference, appealing to a broad circle of musicologists.

The Stockholm Congress had appealed to 110 researchers, most of them active presenters, about half of them from Sweden, the rest distributed rather evenly between Denmark, Norway, Finland and a number of non-Nordic countries.

The conference programme was documented in a booklet consisting of abstracts for keynotes, panels and free papers distributed at the beginning of the congress. It is further planned that three of the four keynotes and some 20 of the free papers shall be published in a volume of proceedings.

One of the main functions of a Nordic Musicological Congress is to be a broad forum for communication of current music research and, equally or even more important, to provide a forum for establishing personal contacts between researchers. A minor (im)practical thing in this respect was that the institutional affiliation of the contributors was not indicated neither in the booklet nor in the e-mail list distributed at the end of the congress.

According to tradition it was announced at the end of the congress that the next one takes place in Denmark, organized by the Danish Musicological Society, probably in August 2015 and hosted by Aalborg University.

Peder Kaj Pedersen

MUSIC AND PUBLIC HEALTH, COPENHAGEN, NOVEMBER 2011

This was the first conference on music and public health held in a Nordic country. The European Public Health Association (EUPHA), Association of Schools of Public Health in the European Region (ASPHER) and the Danish Society of Public Health organized the 4th European Public Health Conference in Copenhagen 10–12 November 2011, with more than 1300 participants and many hundred presentations. The present event at the Royal Library on 9 November was an invited pre-conference (one of 20), arranged in a collaboration between the Department of Communication and Psychology/Music therapy at Aalborg University and the Center for Music and Health at the Norwegian Academy of Music, Oslo.

Music as/in therapy is well established as an evidence-based treatment modality all over the world, so there is a solid knowledge base to how and why music can help people with physiological, psychological, existential, spiritual and social problems and pathologies. 'Music and health' is a broader field where the use of music experiences to promote health and wellbeing in everyday life is studied and promoted. 'Music and public health' is a new, interdisciplinary field where music psychologists, music therapists, musicologists and health professionals are creating a knowledge base for the focused application of music experiences and activities in a public health perspective.

The purpose of this pre-conference was to present state-of-the-art by three internationally wellknown keynote speakers and to give an overview of the Nordic experiences with and perspectives on music as health promotion, and to discuss problems, achievements and ideas.

The program was divided into three sections: (1) International perspectives on music and public health; (2) Perspectives on music and public health as seen from the Centre for Music and Health, Oslo; (3) Scandinavian perspectives on music and health, as seen by leading researchers from Norway, Sweden, Finland and Denmark. Different theoretical and practical models was presented, and recent research results from clinical and non-clinical areas was related to the public health perspective.

Keynote speaker Suzanne B. Hanser (Berklee College of Music) has studied for decades how music therapy can assist in the fields of childbirth, depression, and cancer. In her paper, she examined how evidence-based strategies developed in her clinical practice and documented in research could be translated to the general public, as exemplified in a new book and accompanying CD, *Manage Your Stress and Pain through Music* (co-authored with Dr. Susan Mandel, Berklee Press, 2010). Hanser sees one important role of music in modern health care in bringing homeostasis to the autonomic nervous system, and her vision is the integrating of music therapy into mind-body approaches, giving it a role in the new science of integrative medicine.

Raymond MacDonald (Glasgow Caledonian University) presented in his keynote paper an overview of current conceptions of improvisation, highlighting a number of key themes in relation to improvisation and musical identities within a health care context. Musical identities refer to the multitude of ways in which interactions with music (both listening and playing) can influence our sense of self, and MacDonald demonstrated how participation in improvisation workshops can have health benefits for cancer patients, highlighting the potential of music activities as innovative psychological interventions in a health care setting.

Stephen Clift (Sidney De Haan Research Centre for Music, Arts and Health) departured from the fact that the WHO Commission of the Social Determinants of Health, under the leadership of Michael Marmot, has given no consideration to the role of music, or the wider field of creative arts as potential contributors to positive health and wellbeing. Clift presented evidence from many studies documenting how group singing can promote psychological and social wellbeing and help society to meet a number of key challenges linked to an increasingly elderly population and the growing burden of long-term conditions. The big challenge is how to organize such activities on a sufficient scale to have relevance for public health; and to assess potential cost-savings to health services from a health economics standpoint.

Researchers from the Center for Music and Health, Oslo (Even Ruud, Gro Trondalen, Karette Stensæth, and Torill Vist) gave examples of how the center works to increase public knowledge and awareness of the health potential of music activities, in everyday life as well as in clinical and community work with people suffering from health deficits. Researchers from Sweden (Lars Lilliestam), Norway (Brynjulf Stige), Denmark (Hanne Mette Ridder) and Finland (Suvi Saarikallio) reported from research studies documenting the health benefits of singing, playing and listening to music for 'ordinary people', adolescents and the elderly, and for people with physical or mental problems.

'Health musicking' is a concept integrating the many different perspectives and results of the studies presented. To take part in musical activities and share experiences with other people is a resource with a health dimension and potential well documented in small studies from music therapy, music psychology and music ethnology. The big challenge in a public health perspective is to take the present knowledge into the field of health prophylaxis and prevention. This will require large controlled studies, even longitudinal and cohort studies, and thus cross-disciplinary networking and funding in a much bigger scale than now. The pre-conference provided a sharing of promising results and ideas, and plans for large scale music and public health studies are already growing as a result.

Lars Ole Bonde

Danish Musicological Society, 2011/2012

BOARD

Associate professor, Ph.D., Jens Hesselager, University of Copenhagen, chairman
Part-time lecturer, Ph.D., Bjarke Moe, University of Copenhagen, secretary
Research librarian, cand.mag., Kristoffer Brinch Kjeldby, The Royal Library, treasurer
Associate professor, cand.mag., Peder Kaj Pedersen, University of Aalborg
Associate professor, Ph.D., Thomas Holme Hansen, University of Aarhus
Assistant professor, Ph.D., Sanne Krogh Groth, Roskilde University Centre
Associate professor, Ph.D., Morten Michelsen, University of Copenhagen, deputy
Research assistant, Ph.D., Mads Krogh, University of Aarhus, deputy

The Society's general assembly in 2011 took place on 23 March at the Section of Musicology, University of Copenhagen. On election were Thomas Holme Hansen and Peder Kaj Pedersen – both were reelected. Immediately following the assembly, the society's treasurer, Kirsten Flensborg Jensen, announced her resignation, and deputy Jens Hesselager entered the board in her place. Since Anne Ørbæk Jensen, furthermore, wished to retreat as chairman, the new board thereafter consisted of Jens Hesselager, chairman, Bjarke Moe, secretary, and Peter E. Nissen, treasurer, with Anne Ørbæk Jensen, Peder Kaj Pedersen and Thomas Holme Hansen as ordinary members. In December, however, Peter E. Nissen announced his resignation, and deputy Morten Michelsen entered in his place. This was a rather unstable and temporary situation, particularly as regards the post of the treasurer, and on the following general assembly, on 28 March 2012, a new constellation, listed above, took over.

In the period between the 2011 general assembly and that of 2012 the activities of the Society were at a relatively low ebb. The tradition of hosting an annual symposium was discontinued, at least for the time being – a decision made by the previous board. In its place a few other meetings as well as a one-day thematic symposium were arranged. The Society thus hosted one meeting in 2011, and a programme of three events during the spring of 2012.

On 12 May 2011 the Society arranged a debate evening, featuring Sune Auken, at the Section of Musicology, University of Copenhagen, entitled 'Musikvidenskab i Danmark 2011. Netværk og muligheder' (Musicology in Denmark 2011. Networks and Possibilities). A symposium on Medieval and Renaissance music was held on 10 March 2012, also at the Section of Musicology, University of Copenhagen: 'Kilder i kontekst. Middelalder og renæssance i musikvidenskabens lys' (Sources in Context. Medieval and Renaissance in the Light of Musicology). Invited speakers were Thomas Holme Hansen, Peter Woetmann Christoffersen, Peter Hauge, Astrid Bryder Steffensen, Søren Møller Sørensen, and Bjarke Moe. On the same day as the general assembly, 25 March 2012, the Society hosted an arrangement, 'Jazz i Danmark' (Jazz in Denmark), in which Olav Harsløf and Christian Munch Hansen spoke about their new book, *Jazz i Danmark, 1950-2010*. Finally, on 23 April 2012, a thematic evening, 'Musik og erindringssteder' (Music and Places of Remembering), on the relation between music and the concept of 'lieu de memoire' (Pierre Nora) was held, with Jens Hesselager, Sebastian Olden-Jørgensen, and Bent Holm as invited speakers.

General information on the Society can be found on p. 131 and www.musikforskning.dk.

Jens Hesselager

Reviews

Christian Troelsgård
Byzantine Neumes: A New Introduction to the Middle Byzantine Musical Notation
Monumenta Musicae Byzantinae, Subsidia, 9
Copenhagen: Museum Tusculanum Press, 2011
142 pp., illus., music exx.
ISBN 978-87-635-3158-0
DKK 485, EUR 65

Christian Troelsgård's well-written new introduction covers a wide range of aspects concerning the middle Byzantine musical notation ('*neumes*') – that is, of the Eastern Orthodox Church since *c.*1100 in Byzantium, also known as the East Roman Empire (ended with the fall of Constantinople in 1453). The basic principles of the notation continued well into the nineteenth century having a profound bearing on the musical system in use in the Greek Orthodox rite to this day.

The volume is a most welcome update of H.J.W. Tillyard's *Handbook of the Middle Byzantine Musical Notation* (1935), one of the first publications to appear in the Monumenta Musicae Byzantinae (MMB) series. Together with the philologists Carsten Høeg and Egon Wellesz, Tillyard founded the international centre for the study of Byzantine musical notation in Copenhagen in 1931. They had been interpreting musical neumes since the 1910s, and new findings around the time of World War I led them to convene this founding meeting where, among other topics, the transcription of Middle Byzantine musical notation was discussed. Already in the 1920s, Byzantine studies had been established as a discipline at the University of Copenhagen by Høeg. When Tillyard's *Handbook* was reprinted in 1970, Oliver Strunk, the then director of MMB, admitted in his postscript that the volume had become outdated with respect to many details. In 1993, it was decided that Jørgen Raasted should initiate the work on an up-to-date introduction; however, Raasted died two years later leaving only a five-page sketch. This sketch was the point of departure for Troelsgård, who, at the 1996 MMB Editorial Board Meeting, was given the opportunity to bring the project to an end – he has published widely on Byzantine chant and is a leading capacity within the field. Most of the writing of the present volume was completed in 2000, yet, for various reasons the publication has been delayed a decade. But the waiting has been worthwhile.

Troelsgård's introduction to the deciphering of Middle Byzantine notation is structured through seven chapters and 79 forth-running paragraphs across chapters. The volume introduces Byzantine chant in a wider sense, as it deals with topics such as oral transmission, problems of cheironomy (hand gestures), the relation between poetry and melody, and the many genres and varieties of notational practice within the immensely rich history of Byzantine music.

In Byzantine chant, defined as the liturgical music of the Greek Orthodox Christianity following the Byzantine Rite, there is an intimate relationship between the sacred texts and the melodies. Chapter 1 points to this relationship mentioning that the 'Book of Psalms and other poetic portions of the Bible form the basis for the chant at the Byzantine Offices and Divine Liturgy … The majority of chants transmitted in the musical manuscripts of the Middle Ages, and probably the chant types for which notation was eventually invented, belong, however, to various classes of non-scriptural poetry, which collectively are designated "*tropária*"' (p. 16). These *tropária* were sung as refrains between biblical verses or otherwise as hymns. The chapter touches upon the poetic language (ecclesiastical Greek), textual and musical accents, syntax and syllables. A considerable amount of Byzantine hymns (or *tropária*) was produced to already known melodies – a practice also known in Latin traditions as '*contrafacta*', in Greek context known as '*proshómia*'. A tiny confusion arises here as the title for §5 (p. 20) is 'Automelon – Proshomion', but the term 'automelon' is not explained here. It is revealed, however, in the next chapter on the following page that '*autómela*' refers to a body of model melodies to which the '*proshómia*' were adapted (p. 21).

Chapter 2 (§§7–11) consists of preliminary remarks concerning various problems in relation to working with Byzantine musical notations. The arguments as to when, how, and why a written tradition was established are thoughtful and instructive and point to ways of controlling the chant repertories and to stabilize oral transmission. Troelsgård points to the restoration of Orthodoxy in 843 (after the turbulent period of Iconoclasm) as a basis for a more uniform liturgical and musical practice. Around this time the 'monasteries contributed substantially to the process of re-establishing and consolidating the Byzantine church and society, and very likely it was due to monastic influences that new liturgical books and collection of chants were brought in circulation' (p. 21). Troelsgård's remarks on Byzantine and Western neumatic notations, the unknown origins, and possible musical changes and aesthetics (how did the music sound in the Middle Ages?) are weighed with timely scholarly caution.

In §11, on 'The problem of "scales" and tuning', the musical intervals are compared to those of the equally tempered scale (and not to Turkish or Persian material). Alexander Ellis's cent-system is drawn upon as a pedagogical means, or, so I guess, for introducing the musical structure to new students and colleagues. But this comparison is strikingly *old school* – unlike the standard of the rest of the volume. The 'cent' (technically defined as 0.01 of an equal-tempered semitone), I contend, is neither a culturally neutral nor a scholarly objective measure – its claim to universality is based on the western, equally-tempered scale, which like any other musical phenomenon is historically and culturally positioned. The implied, albeit unintended, cultural bias becomes all too clear in the figure were the Chrysanthine (nineteenth century) intervals are represented in terms of 'deviation' (p. 25). This represents a particular western reading that identifies Byzantine music as other and the equally tempered scale as self, as the possessive pronoun in the following phrase suggests: 'We can be fairly certain that the scale system differed from *our* equally tempered scale' (p. 24, emphasis mine).

Chapter 3 (§§12–16) provides an overview of the Byzantine notational forms. Other than the Middle Byzantine musical notation, notational forms that predated it are mentioned, such as the early 'Ekphonetic' (lectionary) notation, and the 'Theta' notation dating back to the eighth century, and the more developed 'Coislin' and 'Chatres' notations from tenth century. The basic principles of the 'Middle Byzantine' notation were in use for around 650 years until the reform of the Byzantine musical system in the first decades of the nineteenth century, in the text defined as '*c.*1815' – the year when the new system was introduced in the Patriarchal School of Music in Constantinople by the reformists themselves. Whether and to what extend this in practice actually put the old system(s) out of use is subject to scholarly controversy still. Also the modern notational form, the 'New Method' or 'Chrysanthine Notation', is briefly mentioned here (p. 33) and throughout the book. This is a welcome novelty in paleographical approaches to Byzantine music, tending otherwise to draw a firm distinction between what was 'before' the reform (Byzantine and post-Byzantine music), and what was 'after' (modern Greek church music).

Chapter 4 (§§17–22) is focused on ways Byzantine music is transcribed throughout the scholarly discipline commenting critically on the transcription conventions in the MMB *Tran-*

scripta series, where transcriptions of huge portions of manuscripts were published. The inclusive approach employed brings information to the fore about the work of Byzantine musical scholars also outside MMB, such as Petrescu, van Biezen, Raasted, and Stathis. The guidelines for the author's own transcriptions in the volume is also presented: Troelsgård prefers to show the original Byzantine neumes together with the transcribed version in Western staff notation, and the staff notation in use is modified to communicate what the transcriber knows and cannot know about the melodies; for example, the use of note heads without stems and quavers signals that the rhythmic values of the various signs cannot be determined with certainty. These are transcription principles that must be highly recommended as they do not only portray a particular graphic representation of the studied Byzantine notation, but include the transcriber's dialogue with the material and consequently also represent the gaps. Some level of discussion of the many general problems concerning the transcription of the Byzantine musical system into western staff notation (and other notations) would have been welcome at this point, though. Allow me to briefly inform the reader that such a discussion is offered in a new publication of my own, which deals with the late end of the historical spectrum drawing in the main on the discussion about transcription from the field of ethnomusicology (*The Past is Always Present: The Revival of the Byzantine Musical Tradition at Mount Athos* (Lanham, MD: Scarecrow Press, 2012)).

Chapter 5 (§§23–54) introduces each sign of the middle Byzantine musical notation meticulously with dense and detailed information, but a number of easy intelligible tables give an excellent overview: the *ison* (for repeated note), and the interval signs called '*semádia phonetiká*', meaning the signs that have a 'voice' (*phoné*), here referring to 'interval'. These are divided into 'bodies' (signs indicating the stepwise interval of a second) and 'spirits' (signs indicating leaps of a third or more in the melody). No less than six signs indicate an ascending second, each with a distinct quality or accentuation. These and the many other signs combine in many ways, though in practice composers and scribes had to observe specific rules for their application. Often these rules were related to specific genres: 'As a consequence of the use of 'pitch accent', a single *oxeía* or *petasté* [signs for ascending second] is normally followed by a descending interval in the sticheraic and heirmologic genres' (p. 42). A minor error in the first 'conspectus' or table (p. 43), and in the 'Quick Reference Card' (inserted at the back of the book) might cause slight confusion: the signs '*elaphrón*' and '*chamelé*' represent *descending* intervals of a third and a fifth respectively (and *not* ascending), but the transcriptions show the correct descent.

In chapter 6 (§§55–72) Troelsgård deals with Byzantine music theory and practice in more detail addressing modes and modality, modal signatures, and intonation formulas, among other things. A renewed interest in much of this material in Greece today is related to Byzantine musical revivalism at the monasteries of Mount Athos, for example, intonation formulas have been reintroduced in modern musical performance practice (cf. above mentioned Lind, 2012). A number of paragraphs about modulation lead to a very interesting discussion about chromaticism (pp. 72–75), a long standing issue in Byzantine musical scholarship. Based on an assumed parallel with the Gregorian tradition, the founders of MMB 'were in favour of a strictly diatonic interpretation of medieval Byzantine chant' (p. 72). They saw the modern tradition with its chromatic scales and tetrachords as the result of a corrupting orientalization process – 'as an effect of the contact between Greek singers and their Ottoman overlords' (p. 72). Troelsgård questions this view in maintaining that the 'theory of Turkish/Persian influence as a reason for 'introduction' of chromaticism in Byzantine chant seems to be too simple. It appears that Byzantine chant shared practices of melodic alteration already before the Ottoman domination was established' (p. 73, n. 222). Troelsgård then goes on to demonstrating how chromatic 'accidentals' (*phthoraí*) can be located in manuscripts from the fourteenth century onwards and suggests that these signs are related to 'other additions to the sign repertory of the Middle Byzantine notation around the year 1300' (p. 75). A single but well placed reference to an article on 'historical ethnomusicology' by early Indian music researcher Richard Widdess points to the problems of distinguishing between interior and exterior changes in a historical chant tradition. Such interdisciplinary discussion strengthens the arguments considerably, and indicates that Byzantine music research benefits from dialogical contact with studies of other chant traditions from around the globe, early as well as late.

The final chapter (§§73–79) discusses the aspect of 'style' in Byzantine chant, more narrowly defined as the different styles that can be identified in the various parts of the repertoire. The simplest style of chanting is known as 'simple psalmody' and is transmitted orally until the end of the thirteenth century. A slightly more elaborate style is found in the above mentioned '*autómela*' and '*proshómion*' singing and in the *Heirmológion*, a collection of model melodies (*heirmoí*) used for the '*kanón*'. The latter belongs to the earliest repertoire found with musical notation, and is characterized by a great deal of formulaic melodic material. It is syllabic-neumatic in style, a trait it shares with yet another part of the repertory, the *Sticherárion*, referring to the collection of the '*sticherá idiómela*', which is chanted only once a year. This part of the repertoire contains melismatic passages for the longer pieces. The soloist pieces of the *Psaltikón* and the *Asmatikón* have their origin in the cathedral rite of Constantinople. Despite its formulaic character these melodies are 'rather melismatic' (p. 85) in comparison with the other styles. Finally, there are the kalophonic styles, first documented in the fourteenth century, which are characterized by excess melodic elaboration.

This is not an introduction to Byzantine chant as sacred music, but to the study of its musical notation, which narrows the subject considerably. *Byzantine Neumes* deals mainly with the technical aspects of the musical tradition, and it does so thoroughly and convincingly. Yet, I would have loved to see a few comments on religious and spiritual aspects of the Byzantine musical tradition. We read about the so-called 'nonsense syllables' in the kalophonic repertoire (pp. 88–89), but we know so unbearably little about the spiritual meaning of these and other musical phenomena. Also, lurking somewhere behind the back stage curtain is the ghost-like, hard-to-define concept of tradition: what does tradition in a Byzantine-Christian Orthodox context mean? What are the possible relations between the tradition of musical notation and that of Orthodox rite?

The rich bibliography is updated with relevant publications from the period 2000–11 (that is, after the main parts of this volume was written), which serves as a service and an invitation to new scholars and students. The index is divided into three for convenience: one for proper names, one for manuscripts, and one for neumes and subjects. Despite the complex nature of the subject, it is rather easy to get an overview of the volume as a whole. And this owes partly to how the book is structured, partly to how it is presented visually: *Byzantine Neumes* is richly illustrated with notational examples, parts of which are handwritten by Troelsgård himself, and contains reprinting of selected specimen of manuscripts taken from MMB's facsimiles (pp. 95–116), providing a useful and illustrative compendium.

Reviews of academic publications rarely dwell on the design, but here is plenty of reason to make an exception and credit both author and designer. The beautiful layout of the book makes it most inviting. The graphic designer – he deserves mentioning here – Kim Broström, has wisely chosen a red-brown (and not a hot red) to highlight necessary details in the musical notation (the so-called 'red signs'), but also successfully uses this colour for chapter titles to counterpoint the black text (see for example pp. 26–27). This detail and its relation to the overall typesetting caresses the eyes of bibliophiles, palaeographers, and calligraphers, and whispers: read me! Keep me company! And there is more: the hard back cover of the book is kept in the MMB's classy cardboard-grey design to match the previous publications in the series, yet the dust cover creates a striking contrast portraying in aquarelle burnt orange and yellow abstract brush strokes with the hint of dark monumental arches in the background: there's a fire in the old monument! It is striking because it dares presenting the study of Byzantine music in new ways which pinpoints the novelty of the volume: *Byzantine Neumes* brings the palaeographical study of Byzantine music well into the twenty-first century and reconfirms the leading status of MMB. The 'Quick Reference Card' inserted at the back of the book is handy and helpful for the transcriber at work, and the idea to give it a plastic coated finish – really practical when messing with pencil, ink and pen while transcribing – could only have been the product of a mind of many years of scholarly experience and passion.

Tore Tvarnø Lind

Studia Musicologica Regionis Balticae I
ed. Ole Kongsted
Copenhagen: Capella Hafniensis Editions, 2011
304 pp., illus., music exx.
ISBN 978-87-994281-0-6
DKK 400

A new Danish series of musicological studies is now being published from *Capella Hafniensis Editions* in cooperation with The Royal Library (Copenhagen). It is dedicated to publishing articles that are dealing with 'Themen der Ostseeraumkultur' (the culture of the Baltic Sea area; p. 10). Musical culture in the Baltic Sea area as a concept was put forward by the Swedish musicologist Carl-Allan Moberg in 1957, and it was criticized and developed further by among others the members of the research project 'Östersjöområdet som musiklandskap' that was launched in 1990. The present volume works as an 'anthology' bringing together some of the writings of the working group from 1990. Three of the six former members are represented, contributing with nine of the ten articles. To readers who want to get familiar with some of the central concepts of research in 'der Ostseeraum', a publication like this must be welcome.

The editors give no information why this newly initiated journal should have a Latin title. It is in line with the other series that are being (or will soon be) published from the same publisher: *Monumenta Musica Regionis Balticae*, *Ars Baltica Musicalis*, and *Documenta Musica Regionis Balticae*. The 'Hauptsprache' of the series is German, but the current volume includes contributions in English, Swedish, and Danish as well. Thus, the series has both a national and an international profile, and since it covers a large thematic field it should naturally embrace the variety of studies that are conducted by many music scholars worldwide. However, the journal is intended to be a forum 'das offensteht für Beiträge aus allen Ostseeländern, Norwegen eingeschlossen' (open to contributions from all Baltic Sea countries including Norway; p. 10). One wonders, why scholars from outside the region are to be excluded. Over the last decades there has been a growing interested in the musical cultures of the Baltic Sea area – also from scholars outside the region, who have contributed to new perspectives on the field. I am sure they too would welcome a series dedicated to this subject. The volume makes room for different kinds of contributions, for instance lengthy studies, short report-like articles, and source presentations. This seems like a good way of arranging a large-scale volume like this (consisting of more than 300 pages). The contents mainly cover studies from the period 1500–1800, while a couple of articles deal with historiography of the twentieth century.

As mentioned, some of the writings from the members of the 1990 research group has been included in this first volume of the series. The background, the outcome, and the continuation of the project are shortly described by its leader Greger Andersson (pp. 69–74). Two articles by Heinrich W. Schwab (originally published 1989 and 1993) focus on the structure and concept of 'der Ostseeraum'. As a direct response to the writings of Moberg, Schwab suggests (in 'Zur Struktur der "Musikkultur des Ostseeraumes" während des 17. Jahrhunderts' (On the concept of 'musical culture of the Baltic Sea area' in the 17th century; pp. 13–38)) a distinction between three musical cultures: in villages, in cities, and at courts. Based on examples from all three categories, he demonstrates, for instance, the different social conditions under which music and musicians were employed. Another article by Greger Andersson on 'Musikgeschichtschreibung in den Nordischen Ländern am Ende des 20. Jahrhunderts' (music historiography in the Nordic countries in the late 20th century; pp. 87–97) reports some of the different co-operations that were carried through by musicologists in the Baltic Sea area in the 1980s and 1990s. Besides describing the above-mentioned research project that Andersson himself was leader of, he draws attention to the book *Musiken i Norden* from 1997 that was initiated to address the need for a Scandinavian music history as opposed to the individual national music histories. As the editor of the book, Andersson reveals some of the initial considerations that influenced the writing of a music history from a supranational perspective.

In his third article Andersson draws attention to four documents from Lübeck and Stockholm that contribute to throw light on the role of 'Der Stadtmusicus als Hochzeitmusikant' (pp. 75–85). The sources, which are transcribed in full length in the article, give insight into, for instance, how the 'Musikanten' in Lübeck were required to service the citizens differently according to their social rank. Two documents deal with how they were forbidden to play at weddings during the mourning period of the emperor in 1711. Also Ole Kongsted's article on 'Die Musikalien im Archiv der Hansestadt Wismar' (pp. 217–230) presents information on rediscovered (in 1995) sources, in this case eight vocal pieces from the seventeenth century.

An article by Joachim Kremer is concerned with 'die regionale Ausdifferentierung des Kantorats im Ostseeraum' (the regional differentiation of the Kantorat in the Baltic Sea area) and intends to re-evaluate the fundamental question of whether the office of the 'Kantor' was uniform or differentiated in the region (pp. 99–175). The study is based on a new type of sources in this connection, namely biographical writings from the eighteenth century. Especially Johann Mattheson's extensive biographical project in his *Grundlage einer Ehrenpforte* (1740), which he worked on since 1713, is thoroughly investigated in order to assess Mattheson's purposes of collecting life stories of contemporary musicians. He was concerned with the state of music and musical life, and Kremer argues that 'das eigentliche Ziel seiner biographischen Bemühungen … aus einer theologischen Argumentation abgeleitet [ist]' (the actual goal of his biographical efforts derived from a theological argument; p. 120). The honour of music was to be rehabilitated through biographies, 'indem die verschiedenen Lebenswege der Musiker die Weisheit Gottes erkennen lassen' (in which the wisdom of God would be recognized through the musicians' different life paths; p. 121). Through a comparison with other contemporary biographies Kremer shows that Mattheson's biographical writings were complex in terms of contents and style. Mattheson was concerned with 'weitaus mehr als nur Berufsbiographien zu veröffentlichen' (publishing more than just biographies on careers; p. 149). The last part of the article is investigating 'ob das vom Ideal der Gelehrsamkeit bestimmte Kantorat die Regel war oder ein an der musikalischen Praxis ausgerichtetes Kantorat, wie Mattheson es propagierte' (whether the Kantorat, which was characterized by scholarly ideals, was the more common, or the one that was ordered according to the musical practice, the one which Mattheson propagandized for; p. 153). With views on especially Scandinavian grammar schools, Kremer draws attention to many structural differences throughout the region, and concludes: 'Solche regionalen und lokalen Ausdifferenzierungen sind gegeneinander abzugrenzen, so dass sich als historiographische Aufgabe weniger die Darstellung der Einheitlichkeit des Phänomens stellt, sondern die Beschreibung der Vielgestaltigkeit' (Such regional and local differentiations are separate from each other which is why the historiographical task is less about describe the similarities of the phenomenon than describing the diversity; p. 171 f.). Studies of the 'Kantorat' in Denmark are few, and Kremer primarily bases his survey on Bengt Johnsson's *Den danske skolemusiks historie indtil 1739* from 1973. To comply with Kremer's request of describing the variety of the 'Kantorat' in the Baltic Sea area, I would like to mention my own study of the musical life at Copenhagen churches, where the role of the different 'kantorer' varied during the first half of the seventeenth century according to their institutional affiliations or as a result of changing demands for musical activities in the city (Bjarke Moe, *Musikkulturel trafik i København og Rostock. Musikerrekruttering og repertoirefornyelse i første halvdel af 1600-tallet*, Ph.D. diss., University of Copenhagen, 2010).

Ole Kongsted's article on the 'carmen gratulatorium' presents an investigation of printed 'congratulation songs' (pp. 177–87). The study is based on an inspection of the RISM A/I catalogues, which contain (often fragmental) titles of printed music until 1800. Only prints up until 1660 are included in the investigation. The author counts 630 prints containing occasional works under the definition 'ein Musikwerk also, das für die Aufführung zu einem bestimmten Anlass komponiert wurde' (a musical work which was composed in order to be performed at a certain occasion; p. 179). Not all kinds of occasional works are included, though; only music for celebration is counted in. The number of prints found also covers some 'Dedikationswerke', but it is not clear whether they were written for specific occasions. Kongsted sums up some of the formulas used in the printed titles (*Epithalamium in honorem …*, *Cantio in honorem nuptiarum …*) that reveal the contents of the print. However, it is unclear what kind of information is uncovered in the titles of the prints, and whether further source evaluations have been conducted in order to assess the status of a certain print as 'occasional music'. The author emphasizes that not all prints with occasional music will be spotted by looking only at the title of a publication, since the contents of it might not be mentioned specifically on the front page. The results of the investigation covers only printed music, and thereby occasional music in manuscripts is ignored despite its significant contribution to the genre. The extent of these limitations is not further commented on by the author, and it is questionable whether the method is sufficient to give an account of occasional music in general. From the data the author concludes that 'die Hochzeitsmotette in der Renaissance [bildet] eine der häufigsten Formen von Gratulationsmusik' (the wedding motet constitutes one of the most frequent forms of music for celebration; p. 180) with a total number of 513 prints (out of 630). Around 66 per cent of the prints were published 1595–1639. It raises a row of questions as to what could have caused the raise and decline of the number of prints: Was it common to have occasional music printed in the late 16th century, or was it rather becoming a widespread tendency to have music written for special occasions? What role did the printers play? How did the Thirty-Years-War influence the production of occasional music, and how is this related to the production of music prints in general? The genre *Carmen gratulatorium* and more generally 'occasional music' calls for further studies that include more varied sources. An ongoing project at the University of Greifswald led by Peter Tenhaef is at the moment collecting information on extant occasional music related to the Baltic Sea area.[1] Once the catalogue of sources is available, we will be confronted with the variety of material preserved in both prints and manuscripts.

The third article by Kongsted is a survey on the musical life at the royal court of Christian IV (1588–1648) and it sums up the many different situations at court when music was played (pp. 189–215). Thanks to Kongsted's familiarity with the topic, it gives an informative account of the role of music 'at times of feasting and festivity' and 'in everyday life of the king' (p. 207) and how it displayed 'The Secular "rex splendens"'. Also the fourth and last article by Kongsted is concerned with Danish court music. The lengthy study on 'Musikhistoriografien og den danske hofmusik i den nordiske Senrenaissance' (The music historiography and the Danish court music in the Nordic late Renaissance; pp. 231–87) has the purpose of providing a survey of the writings on music at the Danish court from *c.* 1515–*c.* 1650. This seems like an interesting task – and a rather large one, too. Kongsted's many years of research come into light as a large amount of references to the existing literature is presented, especially in relation to the sixteenth century. To scholars who want to devote themselves to the subject many interesting and relevant texts are listed. However, the criterion for Kongsted's selection of literature, on which he bases his examination of the historiographical tendencies, remains unclear. A large number of studies from the past decades are ignored although they would have contributed to throw further light on recent research interests in Danish court music. As the article is presented as part one, the second part of the article, which is to be published in a forthcoming issue, might be concerned with this.

The present volume of this new series looks back upon a corner of musicological research in the musical culture of the Baltic Sea area. Six of the ten contributions in the volume have been published before (the two by Schwab and the four by Kongsted). This makes good sense, since some of them come from minor publications that might be difficult to get hold of. As mentioned earlier, a couple of the articles represent important contributions to the development of the concepts of musical culture in 'der Ostseeraum'. Also Ole Kongsted's article on 'The Secular "Rex Splendens"' that was published in the anthology *Christian IVs Verden* (1988) is now accessible for foreign researchers in an English translation. Much research on music in 'der Ostseeraum' has been accomplished and brought forward to the public during the last three decades. The re-issued writings from the 1980s and 1990s stand as testimonies of the 'state of the art' at that particular moment. It would, however, have been interesting had the editors considered including a survey of current problems and interests in the research of music in the Baltic Sea area. Furthermore, the opportunity of brushing up and bringing the old articles up-to-date could have been seized. As the first publication in a row, it is appropriate with a retrospective volume on the background of the research field. Many of us will certainly look forward to see the coming volumes and read new forward-looking studies.

Bjarke Moe

1 'Gelegenheitsmusik des Ostseeraums vom 16. bis 18. Jahrhundert: Erfassung, Katalogisierung und musikwissenschaftliche Auswertung', www.phil.uni-greifswald.de/bereich2/musik/dfg-projekt-gelegenheitsmusiken-im-ostseeraum.html.

Jørgen Erichsen
Friedrich Kuhlau. Ein deutscher Musiker in Kopenhagen
Hildesheim: Georg Olms Verlag, 2011
416 pp., illus., music exx.
ISBN 978-3-487-14541-9
EUR 39,80

Richard Müller-Dombois
Der deutsch-dänische Komponist Friedrich Kuhlau. Klassik und Frühromantik im Kontext der geistigen, sozialen und politischen Bewegungen Europas. Ein synchrosynoptisches Lese- und Nachschlagebuch
Detmold: Syrinx Verlag, 2004
119 pp.
ISBN 3-00-014132-4
EUR 14

Innerhalb der Zeitspanne von sieben Jahren sind bei zwei deutschen Verlagen zwei Publikationen erschienen, die sich mit dem 1786 in Uelzen geborenen und 1832 in Kopenhagen verstorbenen Musiker und Komponisten Friedrich Kuhlau befassen. Repräsentative Arbeiten in deutscher Sprache waren zuletzt die musikwissenschaftlichen Dissertationen von Karl Graupner (München 1930), Kuhlaus frühe Schaffenszeit betreffend, diejenige von Jörn-L. Beimfohr über Kuhlaus Klavierkonzert (Hamburg 1971) oder Dan Fogs *Thematisch-bibliographischer Katalog* der Kompositionen (1977). Bereits in ihrer differenzierten Titelei weisen die oben genannten Bücher deutliche Unterschiede auf. Angezeigt ist damit, wie sie gelesen und beurteilt werden wollen, was die Autoren vorrangig intendiert haben. Die ältere Arbeit stammt von Dr. phil. Richard Müller-Dombois, von Musikologen geschätzt dank seiner Dissertation über "Die Fürstlich Lippische Hofkapelle" (Regensburg, 1972) als einer aspektreichen Institutionengeschichte. Tätig war er als Musikhistoriker an der neugeschaffenen Musikhochschule Detmold, deren Geschichte er nachgezeichnet hat. Von Musikern wird er verehrt als 'Flöten-Professor', der eine Fülle von Kompositionen für dieses Instrument im Eigenverlag ediert hat. Vorrang genießt hierbei offenbar die 'Uelzener Kuhlau-Edition', die "Wissenschaftlich-praktische Urtext-Gesamtausgabe der Kuhlauschen Flötenwerke".

Auch das hier angezeigte großformatige Buch ist im Eigenverlag erschienen und der "Internationalen Flötistenhauptstadt" Uelzen gewidmet. In seinem Titel wird Kuhlau als "Der deutsch-dänische Komponist" charakterisiert. Informationen über seine Vita und seine Kompositionen stehen allerdings nicht im Zentrum der Darstellung. Anders gesagt: Eine Monographie im Sinne des eingeführten Typus "Leben und Werk" darf man hier nicht erwarten. (Selbst das Literaturverzeichnis zum Stichwort Kuhlau ist mit insgesamt nur sechs deutsch- bzw. dänischsprachigen Publikationen äußerst ärmlich ausgefallen, S. 117). Präsentiert hat der Autor mit diesem Buch ein tabellarisches Nachschlagewerk zu den Lebensdaten des Komponisten, angeordnet nach Jahresübersichten, korreliert mit fünf Rubriken heraustretender historischer Ereignisse in den Bereichen Geschichte der Flöte, Musikgeschichte, Sozial- und Zivilisationsgeschichte, Geistes- und Literaturgeschichte sowie Politische Geschichte. Diese "Nachschlagebuch" will den interessierten Leser, wie es im Vorwort heißt, "weder im üblichen Sinne belehren, noch vertritt es außer dem allerdings grundlegenden Vernetzungs-gedanken eine bestimmte Tendenz". Motiviert werden soll der Leser, "das Verbindende und Trennende zu erkennen und so zu einer aktiven Auseinandersetzung zu gelangen, die allein gewährleistet, dass die historischen Gegebenheiten und deren Umstände wirklich begriffen und internalisiert", also unbewusst zu Eigenem gemacht werden. Zum einen erhebt sich die Frage, wie dies denn zu bewerkstelligen ist, wenn im Blick auf Kuhlau recht wenige Fakten zusammengestellt sind, die zudem ohne Quellennachweis bleiben. Zum anderen wird der Gegensatz zu wissenschaftlichem Erkennen offenkundig, bei dem eben das Bewusst-Machen oberstes Gebot ist. Mit seinem Kuhlaubuch hat es sich der Autor sehr einfach gemacht. Trotz der Vorwarnung durch die Untertitel kann man letztlich nur enttäuscht sein, weil so viele Erwartungen nicht bedient werden.

Dies gilt ebenfalls für die Charakterisierung Kuhlaus als "deutsch-dänischer Komponist". Er ist einer der so bezeichneten "Grenzgänger". Neben Kuhlau trifft dies ebenfalls auf J.A.P. Schulz, F.L.Ae. Kunzen oder C.E.F. Weyse zu. Zu den gesonderten Problemen, welche diese Komponisten der Musikgeschichtsschreibung aufgeben, namentlich wenn letztgenannte sich nicht von der nationalen Priorierung zu lösen vermag, gehört vorzugsweise die Klärung der Frage, welchem Land, welcher Tradition sie mehrheitlich angehören und nach "welcher Elle" sie historiographisch zu bewerten sind. Tatsache ist, dass Kuhlau bereits 1811 die dänische Staatsangehörigkeit beantragt und erhalten hat, und dass er in Dänemark in der Folgezeit zum "Nationalkomponisten" avancierte, während ihm in seinem Herkunftsland neben den kurz vor ihm verstorbenen deutschen Zeitgenossen Beethoven, Schubert und Weber kein nennenswerter Platz zugewiesen wird. Dies ist jedoch zu einem guten Teil auch dadurch bedingt, dass es an kritischen Analysen seiner Kompositionen mangelt. Und solange wir keine europäische Musikgeschichte besitzen, wo die von Grenzgängern erbrachten Leistungen a priori nach einem anderen Maßstab zu beurteilen und zu würdigen sind, wird das Kuhlaubild widersprüchlich bleiben. Zu Dombois' synchron-synoptischen Darstellungsmodell wäre noch anzumerken, dass es sich mit Bezug auf die deutsch-dänischen Grenzgänger ein solches Buch unschwer ein zweites, drittes oder viertes Mal in Druck bringen ließe, würde man nur in der ersten Rubrik Daten und Fakten der genannten Komponisten Schulz, Kunzen oder Weyse einsetzen und auf die Rubrik "Geschichte der Flöte" verzichten. (Im Blick auf Puccini hat der Autor dieses Verfahren in der Tat nochmals praktiziert. Dieses andere "Lese- und Nachschlagebuch" trägt den Titel: "Puccini im Kontext. Weltpanorama seiner Lebenszeit 1858-1924"; Detmold: Syrinx Verlag, 2006/07).

Müller-Dombois gegenüber legt Jørgen Erichsen, seines Zeichens Organist in Aarhus, eine auf reichlich herangezogene Primärquellen gegründete Biographie vor. Konzentriert ist sie auf die Orte von Kuhlaus Leben in Uelzen (*1786) und Lüneburg (seit 1793), seinem Studieren und ersten Wirken in Hamburg (seit 1803), seine Flucht vor der französischen Konskription nach Dänemark und seine langjährige Tätigkeit in Kopenhagen (1810-1832). Schwerpunkte bilden zugleich die Begegnungen und Erfahrungen, die Kuhlau bei seinen diversen Reisen nach Schweden (1815, 1828), nach Berlin und Leipzig (1829), zweimal auch nach Wien (1821, 1825) sowie ebenfalls nach Norwegen (1828) unternommen hat. Den eingebürgerten Typus einer Darstellung von "Leben und Werk" steuerte indes auch Erichsen nicht an. Ausdrücklich hat er auf eine "kritische Beurteilung" der einzelnen Kompositionen "im Großen und Ganzen verzichtet" (S. 19). Deshalb hat er im Titel seines Buches offenbar auch die Kennzeichnung Kuhlaus als "Komponist" vermieden; gesehen wird er als "ein deutscher Musiker in Kopenhagen". Wie nun, soll damit etwa Kuhlaus Bekenntnis zur dänischen Staatszugehörigkeit ausgeblendet werden? Räsoniert hat Erichsen jedenfalls über seine Hervorhebung nicht. Vielleicht ist sie auch nur ein weiteres Zeichen der Dankbarkeit gegenüber der finanziell den Druck des Buches unterstützenden Stadt Uelzen.

Was die Darstellung der Vita Kuhlaus anbelangt, vor allem die Klärung vieler Details, hat sich Erichsen vor allem aufgrund seiner langjährigen Studien im Kopenhagener Staatsarchiv

(Auswertung des Briefwechsel des Theaters, der *Capelprotokoller*, *Resolutioner* und *Reskripter*) und im Landesarchiv (*Skifteretsprotokoller* 1832) bleibende Verdienste erworben, gerade auch dadurch, dass sie nun zugleich in deutscher Übersetzung mitgeteilt sind. Auch sorgen die von ihm ausgewählten Abbildungen (Porträts, Stadt- und Landschaftsbilder, selbst angefertigte Landkarten, Titel-, Noten- und Szenenbilder, Genrebilder, Karikaturen) stets für eine erhöhte Anschaulichkeit.

Durch den erklärten Verzicht, auf die kompositorische Faktur einzugehen, und damit auf eine unumgängliche Auseinandersetzung mit der Wertfrage, wird jedoch bereits im Titel gewollt-ungewollt auf jenes Kernproblem aufmerksam gemacht, das Kuhlau nach wie vor in der deutschen Musikgeschichtsschreibung darstellt. Auf drei Beispiele sei kurz verwiesen. Erstens: Das als op. 7 in Druck gegebene "Klavierkonzert Nr. 1, in C" (1812) versetzt wohl jeden Musikkenner, der es zum ersten Mal hört, in erstauntes Reagieren, weil er sicher ist, diese Komposition in anderer Version schon einmal gehört zu haben. Und es bedarf keiner tiefgehenden Analyse, um sie als eine Adaption des Beethovenschen C-Dur-Konzertes op. 15 zu identifizieren. Der zeitgenössischen Forderung nach kompositorischer "Individualität" eines jeden neuen Werkes, das in die kritische Öffentlichkeit entlassen wird, ist Kuhlau hier keinesfalls nachgekommen. Nichtsdestotrotz wird von Kuhlauforschern erwartet, eine Erklärung dafür zu liefern, wie dieses Opus gattungs- und musikgeschichtlich überhaupt einzuordnen ist (vgl. hierzu Beimfohr, 1971). Zweitens: Mit seiner Musik zu dem Schauspiel "Elverhøj" (1828) hat Kuhlau Furore gemacht. Sie hat ihm entscheidend die Anerkennung als "dänischer Nationalkomponist" eingebracht. Bei Lichte besehen handelt es sich jedoch weniger um eine Komposition als um ein geschickt arrangiertes und instrumentiertes Potpourri von eingängigen und stimmungsgeladenen Tanz- und Volksmelodien. Schwerlich ist diese Schauspielmusik ein Zertifikat für den Komponisten Kuhlau. Drittens: Zu den kompositorischen Besonderheiten Kuhlaus zählt die Tatsache, viele, aber auch höchst kunstfertige Kanons geschrieben zu haben. Dies war zu seiner Zeit durchaus nicht mehr zeitgemäß. Dennoch fand selbst Beethoven daran Interesse und trat anlässlich beider Begegnung in Wien mit dem Kgl. dänischen Hofcompositeur in einen kompositorischen Dialog. Andererseits hat sich Franz Xaver Mozart, Mozarts Sohn, 1819 nach seinem Besuch Kuhlaus in Kopenhagen recht abschätzig über Kuhlaus Komponieren generell wie speziell auch über seine Kanons geäußert: "Er ist ein großer Freund musikalischer Künstlereien, die gewiß, wenn sie nichts als das sind, den Werth dieser edlen Kunst verfehlen. … Dass er also sehr viel Theorie besitzen muss, davon ist dies wohl ein Beweis, aber zum Herzen spricht seine Musik ganz und gar nicht" (S. 175). Da Erichsen es bedauerlicherweise ausgeklammert hat, sich auf die Beschaffenheit der Kuhlauschen Kompositionen einzulassen, erübrigt es sich hier solche Arbeiten aufzulisten, die in den letzten Jahren u.a. auch dessen Kanonkunst des Näheren untersucht und typologisiert haben.

Bleibt schließlich noch darauf hinzuweisen, dass Aktivitäten auf dänischer Seite in den letzten Jahrzehnten (und dies gilt auch für Erichsens Buch und seine Beiträge zu Kuhlaus Vita), ungleich mehr zu Tage zu bringen vermochten als die deutschsprachige Musikwissenschaft, die in der Regel eben allein schon Schwierigkeiten bei der Erfassung dänischer Originalquellen hat und sich kaum mit Kuhlau beschäftigt. Nennenswerte Fortschritte sind dänischerseits insbesondere Gorm Busk zu danken (vgl. etwa die Briefausgabe, die Einzelstudien zu den Klaviersonaten und -sonatinen, zu dem Kantatenfragment zu Schillers "An die Freude", die Editionen der Kanons und einiger Opern, gefördert von japanischen Geldgebern). Zu bedauern ist ein weiteres Mal die Malaise, dass Busks Arbeiten mehrheitlich nicht auf Deutsch oder Englisch erschienen sind, sondern in seiner Muttersprache. Demgemäß werden diese Publikationen nur selten rezipiert und belassen die internationale Kuhlausforschung weiterhin in einer gewissen Stagnation. Zu wünschen wäre, dass Gorm Busk, der Senior der Kuhlauforschung, ähnlich wie Jørgen Erichsen, die Chance erhält, die Summa seiner Studien bei einem Weltverlag in Druck bringen zu können.

Heinrich W. Schwab

Inger Sørensen
Horneman. En kunstnerslægt
Copenhagen: Museum Tusculanums Forlag, 2011
397 pp., illus.
ISBN 978-87-635-3740-7
DKK 298, EUR 40

Et venskab. C.F.E. Hornemans korrespondance med Edvard Grieg 1863-1898
ed. Inger Sørensen
Danish Humanist Texts and Studies, 40
Copenhagen: The Royal Library & Museum Tusculanums Forlag, 2011
166 pp., illus.
ISSN 0105-8746, ISBN 978-87-635-3741-4
DKK 198, EUR 27

The two recently published books on the composer Christian Frederik Emil Horneman (1840–1906) are the third study in a number of nineteenth-century Danish composers by Inger Sørensen; as the previous two – *Hartmann – Et dansk komponistdynasti* (1999) and *J.P.E. Hartmann og hans kreds – en komponistfamilies breve* (1999–2003); and *Niels W. Gade – Et dansk verdensnavn* (2002), and *Niels W. Gade og hans europæiske kreds – en brevveksling 1836-1891* (2008) – also this publication consists of an edition of letters by the composer and a biography. It is astonishing how Sørensen is able to produce and publish this quantity of studies and editions in a time of great difficulties in obtaining funding for studies on Danish music history. In the present case, a private donation from a widow related to the Horneman family has made the study and its publication possible. Also private funding in addition to support from the Royal Library has covered the edition of letters.

For this reason, the patron has had a great influence on the presentation (see Introduction, pp. 7–8), that is, a lavishly illustrated book focusing on three members of the Horneman family which ends with a family tree showing the family up until today. Though this frame of genealogy and memorabilia has restricted the author, it is easy to recognize the structure and flow of the book when one already knows her previous books on Hartmann and Gade.

Sørensen expounds on the three life stories with many anecdotes connected to memorabilia, well-known places, people, and incidents of the time. Christian Horneman was a popular miniature painter in the late eighteenth century, and on his journeys around Europe he met and portrayed people such as the young Beethoven. The story of (Johan Ole) Emil Horneman concentrates on his life as a music publisher and joint owner of the amusement park *Alhambra*. His most well known musical works are presented and in particular his successful companionship with the poet Peter Faber, which resulted in the well-known songs 'Dengang jeg drog afsted' and 'Højt fra træets grønne top', is described. Out of the book's thirteen chapters, eleven are concerned with C.F.E. Horneman recounting his life story extracted mainly from his letters and reviews of his music. His life was characterized by great initiative and creativity: his study in Leipzig, his formation of music societies, his friendship with Edward Grieg, his work as a music publisher and founder of a music school, his involvement in *Koncertforeningen*, and his musical works. Sørensen has done an important job making Horneman's personal papers known and placing them in a historical context. The book is relevant for source studies in Danish music history. The author creates a coherent story of C.F.E. Horneman with interesting and amusing details. Her presentation of the friendship between Horneman and Grieg and Horneman's music pedagogical work offers new aspects to further research. However, it is remarkable that the well-known piano school by his father Emil (*Ny praktisk Pianoforte-Skole for Begyndere og Viderekomne*) is not mentioned at all as that would have provided an obvious link between the persons. The three chapters on Horneman's music lack references to the musical material. The author may have had good reasons for not including any musical analyses of her own but could instead have drawn on those done by others. Though the emphasis in chapter six is on Horneman's personal involvement in *Koncertforeningen*, it seems strange that the author has chosen to expound on the establishment of this important music society as if no one has ever written about it before (see e.g. T. Schousboe, 'Koncertforeningen i København – Et bidrag til det københavnske musiklivs historie i slutningen af det 19. århundrede', *Dansk årbog for musikforskning*, 6 (1968–72), 171–209; the article is mentioned in the bibliography, though there is no reference to it in the text).

These are examples exposing a fundamental problem with the book. The accounts never get deeper than the many incidents and details that the family sources reveal. There is no dialogue with relevant musicological studies related to the Hornemans. Thus the recent dissertation, focusing on C.F.E. Horneman in a discourse on nationalism in music, is only referred to once concerning a minor biographical detail (p. 100; Wasserloos, *Kulturgezeiten. Niels W. Gade und C.F.E. Horneman in Leipzig und Kopenhagen* (Hildesheim, 2004)). There are no theoretical and analytical assessments on the development of the Hornemans' musical styles or use of genres in the light of the time or place, institutions, and ethnicity; and the reception of their works is not connected to relevant academic discussions and perspectives on contemporary art and culture. There are, however, interesting observations: the contradiction between the musical quality of *Gurre* (1900) and the reviewers' critique of the work (p. 267); or the fact that Horneman had his greatest success with his *Kantate ved Universitetets Mindefest for Kong Christian IX* (1906) (p. 276). In light of theories of reception and genre this would have been highly relevant. The book ends with a chapter on the C.F.E. Horneman's personality. This also makes the book look similar to a genealogical study rather than a musicological one on the Horneman family. The generations' different life conditions and the transformation of the family as it entered modern times could be worth while discussing.

The edition of Horneman's letters is, as Sørensen's two previous studies in the series *Danish Humanist Texts and Studies*, published by the National Library of Denmark. While the two previous ones consisted of a much larger number of letters from the collections of the library, this edition of letters is exclusively related to Horneman's correspondence with Edvard Grieg. Most of the introduction to the collection is similar to the part about Grieg and Horneman in the biography, and it provides a good introduction to their relationship. The correspondence includes many amusing and interesting details and relates in an entertaining way the two music characters from the nineteenth century and their way of thinking. From a scholarly perspective, however, this way of publishing letters seems outdated, especially when comparing the study with the fine digital collection of Grieg-letters accessible from the webpage of the *Bergen Public Library*, where 71 of the 90 letters in this book are available (http://bergenbibliotek.no/digitale-samlinger/grieg/om-edvard-grieg/horneman-og-grieg). Here anyone may read the letters in their original handwriting, search on names, words etc., which is not possible in the same useful way in a traditional edition. It seems strange that the Royal Library today chooses to publish letters in this form, because digitization has such a high priority in research libraries. This confirms my impression that the purpose of the collection is first and foremost to tell an entertaining but closed story, but not necessarily providing musicology with the most recent tool for research. That is sad, because when we get access to the last 20 per cent of the letters online, this book will be of little relevance.

Peter E. Nissen

Eva Maria Jensen
Død og evighed i musikken 1890-1920
Copenhagen: Museum Tusculanums Forlag, 2011
356 pp., illus.
ISBN 978-87-635-1089-9
DKK 300, EUR 40

Med denne udgivelse foreligger der en folkeudgave af Eva Maria Jensens meget omfangsrige ph.d.-afhandling *Aufersteh'n, ja aufersteh'n! – død og evighed i musikken i tiden 1890-1920* fra Center for Kunst og Kristendom ved Det Teologiske Fakultet, Københavns Universitet. I den oprindelige afhandling var emnefeltet ikke blot død og evighed i musikken 1890–1920, men også en mere almen redegørelse for programmusikkens beskæftigelse med metafysiske spørgsmål udtrykt gennem især Richard Strauss' *Also sprach Zarathustra* og en række af den polske komponist Mieczyslaw Karlowicz' værker. Med denne indholdsmæssige slankning er det i højere grad lykkedes at fokusere på den intense beskæftigelse med død og uendelighed, som var gældende i musikken og kulturen som sådan omkring år 1900.

Til trods for emnets umiddelbart dystre karakter har Eva Maria Jensens redegørelse langt hen ad vejen karakter af en lystvandring, hvor tidligere tiders mindre tabuiserede forhold til døden kortlægges, og hvor datidens ofte naive eviggheds- og paradisforestillinger udfoldes. Eva Maria Jensen argumenterer overbevisende for at netop koncertsalsmusikken spillede en særlig rolle som et ideelt medium til formidling af religiøse budskaber i en tid hvor kirkens betydning var vigende. Ganske vist var scenekunsten i høj grad præget af Wagners idéer om en kunstreligion – eksemplarisk udtrykt i *Parsifal*. Men hvor scenekunsten så at sige opleves gennem agerende stedfortrædere på scenen, nedbrydes skellet mellem den oplevende og det oplevede i højere grad i værker som f.eks. Mahlers 8. symfoni, *Symphonie der Tausend*, hvor orkestermusik og menneskestemmer fusionerer i hvad Mahler opfattede som lyden af kredsende planeter og sole.

I bogens første store teoretiske afsnit viser Eva Maria Jensen hvordan denne grænsebrydende fordring er en naturlig konsekvens af periodens optagethed af metafysiske spørgsmål, og i forsøget på at udtrykke det uudsigelige viser der sig en række paradokser, som sprænger det traditionelle musikalske værkbegreb. I et forsøg på at gøre det enkelte værks effekt stærkere arbejdes der med synæstesi, hvor musikken som selvstændig kunstart udviskes til fordel for en sammensmeltning med bl.a. visuelle udtryk. Og i et forsøg på at omfatte de største metafysiske emner vokser de enkelte værker til en størrelse, hvor det ikke længere er praktisk muligt at komponere dem, og dermed bliver den uendeligt store musik uendeligt lille. Dette gælder i udtalt grad Skrjabins *Mysterium* og Charles Ives' *Universe Symphony*, og til dels Schönbergs ufuldendte oratorium *Die Jakobsleiter*, som Eva Maria Jensen præsenterer indgående i bogens store tredje del, hvor en række udvalgte værker analyseres med fokus på deres åndelige betydningsindhold.

I særlige tilfælde kan komponisternes beskæftigelse med eskatologiske emner føre til en radikal udvikling af det musikalske sprog. Det er tilfældet med *Die Jakobsleiter*, hvor Schönberg forsøger at beskrive himlen "som et uendeligt sted uden for tid og rum" (s. 208). Dette fører ifølge Eva Maria Jensen til at Schönberg – allerede inden han har formuleret sin teori om dodekafoni – opererer med en tolvtonerække for dermed at opnå den ønskede vægtløse og retningsløse tilstand. I andre tilfælde lader det til at musikken omhandlende død og evighed søger at udvide det traditionelle musikalske tidsbegreb eller selve det fysiske rum musikken udspiller sig i.

Til grund for sin analyse af periodens musik arbejder Eva Maria Jensen med en forestilling om en musikalsk symbolisme i kombination med Carl Dahlhaus' periodebegreb 'det moderne' dækkende årene fra 1890 og frem til 1924. I stedet for det upræcist tilbageskuende begreb 'senromantik' skabes der hermed en virkningsfuld ramme, der rummer periodens originale kunstneriske udtryk såsom impressionisme, ekspressionisme og dekadence. Samtidig bygger Eva Maria Jensen også sin forståelse af perioden på en forestilling om, at musikken er nært sammenhængende med almene kulturelle, kunstneriske og religiøse tendenser i tiden, og med netop denne værkkreds viser det sig at være yderst formålstjenligt. Især er inddragelsen af nyreligiøse bevægelser som teosofi og antroposofi frugtbar i en forståelse af værker af Skrjabin og Schönberg, hvor den teosofiske forestilling om menneskehedens mulige åndelige udvikling til højere bevidsthedsplaner spiller en afgørende rolle.

I både Mahlers 2. symfoni *Opstandelsessymfonien* og Elgars oratorium *The Dream of Gerontius* vises det til gengæld i hvor høj grad denne koncertsalsmusik er knyttet til og påvirket af traditionel liturgisk musik, kirkelige ceremonier og katolske dødsritualer. Eva Maria Jensen argumenterer overbevisende for at Mahler i sin stort anlagte 2. symfoni bruger den tyske digter og teolog Friedrich Klopstocks begravelsessalme *Auferstehn, ja auferstehn wirst du* som nøgle til at forløse den oplevelse af eksistentiel meningsløshed, som især formuleres i symfoniens store tragiske første sats. Med udgangspunkt i salmen, som Mahler omskriver, udmunder symfonien i en kirkelig ceremoniel sfære, hvor koret er blevet til en syngende menighed, orglet sikrer den kirkelige tilknytning og harper og dybe klokker er vigtige instrumenter i udfoldelsen af en himmelsk orkesterklang. Og i den store første del af *The Dream of Gerontius* viser Eva Maria Jensen i hvor høj grad katolikken Elgar har modelleret Gerontius' udstrakte dødsscene efter det katolske ritual for døende. Konkrete bønner, der, som foreskrevet af den katolske kirke, skal fremsiges af henholdsvis den døende og de tilstedeværende ved dødslejet, synges af solist og kor, og ved hjælp af ledemotiver repræsenterende f.eks. 'frygt', 'begravelse' og 'domfældelse' kommenterer og anticiperer orkestret dødsscenens handlingsgang.

Værkanalyserne bygger på en konkret gennemgang af det Eva Maria Jensen kalder 'dødens musikalske rekvisitter' og 'transcendensens musikalske attributter'. Her trækkes tråde tilbage til barokken og især romantiske komponister som Berlioz og Liszt, der med deres brug af bl.a. 'dies irae'-sekvensen og dødens instrument par excellence tamtam'en, var med til at initiere hvad man kunne kalde dødens musikalske vokabularium. Og hvad angår særlige instrumenter til at udtrykke transcendens er det sigende at både rørklokker og celeste blev udviklet som selvstændige orkesterinstrumenter i 1880'erne, hvor interessen for at udtrykke døden og det hinsidige i kunsten var i vækst. Der er også eksempler på hvordan imitation af fuglestemmer og særlige rytmiske motiver bruges som dødsvarsler. Alt i alt har denne gennemgang mest af alt karakter af et katalog, da Eva Maria Jensen ikke går ind i en egentlig tolkning af bevæggrunden for komponisternes valg af musikalske døds- og evighedssymboler. Med tanke på Eva Maria Jensen store overblik over emnet kunne det have været spændende, hvis hun havde underkastet dødens og evighedens orkestrale klange og rytmer en egentlig fænomenologisk analyse.

Hvorvidt den særlige interesse for død og evighed i musikken også har relevans i dag, eller der blot er tale om et isoleret historisk fænomen knyttet til perioden 1890–1920, besvares ikke.

Men med tanke på den store interesse, som især har omgærdet Mahlers musik i de seneste årtier, tyder meget på at emnet også i dag har relevans. I forbindelsen med en gennemgang af barnlige himmelvisioner i Mahlers 3. og 8. Symfoni, hvor engle spiller en central rolle, tillader Eva Maria Jensen sig dog at trække perspektiver frem til i dag. Ligesom på Mahlers tid indgår engle i dag i populærkulturen, og med udgangspunkt i en jungiansk tolkning advokeres der for at engle dengang som nu kan ses som en søgen efter det indre barn, og i videre forstand som en drøm om verden som et problemløst sted. Det kan naturligvis diskuteres hvorvidt dette er tilfældet i dag, men i Mahlers tilfælde lader det tydeligvis til, at barnets naive tro på engle kan bruges som et afsæt til at skabe en i ordets bedste forstand naiv glædesfyldt himmelsk musik.

Esben Tange

Laura Lohman
Umm Kulthum. Artistic Agency and the Shaping of an Arab Legend, 1967–2007
Middletown: Wesleyan University Press, 2010
229 pp., illus.
ISBN 978-0-8195-7071-0
USD 40 (hardback), USD 19.99 (e-book)

Umm Kulthum (?1904–1975) was a highly celebrated Egyptian singer, and still today many listener in the Arab world consider her art the epitome of genuine Arabic musical expression. Her particular way of negotiating the relation between Arabic history and modernity and her iconic status in modern Arabic culture have attracted a great part of interest both in Arabic and Western scholarship.

Laura Lohman's book takes issue with the later part of Umm Kulthum's career and with her rich and diverse posthumous reception. Lohman argues against the widespread notion that the final years of this great Egyptian artist – from the Six Day War in 1967 to her death in 1975 – should be a period of decline after the peak was reached in the 1940s with the artistically advanced neo-classical *qasaʾid*. However, this period in Lohman's life was intensively productive and offered Umm Kulthum 'a valuable opportunity for her to redefine herself as an artist and to shape the way she would be remembered after her death' (p. 3). Lohman is obviously fascinated by Umm Kulthum as a strong-willed female artist with the intention of – and the powers to – influence decidedly on her star-imago and her posthumous reception. Thus she discerns in Umm Kulthum 'a remarkable degree of individual agency', and interprets much of what Umm Kulthum was doing during the particular political and cultural climate after Egypt's defeat in the Six Day War as 'a performance of "self" in the public eye, as a "performed autobiography" encompassing a vast collection of carefully rendered autobiographical acts that were perceived as self-representations' (p. 8).

The first three chapters of the book account for Umm Kulthum's late career viewed from this perspective and focus particularly on the political aspects: her strong support to the Egyptian government after the defeat in the Six Days War (comprising 'charity' concerts in favour of the Egyptian army), her concerts throughout the Arab world in support of the pan-Arabic movement, and her support for the Palestinian liberation movement. The remaining chapters four through six examine Umm Kulthum's reception after her death lead by the question: 'why and how she remained so important?' To this end Lohman scrutinizes a rich and diverse source-material: books, articles, and films which take issue with her life and contributes to the shaping and reshaping of her iconographic status. Particular attention is devoted to issues of idealization, to 'strategies … used to reconcile her unconventional life choices as an Egyptian woman with cultural expectations and perceptions of gender and sexuality' (p. 15), and to the processes that lead to the inclusion of the songs of Umm Kulthum in the repertoire of the Arab cultural heritage (*al-Turath*). For the analysis of this last aspect Lohman considers 'sonic memorialization achieved through radio programming, cover songs and remixes' (p. 15) as well as physical memorials such as the Umm Kulthum museum in Cairo and 'Umm Kulthum Cafees' in Arab and Western cities.

Laura Lohman's *Umm Kulthum. Artistic Agency and the Shaping of an Arab Legend, 1967-2007* is a well-written, well-researched, and well-documented account of an interesting and highly relevant topic. It locates itself in a productive field between music history, popular music studies, music anthropology, and area studies and utilizes skillfully the research potentials thus activated. The book offers a very welcome glimpse into the huge bulk of written sources to Umm Kulthum's life and afterlife; it interrogates wisely from the perspective of recent research in stardom and in the constructed nature of star images, and still it bears the marks of respect for the particular cultural context. Obviously this book fills in a lacuna in the Western literature on Umm Kulthum and represents – as I read it – a much needed supplement to Virginia Danielsen's great book, *The Voice of Egypt. Umm Kulthum, Arabic song, and Egyptian Society in the Twentieth Century* (1997).

My reservations are few and pertain primarily to the interpretative practice. It is not evident to me that Lohman's interpretation of Umm Kulthum's self-enactment in her later years as deliberate acts to control her posthumous reception really contributes to our understanding of 'artistic agency' in a deeper sense including the agencies of the artistic forms and practices in question. And on a broader level I miss a style of writing that invites to partaking in the interpretative process. Even if the author is quoting a great number of her source texts, her book leaves the impression of being basically 'monologic'. The quotations are always strategic and fully covered by the interpretation. The voice of the book is the voice of the author, as far as no other voices with the right to contradict are heard. Maybe it is a matter of style, maybe it is a matter of economical writing? But it is as if the author considers her source materials as transparent for the (wished for) meanings. Even when she admits to the fluidity of their significance (p. 55), she does not take the consequence and quotes to an extent that enables the reader to look over her shoulder and take part in the precarious interpretations. Thus a dialogical use of this book is only possible for readers with access to the original Arabic sources.

Criticism of this kind, however, could be directed against a great part of our academic writing. Here it is triggered by desire to get even closer to the subject of a well-done and deserving scholarly work. The book is warmly recommended for research and study.

Søren Møller Sørensen

Elaine Gould
Behind Bars. The Definitive Guide to Music Notation
London: Faber Music, 2011
xviii + 676 pp., illus.
ISBN 978-0-571-51456-4
GBP 65 (hardback), students GBP 45

With the publication of *Behind Bars* the scanty literature on music notation and music processing has become enriched with what is now the most comprehensive presentation on this subject to date – weighing in at no less than 676 pages. Just 25–30 years ago, such a book would only be able to boast of a very small potential readership, supposedly to be found among members of two now completely extinct professions, namely, the music-engraver's and music-copyist's trades. But times have changed. Today, the production of print-ready music notation has come to be part and parcel of the composer's, the arranger's, and the music scholar's work. We are living in a time of transition, where the time-honoured traditions of craftsmanship in the music-engraver's and music-copyist's trades have vanished at an alarming pace without being replaced by new standards for computer-generated music notation or music processing that live up to the refined aesthetics of the past. This does not mean to say that our day's music software programs are inferior. On the contrary – when they are used by adept hands, the modern music software programs deliver altogether excellent results – and indeed, in many instances, they even surpass the standard set by earlier times' engraved notes. The problem is merely that it requires a great deal of professional expertise to operate a music software program in such a way that the finished product maintains a professional standard. Against this backdrop, *Behind Bars* is a highly relevant publication that will undoubtedly satisfy an urgent need in modern music life.

Music notation is not an entirely unambiguous or exact discipline. Traditional Western music notation builds upon a series of overall conventions around which there is essentially a consensus but you need not delve very far down into notation's manifold nooks and crannies before the sense of general agreement breaks off and becomes superseded by a profusion of different traditions that can be nationally/regionally conditioned or can be associated with the individual music publishers' 'house style'. For this reason, it has been anything but an easy task that Elaine Gould has set her sights on, in compiling this *The Definitive Guide to Music Notation*, as the book's ambitious subordinate title resounds.

Literature on the notation of music up to the present day has focused primarily on note-writing, note-engraving, and the specific notation-related factors that are related to the individual instruments. It is the latter topic that gives rise, moreover, to a gray area situated between instrumentation textbooks and the literature on notation. Finally, there are the often bulky manuals for music software programs, which constitute a whole new genre within the field of literature on notation. The most all-inclusive presentation so far has been Gardner Read's comprehensive *Music Notation. A Manual of Modern Practice* (Crescendo Publishing Co., 1969), which has more or less functioned as the standard reference work up until the present day.

Gould has organized her material in a way that calls to mind Read's *Music Notation*, aside from the fact that Gould has wisely refrained from conducting an historical overview of Western music notation's development from Gregorian chant to the present time. Such a synopsis naturally runs the risk of being cursory and superficial and would also fall outside this book's genuine purpose. Similarly, everything concerning manuscript music has been left out of the discussion here; unfortunately, we are presumably going to have to face up to the fact that in the future, the art of writing music by hand – in much the manner as is the case with ordinary handwriting – is bound be to a discipline that will be cultivated only by very few specialists. What is equally remarkable is that computer music-software programs are not mentioned either, not even by a single word – supposedly in an attempt to make the book as timeless as possible, seeing especially that music-software programs are changing and developing so very rapidly in these years, while there is a different kind of stability that has become the order of the day within notational conventions. This is, at one and the same time, the book's weakness and strength. *Behind Bars* is accordingly, in its entire approach to the topic, the diametrical opposite of a book like Steven Powell's *Music Engraving Today: The*

Art and Practice of Digital Notesetting, which takes its mark in the music-software programs, *Sibelius* and *Finale*, and which, through a comparison of these two programs' facilities, points out how modern music processing can be carried into effect.

Behind Bars is apportioned into three main parts. First, there is an opening section that touches upon general notational conventions (General Conventions). This is followed by a sequence of chapters that treat of the specific notation for the individual instrument groups (Idiomatic Notation). Finally, in the third part, matters of score layout and part preparation are addressed, as well as various aspects related to newer music that do not readily lend themselves to being incorporated into the book's earlier chapters (Layout and Presentation).

Taken as a whole, *Behind Bars* is very well arranged, easy to grasp and easy to work with. Every one of the book's twenty chapters is introduced with an extremely user-friendly table of contents related to the current chapter. Moreover, the running text is supplied with useful cross-references so that the reader can easily find his/her way around in what could otherwise prove to be a very complex world of concepts. It must also be mentioned that this book's own typography and layout as well as the seemingly countless music examples have been executed in an exemplary way.

In her brilliant introduction, Gould takes up a stance as an advocate for the altogether sensible position that one ought to strive as far as possible to follow the prevailing practice rather than try to invent novel notation forms. We should therefore constantly envision ourselves in the musician's chair: for the musician, what is crucial is to be able to recognize – without delay – a music image. Every renewal – no matter how sensible it might seem to be – will tend to disturb the musician's reading of the music. Gould makes no secret of the fact that her exposition is subjective. She openly concedes that she has been influenced by the typographic principles that can be traced back to the music publishers Bärenreiter's and Henle's publications.

The individual notational problems are presented in an easily understandable and clear language, as the author perseveringly reviews various options in a sober-minded fashion. At the same time, she does not shy away from disclosing her own subjective preferences. Several sections end with the sentence, 'Some editions use ...'; here, the author is discreetly pointing out that even though these solutions are absolutely legitimate, the author herself does not recommend them.

The last chapters on the layout and the arrangement of the score and parts are nothing short of outstanding. It is most especially in these chapters that the book makes a contribution with mostly new material. Here, for the very first time, one reads a coherent presentation of one of music typography's most complicated areas, information that has hitherto belonged to the music publishing houses' professional experts but which has been available to only a limited extent in the specialized literature. In the chapter, 'Part Preparation', more than twelve pages are devoted to the sole topic of providing and notating cues. Here, all conceivable situations are examined.

The book's subordinate title, *The Definitive Guide to Music Notation*, is pretentious and bound to give rise to a number of comments: first, it has to be made clear that the notion of 'definitive' is necessarily limited, in the chronological sense, to little more than the past 200 years and, in the geographical sense, to the notation of music from the Western cultural sphere. The notation of music composed prior to Viennese Classicism is, generally speaking, not even touched upon. For example, it is not possible to find any guidance in the practice concerning the notation of figured bass in music from the seventeenth and eighteenth centuries, not to mention in the notation forms that are associated with medieval and Renaissance music. It is, perhaps, easy enough to understand why the author has resisted from treating of the older music's notation – that is to say, music from before *c.*1600: an adequate treatment of this complex topic could easily swell up to a self-contained treatise, on a par with Willi Apel's *The Notation of Polyphonic Music 900–1600,* but a few pages about figured bass notation would certainly not have been out of place here.

If it can be said that the book has a chronological limitation – looking backwards – to around 1780–1800, then the other end of the time scale is, naturally, limited to 2011. This seemingly self-evident fact deserves attention, especially because the author devotes no small portion of the book to the newer music's notation forms which, in contrast to the traditional notation, have – for the most part – still not established themselves as fixed notational conventions. Therefore the book's treatment of newer notation forms might quickly prove to have become obsolete. One might ask whether or not the new music's notation practice deserves – in the same manner as appears to be the case with the older music – to be treated in a separate publication. In all fairness, it must be mentioned that the book's author is an expert in the notation of newer and contemporary music.

The book's closing bibliography – a single page headed 'Further Reading' – is, 'highly selective' – twelve titles all in all (only English-language sources are listed here), seven of which have to do with the proper topic of music engraving and notation. Among these seven titles we do not find some of the most recommendable books on music notation: Read's previously mentioned *Music Notation. A Manual of Modern Practice* (1969); Albert C. Vinci's succinct but nonetheless excellent *Fundamentals of Traditional Musical Notation* (The Kent State University Press, 1985; published in German as *Die Notenschrift. Grundlagen der traditionellen Musiknotation*, Bärenreiter, 1988); and Herbert Chlapik's *Die Praxis des Notengraphikers* (Doblinger, 1987). Can it be that the publishing house has pressured the author to omit those titles that, within the compass of the very scanty literature on the topic, comprise the few which, in certain areas, at least, could be thought to be competing with *Behind Bars*? Should the reader feel inspired to become better acquainted with musical notation, there is, on the Danish Centre for Music Publication's website, a bibliography related specifically to the publishing of music, with a special section related to note-setting and notation: www. kb.dk/da/kb/nb/mta/dcm/udgivelser/bibliografi.html

Behind Bars is an altogether splendid and highly recommendable book. Nevertheless, it cannot be overlooked that this book, to a great degree, reflects a specifically Anglo-Saxon practice. The book is evidently targeted at the English readership, while users from other parts of the world are left in the lurch. And that is a shame. With a few strategic expansions, it would have been possible for this book to address itself to a much wider audience. For example, a summary of instrument names, tempo indications, expression marks and performance-technique instructions and their abbreviations in English, German, French, and Italian would have been very useful. On the whole, the book ought to have been making a running examination of the prevalent terminology in these main languages that are customarily used in the sphere of music composition and performance. Another area that the author has neglected to address is – as has already been mentioned – the practice of figured bass notation. With the inclusion of the expansions suggested here, the next edition of the book could bear the subordinate title, *European Music Notation from ca. 1600 to Present Time*.

Behind Bars might very well turn out to be the new standard reference work within the field of music notation – and hopefully the book will be successful in contributing to raising the standard within the countless typographically substandard music notation publications that are flourishing these years – especially on the Internet.

Niels Bo Foltmann

Mark Slobin
Folk Music: A Very Short Introduction
Oxford & New York: Oxford University Press, 2011
Very Short Introductions, vol. 257
144 pp., illus.
ISBN 978-0-19-539502-0
GBP 7.99

Who hasn't eight dollars? *Folk Music: A Very Short Introduction* is one of those books which must be recommended reading for students, researchers, and enthusiasts of all kinds of music. Slobin, former president of the Society for Ethnomusicology and one of North America's most widely experienced ethnomusicologists, presents in scholarly lucid and stimulating fashion the world of folk music from a range of different angles, discusses music from every corner of the globe, and throws open the doors on folk music as a remarkably diverse and ever-changing music. He draws on his own experience from his first fieldwork in Afghanistan in 1967 and his later work on the heritage of the Eastern European Jews.

Through six sturdy chapters various issues and perspectives salient to the study, knowledge, and experience of folk music are touched upon. In the first paragraph Slobin elegantly finds his way around defining folk music: 'This Very Short Introduction … will not offer anything like a definition of "folk music," relying instead on the principle of "we know it when we hear it." Understandings of the term have varied so widely over space and time that no single summary sentence can pin it down' (p. 1). With his inclusive approach and focus on the people who perform, listen, invent, and feel the music in everyday life, Slobin partakes in making folk music and musical scholarship matter profoundly – also beyond the sphere of musicology and folk music connoisseur-ship.

The second chapter is devoted to 'actual folk music … songs that speak directly to people's reasons for singing' (p. 21), addressing close to universal experiences and anxieties of de-territorialization and separation of those who must leave their loved ones for reasons of war, work or refugee status. One of Slobin's own recordings from 1968, a *falak* from Badakhshan in northeastern Afghanistan illustrates the point. *Falak* means heavens or fate in the local Persian dialect spoken in Afghanistan, and for the ethnic Tajik, life is a constant struggle against this fate. In the actual *falak*, which 'basically stays in the anguished lost-love mode' (p. 22), the references to displacement and nostalgia takes on an almost prophetic character, as Afghanistan in 1978, ten years after the recording, suffered from invasions, occupations, shifts of political power, and the majority of the population moving in and out of refugee camps through more than thirty years. Slobin pays considerable attention to the details of the meaning of the text, the instruments, the melody and sound of the song, articulation, and performance practice.

Chapter three addresses the intervening in folk music life of the intelligentsia, the 'ill-assorted group of … the educated elite of thinkers, scholars, artists, and upper-class amateurs' (p. 51). Slobin defines two important trends in the early nineteenth century as central for this intervention: identity-seeking and institution-building which were coupled by two major agendas of the time: nationalism and universalism. Germany, 'fragmented into dozens of little states until 1860, needed a common purpose in the quest for unity, to be founded on the *volk*, a complex compound of sentiments and semantics. Nationalists across Europe eagerly touted folk music as the "spirit" of the hard-to-define concept the "nation"' (p. 52).

The English amateur antiquarian William Thomas coined the term 'folklore' in 1846, replacing terms like 'popular antiquities' and made possible words like 'folk song' and 'folk music', as well as the founding of the first scholarly institutions such as the American Folklore Society in 1888. The disciplines of linguistics, anthropology, and music became the ancestors of today's ethnomusicology.

Chapter four addresses how folk music has been collected and circulated in writing, recording and other formats. The basic philosophy of the early twentieth century of collecting was to make standardized samples as 'clean' as possible for 'quick comparison across a huge range of objects' (p. 69). Over time collectors became more sensitive and sophisticated in their way of approaching, gathering, and interpreting what they heard and observed. One thing is scholars' recordings, another how the music has been picked up and circulated in everyday life, and how performers have continually popularized and re-folklorized folk tunes.

In chapter five, focus is directed at movements and stars within folk music. Folk music is central to regional pride and ethnic and individual identity, to resistance, political uprisings, and movement-formation. Music 'channels strong sentiments, thus circulating into many kinds of movements, conservative and progressive, religious and radical ... Homesickness and protest, lovesickness and religious fervor can flow through the repertoire of a single singer or community at a particular moment without contradiction' (p. 87). In North America, such songs have been rising to the surface during slavery in the 1840s, in the social turbulence of the 1930s and 1950s. Into the heart of folk music practice goes a quotation of social activist and singer-song writer Pete Seeger, worth repeating: 'like hymns and patriotic songs, union songs are songs with a message ... unlike most hymns and patriotic songs, union songs are usually composed by amateurs to suit a particular occasion, and have a short life. More often than not, they are simply new words to an older melody' (p. 88).

In the final chapter, Slobin offers a short survey of three basic categories that characterize much twenty-first century folk music: *The Circuit* describes the organization, initiatives, education, networking, advocacy, and development of the folk music 'field'. 'It's a long way from earlier circuits, such as Woody Guthrie's dustbowl odyssey and Pete Seeger's union halls' (p. 109) to the extremely formalization of the folk music circuit, such as the World Music Expo (WOMEX). *The System* describes another set of networks covering a dense layer of influential 'official' transnational organizations, aiming in high-flown rhetoric to 'safeguard' and 'protect' traditional music. For UNESCO, the operative term is intangible cultural heritage, which it defined in 2003: 'the practices, representations, expressions, as well as the knowledge and skills, that communities, groups and, in some cases, individuals recognize as part of their cultural heritage' (p. 112). *As for the Tourist*, Slobin points to important aspects of responsibility and agendas of tourists, agents, and the locals alike, questions of otherness, heritage, and staged authenticity.

The book is exciting, even entertaining, reading, for example where Slobin describes the bossy, maximum control approach to field recording of song catcher Francis Densmore (the picture of her firm posture while recording an Indian chief singing is well-known): 'She was blunt about who was in charge: "The singer must never be allowed to think that he is in charge of the work. A strict hold must be kept on them".' (p. 68). References are placed at the back of the book, easy enough to locate. Suggestions for further reading and a list of internet resources help the reader to look further into the world of folk music.

Out of the many *Very Short Introductions*, five volumes so far are on music, the others being Nicholas Cook on music (vol. 2), Philip Bohlman on world music (vol. 65), Kathryn Kalinak on film music (vol. 231), and Thomas Forrest Kelly on early music (vol. 265). The strength of all of them is that they do in fact open up for the vast soundscapes that the world's societies are producing and participating in. Yet, one wonders what music will be introduced in the very short form the next time. Introductions to heavy metal or rap music are badly needed.

Condensing the vast and variegated world of folk music to a limited number of very small pages is not an easy task. But this only pays credit to Slobin's format. This small introduction to folk music is nothing less than a masterpiece, a joy to read as it invites for further thinking and studying, and it fits nicely into almost any pocket.

Tore Tvarnø Lind

Bibliography 2011

Anne Ørbæk Jensen

The bibliography is primarily based on questionnaires. It has a dual purpose: to register on the one hand the scholarly work of Danish musicologists, and on the other the publications of music researchers from abroad dealing with Danish music. It includes only titles published in the year with which the bibliography is concerned, as well as addenda to the bibliography for the preceding year. As a rule the following types of work are not included: unprinted university theses, newspaper articles, reviews, CD booklets, and encyclopedia entries.

I. BIBLIOGRAPHICAL PUBLICATIONS

Jensen, Anne Ørbæk, 'Bibliography 2010', *Danish Yearbook of Musicology*, 38 (2010/11), 122–36.

Raben, Erik, 'Diskografi over danske jazzindspilninger 1945-2000', in Olav Harsløf and Finn Slumstrup (eds.), *Jazz i Danmark 1950-2010* (København: Politiken, 2011), 576–606.

Aagaard, René, website http://the-discographer.dk/, contains illustrated discographies on Danish artists such as *Teddy Petersen*, no pag.; *Erik Tuxen*, no pag.; *Max Hansen*, 56 pp.; *Ellen Beck,* 13 pp.; *Emilie Ulrich*, 11 pp.; *Ida Møller*, 31 pp.; *Ingeborg Steffensen*, 32 pp.; *Johanne Brun*, 32 pp.; *Margrethe Lendrop,* 11 pp.; *Per Biørn*, 46 pp.; *Thyge Thygesen and Margherita Flor,* no pag.; *Albert Vaguet*, 94 pp.; *Applaudando-Record*, 90 pp.; *Danske kunstnere udgivet på Edison Records,* 8 pp.; *Blue Boys,* 33 pp.; *Four Jacks,* 11 pp.

II. YEARBOOKS, CONFERENCE REPORTS, FESTSCHRIFTEN, ANTHOLOGIES ETC.

Danish Yearbook of Musicology, 38 (2010/11), ed. Michael Fjeldsøe, Peter Hauge, and Thomas Holme Hansen (Copenhagen: Danish Musicological Society / Aarhus University Press, 2011), 141 pp.

Nordisk musikkpedagogisk forskning – Årbok. Nordic Research in Music Education – Yearbook, 12 (2010), ed. Sven-Erik Holgersen and Siw Graabræk Nielsen (Oslo: Norges Musikkhøgskole, 2010), 217 pp.

III. MUSICAL HISTORY
General

Andersson, Greger, 'Östersjöområdet som musiklandskap. Några refleksioner kring projektet och dess utveckling', in Ole Kongsted (ed.), *Studia Musicologica Regionis Balticae I* (København: Capella Hafniensis and Det Kongelige Bibliotek, 2011), 69–74.

Balslev-Clausen, Peter, 'Luthers salmer i danske salmebøger 1528-2002', *Hymnologi*, 40/1-2 (Apr. 2011), 11–30.

Balslev-Clausen, Peter, 'Martin Luthers salmer i sønderjyske salmebøger 1528-1953', *Hymnologi*, 40/1-2 (Apr. 2011), 31–42.

Balslev-Clausen, Peter, 'Reformation og salmemelodier. Et bidrag til forståelsen af, hvordan reformationen blev oplevet', in Mattias Lundberg and Sven-Åke Selander (eds.), *Melos och logos. Festskrift till Folke Bohlin* (Skellefteå: Artos, 2011), 35–48.

Brincker, Jens, *Komponistbasen. Et webleksikon in-progress over danske komponister i ord, lyd og billeder*. Online publication: http://www.komponistforeningen.dk/node/24 (2011–).

Dürrfeld, Peter, *Gud i musikken* (København: Kristeligt Dagblad, 2011), 255 pp.

Jensen, Eva Maria, 'Recepcja Chopina w Danii – rys historyczny i stan wspolczesnyh', in Zofia Budrewicz, Maria Sienko, and Romualda Lawronska (eds.), *Chopin w polskiej szkole i kulturze* (Krakow: Wydawnictwo Naukowe Uniwersytetu Pedagogicznego, 2011), 404–25.

Nissen, Peter E., 'Kirkemusikforskning i tiden: En undersøgelse af kirkemusikforskningen i Skandinavien', in Mattias Lundberg and Sven-Åke Selander (eds.), *Melos och logos. Festskrift till Folke Bohlin* (Skellefteå: Artos, 2011), 285–94.

Preisler, Ebbe, *Om lidt er sangen klar. Den danske lejlighedssang fra Kingo til Rap* (Knebel: Vistoft, 2011), 432 pp.

Schwab, Heinrich W., 'Der Ostseeraum. Beobachtungen aus seiner Musikgeschichte und Anregungen zu einem musikhistoriographischen Konzept', in Ole Kongsted (ed.), *Studia Musicologica Regionis Balticae I* (København: Capella Hafniensis and Det Kongelige Bibliotek, 2011), 39–68.

Before *c.* 1600

Christoffersen, Peter Woetmann, 'The restoration of Antoine Busnoys' four-part Flemish song "In mijnen sijn" – An experiment in sound, imitation technique, and the setting of a popular tune', *Danish Musicology Online*, 2 (2011), 21–51. Online publication: http://www.danishmusicologyonline.dk/arkiv/arkiv_dmo/dmo_02/dmo_02_artikel_02.pdf

Koldau, Linda Maria, 'Liturgie und Lebenswirklichkeit. Die spätmittelalterliche Kultur der Lüneburger Klöster', *Heimatkalender für Stadt und Kreis Uelzen*, 79 (2011), 47–60.

Petersen, Nils Holger, 'The Concept of Liturgical Drama. Coussemaker and Modern Scholarship', in Barbara Haggh and Frédéric Billiet (eds.), *Ars musica septentrionalis. De l'interprétation du patrimoine musical à l'historiographie* (Paris: Presses de l'Université Paris-Sorbonne, 2011), 59–73.

Schiødt, Nanna, 'From Byzantium to Italy. Castrato singers from the 4th to the 20th centuries', in Nina-Maria Wanek (ed.), *Psaltike. Neue Studien zur Byzantinischen Musik. Festschrift für Gerda Wolfram* (Wien: Praesens, 2011), 301–11.

Troelsgård, Christian, *Byzantine Neumes. A New Introduction to the Middle Byzantine Musical Notation* (Monumenta Musicae Byzantinae, Subsidia, 9; Copenhagen: Museum Tusculanum, 2011), 142 pp.

Troelsgård, Christian, 'I trattati bizantini di teoria musicale', in Giacomo Baroffio, Vera Minazzi, and Ruini Cesarino (eds.), *Atlante storico della musica nel medioevo* (Milano: Jaca book, 2011), 72–76.

Troelsgård, Christian, 'When did the practice of eunuch singers in Byzantine chant begin? Some notes on the interpretation of the early sources', in Nina-Maria Wanek (ed.), *Psaltike. Neue Studien zur Byzantinischen Musik. Festschrift für Gerda Wolfram* (Wien: Praesens, 2011), 345–50.

C. 1600 till *c.* 1910

Adams, Andrew and Bradley Martin, *Forgotten Romantic: The Life and Works of Edmund Neupert (1842–1888)*. Online publication: http://www.griegsociety.org/default.asp?kat=1046&id=5163&sp=1 (2011), 69 pp.

Andersen, Rune, *An 'authentic' Peer Gynt music? A source-critical study of Edvard Grieg's Opus 23 – some aspects*. Online publication: http://www.griegsociety.org/default.asp?kat=1046&id=5161&sp=1 (2011), 10 pp.

Appold, Juliette, *Edvard Grieg, Niels Gade and Johann Peter Emilius Hartmann. Musical reverences in selected piano works*. Online publication: http://www.griegsociety.org/default.asp?kat=1046&id=5175&sp=1 (2011), 19 pp.

Bergsagel, John, *"… an indefinable longing drove me towards Copenhagen". Opening address, The International Edvard Grieg Society Conference, Scheffergården, Copenhagen, 11 August, 2011*. Online publication: http://www.griegsociety.org/default.asp?kat=1046&id=5162&sp=1 (2011), 16 pp.

Busk, Gorm, 'Kuhlau's Model Technique and Musical Style', *IFKS Newsletter* (2010). Online publication: http://www.kuhlau.gr.jp/e/e_library/ee_impotant_article_from_newsletter/ee_kuhlaus_modeltechnique.html

Dreyer, Kirsten, 'Det er en deilig Fætter, den Ole! H.C. Andersen og Ole Bull', *Magasin fra Det Kongelige Bibliotek*, 24/2 (June 2011), 38–54.

Erichsen, Jørgen, *Friedrich Kuhlau. Ein deutscher Musiker in Kopenhagen. Eine Biographie nach zeitgenössischen Dokumenten* (Hildesheim: Georg Olms, 2011), 352 pp.

Erichsen, Jørgen, *Friedrich Kuhlau*. Online publication: http://www.josebamus.dk/Kuhlau/Kuhlau-4.htm (2011)

Foltmann, Niels Bo, 'Carl Nielsens "Maskarade" og Det Kongelige Teaters scenemusik til Holbergs komedier', *Fund og Forskning i Det Kongelige Biblioteks samlinger*, 50 (2011), 371–86.

Gero, Olga V., *Duchovnye teksty v muzyke Bukstechude* (Moskva: Klassika XXI, 2010), 305 pp.

Grage, Joachim, 'Intermedial Reference as Metareference. Hans Christian Andersen's Musical Novels', in Walter Bernhart and Werner Wolf (eds.), *Self-Reference in Literature and Music* (Word and Music Studies 11; Amsterdam: Rodopi, 2010), 175–88.

Grimley, Daniel, 'Carl Nielsen's Carnival: Time, Space and the Politics of Identity in *Maskarade*', in Rachel Cowgill, David Cooper, and Clive Brown (eds.), *Art and Ideology in European Opera, Essays in Honour of Julian Rushton* (Woodbridge: Boydell, 2010), 241–61.

Grüner, Wulfhard von and Volker Rehberg, *Johann Abraham Peter Schulz. Liedermann des Volkes. Leben, Umfeld und Schaffen. Eine Reflexion* (Schwedt/Oder: Freund und Förderer der Musik- und Kunstschule "J.A.P. Schulz" der Stadt Schwedt, 2010), 184 pp.

Hauge, Peter, 'Johann Adolph Scheibe (1708-76) and Copenhagen', *Fund og Forskning i Det Kongelige Biblioteks samlinger*, 50 (2011), 315–44.

Hauge, Peter, 'John Dowland's employment at the royal Danish court. Musician, agent – and spy?', in Marika Keblusek and Badeloch Vera Noldus (eds.), *Double Agents: Cultural and Political Brokerage in Early Modern Europe* (Studies in Medieval and Reformation Traditions, 154; Leiden: Brill, 2011), 193–212.

Hauge, Peter, 'Michael Praetorius's Connections to the Danish Court', in Susanne Rode-Breymann and Arne Spohr (eds.), *Michael Praetorius. Vermittler europäischer Musiktraditionen um 1600* (Hildesheim: Georg Olms, 2011), 27–43.

Heiner, Jørgen, '"Jeg elsker denne Mester overalt". Om August Enna og H.C. Andersen', *Anderseniana*, 2010, 177–205.

Hesselager, Jens, 'Operatic or Theatrical? Orchestral Framings of the Voice in the Melodrama *Sept heures* (1829)', in Sarah Hibberd (ed.), *Melodramatic voices: understanding music drama* (Farnham: Ashgate, 2011), 27–44.

Jensen, Anne Ørbæk, 'En nordisk sangforening', in Mattias Lundberg and Sven-Åke Selander (eds.), *Melos och logos. Festskrift till Folke Bohlin* (Skellefteå: Artos, 2011), 401–12.

Jensen, Eva Maria, *Død og evighed i musikken 1890-1920* (København: Museum Tusculanum, 2011), 356 pp.

Jensen, Niels Martin, 'Fire visemelodier. Melodierne og deres baggrund', in Jens Keld and Marita Akhøj Nielsen (eds.), *Jens Steen Sehesteds digtning* 1: Tekster ([København]: Det Danske Sprog- og Litteraturselskab, 2011), 311–35 + 1 cd.

Jensen, Niels Martin, 'When Is a Solo Sonata Not a Solo Sonata? Corelli's Op. V Considered in the Light of the Genre's Tradition', in Peter Walls (ed.), *Baroque Music* (The Library of Essays on Music Performance Practice; Farnham: Ashgate, 2011), 457–76.

Koldau, Linda Maria, 'Singing Luther's Praises in 1883 with L. Meinardus', *Lutheran Quarterly*, 25/3 (Autumn 2011), 279–97.

Kongsted, Ole, 'Das "carmen gratulatorium" als vokalpolyphone Gattung in Nordeuropa während der Spätrenaissance und des Frühbarock', in Ole Kongsted (ed.), *Studia Musicologica Regionis Balticae I* (København: Capella Hafniensis and Det Kongelige Bibliotek, 2011), 177–87.

Kongsted, Ole, 'Die Musikalien im Archiv der Hansestadt Wismar', in Ole Kongsted (ed.), *Studia Musicologica Regionis Balticae I* (København: Capella Hafniensis and Det Kongelige Bibliotek, 2011), 217–30.

Kongsted, Ole, 'Musikhistoriografien og den danske hofmusik i den nordiske Senrenaissance. En forskningsberetning I', in Ole Kongsted (ed.), *Studia Musicologica Regionis Balticae I* (København: Capella Hafniensis and Det Kongelige Bibliotek, 2011), 231–87.

Kongsted, Ole, 'The Secular "rex splendens". Music as Representative Art at the Court of Christian IV', in Ole Kongsted (ed.), *Studia Musicologica Regionis Balticae I* (København: Capella Hafniensis and Det Kongelige Bibliotek, 2011), 189–215.

Kremer, Joachim, 'Biographien als Indikatoren. Johann Matthesons *Ehrenpforten*-Projekt und die regionale Ausdifferenzierung des Kantorats im Ostseeram', in Ole Kongsted (ed.), *Studia Musicologica Regionis Balticae I* (København: Capella Hafniensis and Det Kongelige Bibliotek, 2011), 99–175.

Küster, Konrad, 'Fame, politics and personal relationship. Whom did Düben know in the Baltic area?', in Erik Kjellberg (ed.), *The dissemination of music in seventeenth-century Europe. Celebrating the Düben collection* (Bern etc.: Peter Lang, 2010), 149–71.

Moe, Bjarke, 'Italian Music at the Danish Court during the Reign of Christian IV. Presenting a picture of cultural transformation', *Danish Yearbook of Musicology*, 38 (2010/11), 15–32.

Moe, Bjarke, 'København og musikken dér i det syttende århundrede', *Custos. Tidsskrift for tidlig musik*, 9/3 (Nov. 2011), 10–13.

Nissen, Peter E., 'Franz Liszt og de danske pianister: I anledning af Franz Liszts 200-års fødselsdag 2011', *Personalhistorisk Tidsskrift*, 131/2 (2011), 83–107.

Nissen, Peter E., 'Kirchenmusik in Kopenhagen 1840-1920: Nationale Traditionen und internationale Einflüsse', in Helmut Loos (ed.), *Musik-Stadt. Traditionen und Perspektiven urbaner Musikkulturen. Bericht über den XIV. Internationalen Kongress der Gesellschaft für Musikforschung vom 28. September bis 3. Oktober 2008 am Institut für Musikwissenschaft der Universität Leipzig*, 1 (Leipzig: Gudrun Schröder, 2011), 546–56.

Parly, Nila, *Vocal Victories. Wagner's female characters from Senta to Kundry* (København: Museum Tusculanum, 2011), 431 pp.

Rasmussen, Karl Aage, *Tilnærmelser til Gustav Mahler* (København: Gyldendal, 2011), 203 pp.

Roed, Susan Skovborg, *Gustav Mahler – gennem mørke til lys* (Vordingborg: Attika, 2011), 127 pp.

Schlenkert, Helge, *Musiklivet i den danske guldalder* (Herlev: Edition Karpen, 2011), 323 pp.

Schwab, Heinrich W., 'Zur Struktur der "Musikkultur des Ostseeraumes" während des 17. Jahrhunderts', in Ole Kongsted (ed.), *Studia Musicologica Regionis Balticae I* (København: Capella Hafniensis and Det Kongelige Bibliotek, 2011), 13–38.

Schwab, Heinrich, W., ‚Wenn „Brüder einträchtig beieinander wohnen". Zur bildlichen Darstellung Buxtehudes auf dem Gemälde von Johannes Voorhout (1674)', in Wolfgang Sandberger and Volker Scherliess (eds.), *Dieterich Buxtehude. Text – Kontext – Rezeption. Bericht über das Symposion an der Musikhochschule Lübeck, 10. - 12. Mai 2007* (Kassel et al.: Bärenreiter, 2011), 11–32.

Sørensen, Inger, *Horneman. En kunstnerslægt* (København: Museum Tusculanum, 2011), 397 pp.

Vis, Jurjen, *Fuglsang as a musical crossroad: paradise and paradise lost. Röntgen, de Neergaard, Grieg and Fuglsang*. Online publication: http://www.griegsociety.org/default.asp?kat=1046& id=5160&sp=1 (2011), 16 pp.

Wasserloos, Yvonne, 'Reformen und Revisionen. Musikalischer Kulturtransfer von Leipzig nach Kopenhagen im 19. Jahrhundert', *EGO – Europäische Geschichte Online* (Dec. 2010). Online publication: http://www.ieg-ego.eu/de/threads/modelle-und-stereotypen/germano-philie-und-germanophobie/deutsche-musik-in-europa/yvonne-wasserloos-musikalischer-kulturtransfer-von-leipzig-nach-kopenhagen-im-19-jahrhundert

Wasserloos, Yvonne, 'Die Dänen in Leipzig. Formen des Kulturtransfers im 19. Jahrhundert', in Stefan Keym and Katrin Stöck (eds.), *Musik in Leipzig, Wien und anderen Städten im 19. und 20. Jahrhundert* (Musik-Stadt, 3; Leipzig: Schröder, 2011), 165–81.

AFTER *c.* 1910

Balslev-Clausen, Peter, 'Luthers salmer i vækkelsesbevægelsernes sang- og salmebøger 1890-2000', *Hymnologi*, 40/1–2 (Apr. 2011), 46–51.

Balslev-Clausen, Peter, 'Luthers salmer i danske skolesangbøger 1875-1975', *Hymnologi*, 40/1–2 (Apr. 2011), 52–59.

Bergh, Ilja, *En egocentrikers eskapader. Livet i det høje toneleje* (Frederiksberg: Bianco Luno, 2010), 174 pp.

Bonde, Lars Ole, 'Snehvides spejl – opera af Niels Martinsen og Eva Littauer', *Peripeti* (Aug. 2011). Online publication: http://www.peripeti.dk/2011/08/26/smukt-grimt-og-grumt/#more-1329

Buene, Eivind, '…det som er uendelig anderledes', *Seismograf/dmt*, 22.12.2011. Online publication: http://seismograf.org/essay/eivind-buene-det-som-er-uendelig-anderledes

Cornelius, Jens, 'Biografi', 'Tidslinie', 'Værkfortegnelse', 'Diskografi', 'Værkgennemgange', 'Lyt til musikken', 'Links', and 'Kilder', *Ludolf Nielsen (1876-1939) – komponist*. Online publication: http://www.ludolfnielsen.dk/ (2011)

Fabricius, Peter, Valdemar Lønsted and Morten Zeuthen, *Anton Kontra – historien om en kunstner* (København: Gyldendal, 2010), 220 pp. + 1 dvd.

Fjeldsøe, Michael, 'Related European Symphonists? Carl Nielsen and Vagn Holmboe in Relation to George Enescu', in Liliana Birnat, Carmen Maria Carneci, and Mariana Petrescu (eds.), *"George Enescu" International Musicology Symposium 2009* (Bucharest: Editura Muzicala, 2011), 52–66.

Fjeldsøe, Michael, 'Ruth Berlau und 'ihre' Arbeitertheater. Zur Kopenhagener "Mutter"-Inszenierung 1935', *Dreigroschenheft*, 2011/4, 12–19.

Fjeldsøe, Michael, 'Crossroads – an interview with Benjamin Yusupov', *Danish Musicology Online*, 3 (2011). Online publication: http://www.danishmusicologyonline.dk/arkiv/arkiv_dmo/dmo_03/dmo_03_artikel_04.pdf, 5 pp.

Fundal, Karsten, 'Egoets opløsning', *Seismograf/dmt*, 22.12.2011. Online publication: http://seismograf.org/artikel/karsten-fundal-egoets-oploesning

Grimley, Daniel, *Carl Nielsen and the Idea of Modernism* (Woodbridge: Boydell, 2010), xix + 314 pp.

Hansen, Thomas Holme, *Knud Jeppesen katalog. Skriftlige arbejder, kompositioner og editioner – diskografi og bibliografi* (København: *Fund og Forskning Online*, Det Kongelige Bibliotek, 2011). Online publication: http://www.kb.dk/da/publikationer/online/fund_og_forskning/download/kjkatalog.pdf, 136 pp.

Hansen, Thomas Holme, *Knud Jeppesen (1892-1974)* (København: Det Kongelige Bibliotek, 2011). Online publication: http://www.kb.dk/da/nb/tema/fokus/jeppesen/index.html

Holm, Peder, *Musiker* (S.l.: S.n., 2011), 126 pp.

Jensen, Eva Maria, 'En dame fejres. Krystyna Moszumanska-Nazars 80 års jubilæum', *Kalliopes hjørne* (2011). Online publication: http://www.kvinderimusik.dk/kalliopes-hjørne-7.html, 5 pp.

Jensen, Eva Maria, 'Onuté Narbutaité, litauisk komponist og hendes musik', *Kalliopes hjørne* (2011). Online publication: http://www.kvinderimusik.dk/kalliopes-hjørne-7. html, 6 pp.

Kreutzfeld, Jacob and Mads Kullberg, 'Simple Interactions. Lydkunst fra Japan', *Seismograf/ dmt*, 19.09.2011. Online publication: http://seismograf.org/artikel/simple-interactions-ja- pansk-lydkunst

Kring, Gert Walter, *Det var os der spilled'. Musikere i Sydvestjylland 1901-2001* (S.l.: Dansk Musiker Forbund, 2011), 406 pp.

Nielsen, Puk Elmstrøm, 'Alsangen 1940', *Passage*, 65 (2010), 80–97.

Palsmar, Henrik, 'Nielsens Tre Motetter – et bud på en 7. symfoni?', *Dansk Musik Tidsskrift*, 84 (June 2010), 29–33.

Petersen, Nils Holger, 'Sophocles, Christianity, and Modernism. Medievalist Devotion and Neoclassicism in Stravinsky's *Oedipus Rex* (1926–27)', in Dina De Rentiis and Christoph Houswitschka (eds.), *Healers and Redeemers. The Reception and Transformation of their Me- dieval and Late Antique Representations in Literature, Film and Music* (Trier: Wissenschaft- licher Verlag Trier, 2010), 161–79.

Ragge, Melanie, 'New Perspectives from Old Manuscripts' [About Carl Nielsen's wind quin- tet], *The Double Reed*, 33/2 (2010), 35–41.

Rasmussen, Karl Aage, *Musik i det tyvende århundrede – en fortælling* (København: Gyldendal, 2011), 367 pp.

Rasmussen, Karl Aage, 'Hjemfalden', *Seismograf/dmt*, 22.12.2011. Online publication: http:// seismograf.org/essay/karl-aage-rasmussen-hjemfalden

Spence, Marcia, 'Nielsen's Wind Quintet - A Critical Performance Edition', *Horn Call: Journal of the International Horn Society*, 40/2 (Feb. 2010), 91–95.

Wichmann, Malene, 'Den glemte modernist', *Dansk Musik Tidsskrift*, 84 (June 2010), 24–28.

IV. SYSTEMATIC MUSICOLOGY
MUSICOLOGY

Andersson, Greger, 'Regionale, nationale und supranationale Projekte. Musikgeschichts- schreibung in den nordischen Ländern am Ende des 20. Jahrhunderts – eine Übersicht', in Ole Kongsted (ed.), *Studia Musicologica Regionis Balticae I* (København: Capella Hafniensis and Det Kongelige Bibliotek, 2011), 87–97.

Kolltveit, Gjermund, 'Studies of Ancient Nordic Music, 1915–1940', in Sam Mirelman (ed.), *The Historiography of Music in Global Perspective* (Gorgias Précis Portfolios, 9; Piscataway: Gorgias, 2010), 145–75.

Lund, Cajsa S., 'Music Archaeology in Scandinavia, 1800–1990', in Sam Mirelman (ed.), *The Historiography of Music in Global Perspective* (Gorgias Précis Portfolios, 9; Piscataway: Gorgias, 2010), 177–207.

Pedersen, Peder Kaj, 'Musicology as Independent Research?', *Danish Yearbook of Musicology*, 38 (2010/11), 9–13.

THEORY AND ANALYSIS

Hansen, Niels Christian, 'Luciano Berio's "Sequenza V" Analyzed along the Lines of Four Analytical Dimensions Proposed by the Composer', *Journal of Music and Meaning*, 9 (Winter 2010), Section 1. Online publication: http://jmm9.musicandmeaning.net/#post2.

Hansen, Niels Christian, 'The Legacy of Lerdahl and Jackendoff's *A Generative Theory of Tonal Music*. Bridging a significant event in the history of music theory and recent developments in cognitive music research', *Danish Yearbook of Musicology*, 38 (2010/11), 33–55.

Petersen, Nils Holger, 'Quotation and Framing. Re-contextualization and Intertextuality as Newness in George Crumb's Black Angels', *Contemporary Music Review*, 29/3 (2010), 309–21.

AESTHETICS AND PHILOSOPHY

Christensen, Erik and Eva Fock, *Musik og film – på tværs*. Online publication: http://vbn.aau.dk/files/52987927/Musik_og_film_p_tv_rs_EC_EF.pdf, (2010), 72 pp.

Graakjær, Nicolai Jørgensgaard, 'McJingles - Om musik i tv-reklamer for McDonald's-kampagnen I'm lovin' it', *Akademisk kvarter* 2 (Spring 2011), 250-62. Online publication: http://www.akademiskkvarter.hum.aau.dk/pdf/vol2/Nicolai_J_Graakjaer_V2.pdf

Graakjær, Nicolai Jørgensgaard, *Musik i tv-reklamer – Teori og analyse* (Frederiksberg: Samfundslitteratur, 2011), 198 pp.

Graakjær, Nicolai Jørgensgaard, 'Musical Meaning in TV-commercials: A Case of Cheesy Music', *Popular Music Online*, 5 (2011). Online publication: http://www.popular-musicology-online.com/issues/05/nicolai-01.html

Hansen, Anne-Marie, Hans Jørgen Andersen, and Pirkko Liisa Raudaskoski, 'Investigating User Collaboration in Music Based Games', in Jacob Buur (ed.), *Participatory Innovation Conference 13th–15th January 2011* (Sønderborg: Syddansk Universitet, 2011), 69–75.

Hansen, Anne-Marie, Hans Jørgen Andersen, and Pirkko Liisa Raudaskoski, 'Play Fluency in Music Improvisation Games for Novices', *Proceedings of the International Conference on New Interfaces for Musical Expression, 30 May – 1 June 2011, Oslo, Norway*. Online publication: http://vbn.aau.dk/files/55234342/G03_Hansen.pdf, 4 pp.

Hjortkjær, Jens, *Toward a cognitive theory of musical tension*. Ph.D. thesis (Copenhagen: Faculty of Humanities, University of Copenhagen, 2011), x + 330 pp.

Jensen, Kristoffer, 'Pitch Gestures in Generative Modeling of Music', in Kristoffer Jensen, Sølvi Ystad, Mitsuko Aramaki, and Richard Kronland-Martinet (eds.), *Exploring Music Contents. 7th International Symposium, CMMR 2010, Málaga, Spain, June 21–24, 2010*. Revised papers (Heidelberg: Springer, 2011), 51–59.

Kirkegaard, Annemette, 'Spillet mellem det lokale og det globale – hvilke udfordringer stiller det til musikforskning i 2011? Musikvidenskabelige perspektiver på mødet mellem global musikkultur og lokale musikmiljøer', *Svensk tidskrift för musikforskning*, 93 (2011), 11–31.

Kjærgaard, Jørgen, 'Hymns in Modern Society', *Hymnologi*, 40/1–2 (Apr. 2011), 65–74.

Koldau, Linda Maria, 'U-Boot-Filme und ihre Musik', in Stephan Huck (ed.), *100 Jahre U-Boote in deutschen Marinen. Ereignisse – Technik – Mentalitäten – Rezeption* (Bochum: Dieter Winkler, 2011), 187–99.

Koldau, Linda Maria, 'Why Submarines? Interdisciplinary Approaches to a Cultural Myth of War', *Journal of War and Culture Studies*, 4/1 (2011), 65–78.

Koppel, Benjamin and Casper Rongsted, *Ud af musikken* (København: Gyldendal Business, 2011), 255 pp.

Kreutzfeldt, Jacob, 'Lyden af den metropole opgang. En undersøgelse af akustisk territorialitet på Københavns Hovedbanegård', *Kulturo*, 17/32 (2011), 5–12.

Kreutzfeldt, Jacob, 'Acoustic Territoriality – City planning and the politics of urban sound', in Frans Mossberg (ed.), *Ljudmiljö, hälsa och stadsbyggnad. Texter från ett symposium den 7 maj 2010 arrangerat av Ljudmiljöcentrum vid Lunds Universitet i samarbete med SLU Alnarp* (Lund: Ljudmiljöcentrum, 2011), 63–77. Online publication: http://www.ljudcentrum.lu.se/

Kringelbach, Morten L. and Peter Vuust, 'The pleasure of making meaning of music', *Interdisciplinary Science Reviews*, 35/2 (2010), 168–85.

117

Krogh, Mads, Ansa Lønstrup, Charlotte Rørdam Larsen, Steen Kaargaard Nielsen, Birgitte Stougaard Pedersen, Iben Have, and Anette Vandsø, *LYdT – Et akustemologisk manifest.* Online publication: http://ak.au.dk/fileadmin/www.ak.au.dk/MANIFEST_Nyt_LYdT.pdf (2010), 5 pp.

Köritz, Tim and Markus Utz, 'Skandinavische Chormusik. Singen als Volkssport in Skandinavien', *Musik und Gottesdienst*, 63/3 (2011), 94–101.

Meedom, Peter Johan, 'Det uhåndgribelige medium. Noter til musikken som mellemrum og medium ledsaget af Tim Heckers *Radio Amor* og William Basinskis *The Disintegration Loops I-IV*', *Kulturo*, 17/32 (2011), 64–70.

Nielsen, Steen Kaargaard, 'En søndag i studiet med Goddard. Original Broadway Cast-albummet som fonografisk genre II', *Danish Musicology Online*, 3 (2011). Online publication: http://www.danishmusicologyonline.dk/arkiv/arkiv_dmo/dmo_03/dmo_03_artikel_02.pdf , 29 pp.

Olesen, Jonas, 'Optisk syntese. Om konstruktionen af en optisk synthesizer til oversættelse af billeder til lyd', *Seismograf/dmt*, 12.3.2011. Online publication: http://seismograf.org/artikel/jonas-olesen-optisk-syntese

Paulsen, Ove, 'Hymnologi – Nordisk tidsskrift og formidling i Norden', *Hymnologi*, 40/3–4 (Oct. 2011), 128–35.

Pedersen, Birgitte Stougaard, 'Lydens produktive paradokser: Om fænomenologiske potentialer og åbne betydningsrum i lyd, sprog og litteratur', *Kulturo*, 17/32 (2011), 35–41.

Petersen, Nils Holger, 'Introduction', in Andreas Bücker, Eyolf Østrem, and Nils Holger Petersen (eds.), *Resonances. Historical Essays on Continuity and Change* (Turnhout: Brepols, 2011), 1–19.

Steinskog, Erik, 'Diva Forever – The Operatic Voice between Reproduction and Reception', *Danish Musicology Online*, 2 (2011), 5–20. Online publication: http://www.danishmusicologyonline.dk/arkiv/arkiv_dmo/dmo_02/dmo_02_artikel_01.pdf

Stöber, Birgit, *New media and music products: "Any place and any time". The Digital Concert Hall in a media geographical perspective* (Creative Encounters, 54; Copenhagen: Copenhagen Business School, 2011). Online publication: http://openarchive.cbs.dk/xmlui/bitstream/handle/10398/8253/54-BS-%20New%20media%20and%20music%20productsx.pdf?sequence=1, 24 pp.

Søchting, Rune, 'Stedsspecifik lyd. 2 æstetiske strategier for hvordan lydens rumlige aspekt integreres i værksammenhængen', *Seismograf/dmt*, 18.9.2011. Online publication: http://seismograf.org/artikel/stedsspecifik-lyd

Sørensen, Søren Møller, 'Musens kammerpige. Musikæstetik mellem følelsesæstetik, klanglære og retorik. J.G. Sulzer, J.N. Forkel og H.Chr. Koch', *Danish Musicology Online*, 2 (2011), 79–111. Online publication: http://www.danishmusicologyonline.dk/arkiv/arkiv_dmo/dmo_02/dmo_02_artikel_04.pdf

Vandsø, Anette, 'Det performerendes performativitet. Medie og betydningskritik i 4'33"', *Peripeti – Tidsskrift for dramaturgiske studier* (Special issue, 2011), 157–73.

Vandsø, Anette, 'Listening to the World. Sound, Media and Intermediality in Contemporary Sound Art', *SoundEffects – An Interdisciplinary Journal of Sound and Sound Experience*, 1 (Nov. 2011), 68–81. Online publication: http://www.soundeffects.dk/article/view/4071/5011

PEDAGOGY AND MUSIC THERAPY

Bergström-Isacsson, Märith, *Music and Vibroacoustic Stimulation in People with Rett Syndrome: A Neurophysiological Study.* Ph.D. thesis (Aalborg: Department of Communication and Psychology, Faculty of Humanities, Aalborg University, 2011), 199 pp. Online publication: http://vbn.aau.dk/files/57708319/M_rith_Bergstr_m_Isacsson.pdf

Bertelsen, Maria Blum and Lise Høy Laursen, *Musik i øjeblikket. En håndbog om musik i ældreplejen* (Frederiksberg: Unitas, 2011), 95 pp.

Bloch, Anne and Michael Sundorph, *Musik og drama. Pædagogisk arbejde med forskellige målgrupper* (Frederiksværk: Nautilus, 2011), 341 pp.

Bonde, Lars Ole and Marianne Bode, 'Din ven til det sidste. Musikterapi på hospice og i palliativ pleje', in Michael Hvid Jacobsen and Helle Rex (eds.), *Humanistisk palliation. Teori, metode, etik og praksis* (København: Hans Reitzel, 2011), 255–69.

Bonde, Lars Ole, 'Health Music(k)ing – Music Therapy or Music and Health? A Model, Empirical Examples and Personal Reflections', *Music and arts in action*, 3/2 (June 2011), 120–40.

Bonde, Lars Ole and Karette Stensæth, *Musikk, helse, identitet* (Skriftserie fra Senter for musikk og helse; Oslo: Norges Musikkhøgskole, 2011), 130 pp.

Bonde, Lars Ole, 'Musiklytning og indre billeder som klinisk vurderingsredskab. Assessment i receptiv gruppemusikterapi med ambulante psykiatriske patienter', *Musikterapi i psykiatrien. Årsskrift*, 6 (2011), 38–55. Online publication: http://ojs.statsbiblioteket.dk/index.php/mip/issue/view/736

Bonde, Lars Ole, 'Musikterapi i psykiatrien – ny international forskningslitteratur 2008-11', *Musikterapi i psykiatrien. Årsskrift*, 6 (2011), 151–55. Online publication: http://ojs.statsbiblioteket.dk/index.php/mip/issue/view/736

Bonde, Lars Ole, Cheryl Dileo, and Denise Grocke (eds.), 'Special Section: In Memory of Tony Wigram (1953-2011)', with contributions from Helen Odell-Miller, Denise Grocke, Jos De Backer, Monika Nöcker-Ribaupierre, Gro Trondalen, Cochavit Elefant, Felicity Baker, Inge Nygaard Pedersen, Ulla Holck, Stine L. Jacobsen, Christian Gold, Lars Ole Bonde, and Tony Wigram, *Voices, A World Forum for Music Therapy*, 11/3 (2011). Online publication: https://normt.uib.no/index.php/voices/issue/view/70

Brink-Jensen, Line, 'Nonspecifikke faktorer i terapeutisk behandling', *Dansk Musikterapi*, 7/2 (2010), 19–23.

Frommelt, Maja, 'Musikterapi med mennesker ramt af ekspressiv afasi', *Dansk Musikterapi*, 8/1 (2011), 3–10.

Hannibal, Niels, Brian Petersen, Mette Windfeld, and Søren Skadhede, 'Gruppemusikterapi i dagbehandlingsregi: Opsamling på perioden 2003 til 2010', *Musikterapi i psykiatrien. Årsskrift*, 6 (2011), 26–37. Online publication: http://ojs.statsbiblioteket.dk/index.php/mip/issue/view/736

Hansen, Susanne Brødsgaard, 'Musikreminiscens, demens og agiteret adfærd', *Dansk Musikterapi*, 7/2 (2010), 12–17.

Hansen, Susanne Brødsgaard, 'Pilotprojekt om musikreminiscens, demens og agiteret adfærd', *Musikterapi i psykiatrien. Årsskrift*, 6 (2011), 102–15. Online publication: http://ojs.statsbiblioteket.dk/index.php/mip/issue/view/736

Holck, Ulla, 'Det tidlige samspil og musikterapi', *Livsbladet* (May 2011), 11–15.

Holck, Ulla, 'Forskning i musikterapi – børn med en Autisme Spektrum Forstyrrelse', *Dansk musikterapi*, 8/2 (2011), 27–35.

Holck, Ulla, 'Supervision af novicemusikterapeuter i arbejde med børn med betydelige og varige funktionsnedsættelser', in Karette Stensæth and Lars Ole Bonde (eds.), *Musikk, helse, identitet* (Skriftserie fra Senter for musikk og helse; Oslo: Norges Musikkhøgskole, 2011), 89–104.

Holck, Ulla and Hanne Mette Ochsner Ridder, 'A Tribute to Tony Wigram 13 August 1953 – 24 June 2011', *Approaches. Music Therapy and Special Education*, 3/2 (2011), 62–66.

Holgersen, Sven-Erik, 'Færdighedsdimensionen. Færdighed og kropsligt betinget læring i sammenlignende fagdidaktisk perspektiv med særligt henblik på musisk-æstetiske fag', in

Ellen Krogh and Frede V. Nielsen (eds.), *Sammenlignende fagdidaktik* (Cursiv, 7; Køben-havn: Institut for Didaktik, Danmarks Pædagogiske Universitetsskole, Aarhus Universitet, 2011), 119–35. Online publication: http://www.dpu.dk/fileadmin/www.dpu.dk/institutfor-didaktik/cursivskriftserie/Cursiv_7.pdf

Holm, Tina Rudebeck and Hanne Halskov, 'Relation og vibration – Ny tværfaglig indsats', *Dansk Musikterapi*, 8/1 (2010), 14–22.

Holst, Finn, *Faglighed, interaktion og samarbejde. Evaluerings- og udviklingsrapport. Dan-Mus projektet 2009-2010, Rosenlundskolen, Ballerup Kommune.* Online publication: http://pure. au.dk/portal/files/32963866/DANMUS_RAPPORT_Finn_Holst_2010.pdf (2010), 49 pp.

Holst, Finn, 'Musiklærerkompetence mellem teori og praksis', *Nordisk musikkpedagogisk forsk-ning. Årbok*, 12 (2011), 135–48.

Jensen, Bent, 'Brugerundersøgelse om musikterapi i Socialpsykiatrien i Aarhus Kommune', *Musikterapi i psykiatrien. Årsskrift*, 6 (2011), 116–29. Online publication: http://ojs.statsbib-lioteket.dk/index.php/mip/issue/view/736

Jensen, Karina Erland, Heidi Lerche, and Elisabeth Kloster, 'Musik og mennesker – Carl Maria Savery', *Dansk Musikterapi*, 7/2 (2010), 3–8.

Kærså, Lotte, 'Kun det bedste er godt nok', *Grundmotorik*, 7/3 (2011), 43–47.

Lindvang, Charlotte, 'At gøre sig parat til det mulige møde', *Dansk Musikterapi*, 8/2 (2011), 14–21.

Lund, Helle and Charlotte Fønsbo, 'Musiklyttegrupper – en empirisk undersøgelse af an-vendte metoder i psykiatrien', *Musikterapi i psykiatrien. Årsskrift*, 6 (2011), 86–101. Online publication: http://ojs.statsbiblioteket.dk/index.php/mip/issue/view/736

Nadia, Mia and Jens Nielsen, *Skolekoncerter i Danmark. En undersøgelse udført for Statens Kunstråds Musikudvalg* (København: CBS, 2010), 188 pp. Online publication: http://www. kunst.dk/fileadmin/user_upload/dokumenter/Kunstraadet/Skolekoncerter_i_Danmark.pdf

Nielsen, Frede V., '"Man underviser altid i noget". Noter om didaktikkens indholdsbegreb', in Kari Kragh Blume Dahl, Jeppe Læssøe, and Venka Simovska (eds.), *Essays om dannelse, didaktik og handlekompetence. Inspireret af Karsten Schnack* (København: Danmarks Pædago-giske Universitetsskole, Aarhus Universitet, 2011), 9–18.

Nielsen, Frede V., 'Musikfaget i Danmark 1970-2010. En undersøgelse, dens resultater og re-ception', in Monica Lindgren, Anna Frisk, Ingemar Henningsson, and Johan Öberg (eds.), *Musik och kunskapsbildning. En festskrift till Bengt Olsson* (Göteborg: ArtMonitor, Konstnär-liga fakulteten, Göteborgs Universitet, 2011), 137–46.

Nielsen, Frede V., 'Sammenlignende fagdidaktik. Genstandsfelt, perspektiver og dimensioner', in Ellen Krogh and Frede V. Nielsen (eds.), *Sammenlignende fagdidaktik* (Cursiv, 7; Køben-havn: Institut for Didaktik, Danmarks Pædagogiske Universitetsskole, Aarhus Universitet, 2011), 11–32. Online publication: http://www.dpu.dk/fileadmin/www.dpu.dk/institutfordi-daktik/cursivskriftserie/Cursiv_7.pdf

Pedersen, Inge Nygaard, 'Brug af kreative medier i supervision af modoverføringsoplevelser i musikterapi i psykiatrien. Hvordan håndteres sådanne oplevelser så de bliver klinisk re-levante?', *Musikterapi i psykiatrien. Årsskrift*, 6 (2011), 6–25. Online publication: http://ojs. statsbiblioteket.dk/index.php/mip/issue/view/736

Pedersen, Inge Nygaard, 'Voice improvisation based on imaginations as an expression of the self. Focus on raising self awareness through voice work in music therapy', in Felicity Baker and Sylka Uhlig (eds.), *Voicework in Music Therapy. Research and Practice* (London: Jessica Kingsley Publishers, 2011), 287–301.

Pedersen, Peder Kaj, '"Rhythmic Music" in Danish music education', *Leading Music Education International Conference, The University of Western Ontario, London May 28 – June 1, 2011.* Online publication: http://ir.lib.uwo.ca/lme/May30/Program/11/ (2011), 15 pp.

Petersen, Bjørn, *Advances in music and speech perception after Cochlear implantation*. Ph.D. thesis (Aarhus: Faculty of Health Sciences, Aarhus University, 2011), 130 pp.

Pio, Frederik, 'The concept of "Bildung". Response to Øivind Varkøy', *Philosophy of Music Education Review*, 18/1 (2010), 97–101.

Ridder, Hanne Mette Ochsner, 'Einzelmusiktherapie bei Demenz: Cueing, Regulierung und Validation', in Thomas Wosch (ed.), *Musik und Alter. Grundlagen, Institutionen und Praxis der Musiktherapie im Alter und bei Demenz* (Stuttgart: Kohlhammer, 2011), 178–88.

Ridder, Hanne Mette Ochsner, 'How can singing in music therapy influence social engagement for people with dementia? Insights from the polyvagal theory', in Felicity Baker and Sylka Uhlig (eds.), *Voicework in Music Therapy. Research and Practice* (London: Jessica Kingsley Publishers, 2011), 130–46.

Ridder, Hanne Mette Ochsner, 'Musikkterapi i palliativ omsorg på plejehjem', *Omsorg*, 2 (July 2011), 27–36.

Ridder, Hanne Mette Ochsner, 'Singen in der Musiktherapie mit Menschen mit Demenz: Neuropsychologische, psychophysiologische und psychodynamische Grundlagen und Perspektiven', in Thomas Wosch (ed.), *Musik und Alter. Grundlagen, Institutionen und Praxis der Musiktherapie im Alter und bei Demenz* (Stuttgart: Kohlhammer, 2011), 44–64.

Ridder, Hanne Mette Ochsner, 'Musikterapi med demensramte: hukommelse, identitet og musikreminiscens', in Karette Stensæth and Lars Ole Bonde (eds.), Musikk, helse, identitet. Skriftserie fra Senter for musikk og helse (Oslo: NMH-publikationer, 2011), 61–83.

Ridder, Hanne Mette and Aase Hyldgaard, 'Musikterapi og magtanvendelse i gerontpsykiatrien. Protokol til en undersøgelse', *Musikterapi i psykiatrien. Årsskrift*, 6 (2011), 68–85. Online publication: http://ojs.statsbiblioteket.dk/index.php/mip/issue/view/736

Rydahl, Henrik, 'Det sociale i musik hjælper – samfundsmusikterapi og interkommunikation. Et essay', *Musikterapi i psykiatrien. Årsskrift*, 6 (2011), 130–48. Online publication: http://ojs. statsbiblioteket.dk/index.php/mip/issue/view/736

Schou, Karin, Inge Nygaard Pedersen, and Lars Ole Bonde, 'Musiklytning til patienter i skærmning. Pilotundersøgelse på Musikterapiklinikken Aalborg Psykiatriske Sygehus', *Musikterapi i psykiatrien. Årsskrift*, 6 (2011), 56–67. Online publication: http://ojs.statsbiblioteket.dk/index.php/mip/issue/view/736

Schwantes, Melody, *Music Therapy's Effects on Mexican Migrant Farmworkers' Levels of Depression, Anxiety and Social Isolation: A Mixed Methods Randomized Control Trial Utilizing Participatory Action Research*. Ph.D. thesis (Aalborg: Doctoral School of the Humanities, Aalborg University, 2011), 425 pp.

Villarreal, Eduardo Adrian Garza, *Cognitive and Emotional Processing of Music and its Effect on Pain*. Ph.D. thesis (Aarhus: Faculty of Health Sciences, Aarhus University and Royal Academy of Music, Aarhus/Aalborg, 2011), 170 pp.

Vuust, Peter, Eduardo Garza, Elvira Brattico, Sakari Leino, and Leif Østergaard, 'Distinct neural generators of the MMN and the ERAN to chord violations. A multiple source analysis study', *Brain Research*, 1389 (5.3.2011), 103–14.

Vuust, Peter, Elvira Brattico, Enrico Glerean, Miia Seppänen, Satu Pakarinen, Mari Tervaniemi, and Risto Näätänen, 'New fast mismatch negativity paradigm for determining the neural prerequisites for musical ability', *Cortex*, 47/9 (Oct. 2011), 1091–98.

Vuust, Peter, Mikkel Wallentin, Kim Mouridsen, Leif Østergaard, and Andreas Roepstorff, 'Tapping polyrhythms in music activates language areas', *Neuroscience letters*, 494/3 (May 2011), 211–16.

Wigram, Tony and Julie Sutton, 'A Dialogue with Prof. Tony Wigram. Considering Music Therapy Research in a Changing World: review of publications and their related links with the development of the music therapy profession over three decades', *British Journal of Music Therapy*, 25/1 (2011), 8–31.

Wigram, Tony, Jeff Hooper, Derek Carson, and Bill Lindsay, 'The practical implication of comparing how adults with and without intellectual disability respond to music', *British Journal of Learning Disabilities*, 39/1 (Mar. 2011), 22–28.

RESEARCH ON INSTRUMENTS AND PERFORMANCE PRACTICE

Christiansen, Toke Lund, *Kender du Pan. Fløjtespillets historie i Danmark 1800-1930* (Valby: Eget forlag, 2011), 170 pp. Online publication: http://www.kenderdupan.dk/templates/musik/Kender%20du%20Pan,%202010.pdf

Exner, Johannes, 'Om Nørrelandskirkens "nye" orgel', *Orglet*, 79 (Dec. 2011), 28–31.

Holmboe, Rasmus, 'Klaverets tunge tradition', *Seismograf/dmt*, 12.3.2011. Online publication: http://seismograf.org/artikel/klaverets-tunge-tradition

Kengen, Knud-Erik, 'Hellig Kors Kirkes orgel – en succeshistorie om et usædvanligt genbrug', *Orglet*, 78 (June 2011), 21–25.

Kynde, Lars, 'Kompositionsmaskiner', *Seismograf/dmt*, 12.3.2011. Online publication: http://seismograf.org/artikel/lars-kynde-kompositionsmaskiner

Lumholdt, Kristian, 'Et César Franck-orgel i København anno 1915', *Orglet*, 78 (June 2011), 4–9.

Nørfelt, Henrik Fibiger, 'Organist Erik Eriksens rejseberetning fra studietur til Nordtyskland i foråret 1931', *Orglet*, 78 (June 2011), 26–32.

Nørfelt, Henrik Fibiger, 'Georg Jann om Stellwagen-orglets genopførelse efter 1950', *Orglet*, 79 (Dec. 2011), 4–19.

Olesen, Ole Beuchert, 'Orgler [i Svendborg, St. Nikolaj Kirke]', in Birgitte Bøggild Johannsen (ed.), *Danmarks Kirker*, 1/2–3, *Svendborg Amt* (København: Nationalmuseet, 2011), 202–6.

Preussler, Gitte Støvring, Svend Prip, and Johannes Exner, *Orgelindvielse. Nørrelandskirken* (Holstebro: Nørrelandskirken, 2011), 67 pp.

Prip, Svend, 'Marcussen/Andersen-orglet i Trinitatis Kirke, København', *Orglet*, 78 (June 2011), 10–20.

Prip, Svend, 'Orglet i Nørrelandskirken, Holstebro', *Orglet*, 79 (Dec. 2011), 21–27.

Riis, Morten, 'Den fejlende musikmaskine', *Seismograf/dmt*, 12.3.2011. Online publication: http://seismograf.org/artikel/morten-riis-den-fejlende-musikmaskine

Spang-Hanssen, Ulrik, *Om at genoplive en dinosaurus. Om det nye Klais-orgel i Symfonisk Sal, Musikhuset Aarhus*. Online publication: http://www.aarhussymfoni.dk/da-DK/Aarhus-Symfoniorkester/Klaisorglet-i-Symfonisk-Sal.aspx (2010), 24 pp.

Spang-Hanssen, Ulrik and Lea Maria Lucas Wierød, 'Hvor frit er egentlig frit? Et forsøg på en kvantificering af rubatopraksis i vestlig, klassisk musik', *Danish Musicology Online*, 3 (2011). Online publication: http://www.danishmusicologyonline.dk/arkiv/arkiv_dmo/dmo_03/dmo_03_artikel_03.pdf, 21 pp.

POPULAR MUSIC

Berthelsen, Per, *Sume – en grønlandsk rocklegende* (Nuussuaq: Milik, 2010), 97 pp. Also in Greelandic: *Kalaallit rockertarnermikkut tusaamasarsuit*.

Birch, David Pepe, *Master Fatman* (København: Lindhardt og Ringhof, 2011), 240 pp.

Blak, Poul (ed.), *Flemming Bamse Jørgensen fortæller sit liv til Poul Blak* (Højbjerg: Hovedland, 2011), 279 pp.

Dybo, Tor, 'Jazz research in Scandinavia', *Jazzforschung*, 42 (2010), 111–27.

Elers, Pia, *Nattegn. Et portræt af Johnny Madsen* (København: People's Press, 2011), 310 pp.

Enemark, Einar and Anders Houmøller Thomsen, *Manden der var MC Einar* (København: People's Press, 2011), 201 pp.

Frandsen, Kjeld, '1960'erne', in Olav Harsløf and Finn Slumstrup (eds.), *Jazz i Danmark 1950-2010* (København: Politiken, 2011), 68–133.

Frandsen, Kjeld, Jens Jørn Gjedsted, Olav Harsløf, Ole Izard Høyer, Ole Matthiessen, Tore Mortensen, Christian Munch-Hansen, and Finn Slumstrup, 'Dansk jazz i oo'erne', in Olav Harsløf and Finn Slumstrup (eds.), *Jazz i Danmark 1950-2010* (København: Politiken, 2011), 552–75.

Gjedsted, Jens Jørn, '1970'erne', in Olav Harsløf and Finn Slumstrup (eds.), *Jazz i Danmark 1950-2010* (København: Politiken, 2011), 134–269.

Gjurup, Thomas, *Hit House. Da Frederiksberg var rockens centrum* (Frederiksberg: Her & Nu, 2011), 124 pp.

Gjurup, Thomas, *Hvidovre rock. Fra pigtråd til heavy metal. En scrapbog om 1960-1980* (Roskilde and Hvidovre: Roskilde Museum i samarbejde med Danmarks Rockmuseum og Forstadsmuseet i Hvidovre, 2011), 174 pp.

Hansen, Anders Høg, *Bob Dylan. Kærlighed, krig og historie 1961-1967* (Frederiksberg: Frydenlund, 2011), 175 pp.

Harsløf, Olav, 'Indledning', in Olav Harsløf and Finn Slumstrup (eds.), *Jazz i Danmark 1950-2010* (København: Politiken, 2011), 6–21.

Hellhund, Herbert, 'Der Norden, eine Himmelrichtung oder eine Ästhetik – ECM und der Jazz Skandinaviens', in Rainer Kern and Susanne Binas-Preisendörfer (eds.), *Der blaue Klang. Musik, Literatur, Film, Tonspuren. Der Wirkungskreis von ECM und der europäisch-amerikanische Musikdialog* (Hofheim: Wolke , 2010), 35–42.

Jørgensen, Karsten, *Scener fra et stenbrud. 20 store rocktragedier fra Robert Johnson til Michael Jackson* (København: Rosenkilde & Bahnhof, 2011), 547 pp.

Klitgaard, Gitte, *Grete Klitgaard – min stolthed, min stjerne, min mor* (København: Books on Demand, 2011), 146 pp.

Korsgaard, Mathias Bonde, 'Den interaktive musikvideo', *16:9. Danmarks klogeste filmtidsskrift*, 9/41 (Apr. 2011). Online publication: http://www.16-9.dk/2011-04/side05_feature2.htm

Krabbenhøft, Jørgen and Knud Ørsted, *The Hitmakers. En pigtrådsgruppes historie* (S.l.: Legimus, 2011), 114 pp.

Krogh, Mads and Birgitte Stougaard Pedersen, 'Verbale klask, klagen og klynk. Retoriske strategier mellem hardcore og "klynke-rap"', *Danish Yearbook of Musicology*, 38 (2010/11), 57–73.

Krogh, Mads, 'On hip hop criticism and the constitution of hip hop culture in Denmark', *Popular Musicology Online*, 5 (2011). Online publication: http://www.popular-musicology-online.com/issues/05/krogh.html

Kaae, Peer, *Tommy, en biografi* (København: People's Press, 2010), 215 pp.

Lewis, Mark W., *The diffusion of black gospel music in postmodern Denmark* (Asbury Theological Seminary series in world Christian revitalization movements in intercultural studies 3; Lexington, KY: Emeth Press, 2010), 199 pp.

Lund, Jacob D. and Peter Rewers, *Solisten. Historien om Kim Larsen* (København: Gyldendal, 2011), 278 pp.

Marling, Gitte and Hans Kiib, *Instant city – Roskilde Festival* (Art and Urbanism Series 3; Aalborg: Aalborg Universitetsforlag, 2011), 403 pp.

Matthiessen, Ole, '1990'erne', in Olav Harsløf and Finn Slumstrup (eds.), *Jazz i Danmark 1950-2010* (København: Politiken, 2011), 404–551.

Mortensen, Tore and Ole Izard Høyer, '1950'erne', in Olav Harsløf and Finn Slumstrup (eds.), *Jazz i Danmark 1950-2010* (København: Politiken, 2011), 23–67.

Movin, Lars, *Downtown. En New York-Krønike* (København: Information, 2010), 688 pp.

Munch-Hansen, Christian, '1980'erne', in Olav Harsløf and Finn Slumstrup (eds.), *Jazz i Danmark 1950-2010* (København: Politiken, 2011), 270–403.

Nielsen, Jens-Emil, *Rock'n'roll. Musik eller galskab? Dansk rock 1956-1960* (Frederiksberg: Her & Nu, 2010), 65 pp.

Nielsen, Jens-Emil, *Pigtrådsmusik. Dansk rock 1960-1966* (Frederiksberg: Her & Nu, 2011), 117 pp.

Nielsen, Niels Kayser, 'Sange fra Vestkysten – en overset side af populærmusikken i Danmark', *Kulturstudier*, 2/1 (May 2011), 116–33. Online publication: http://ojs.statsbiblioteket.dk/index.php/fn/article/view/5192

Overgaard, Jakob Thorkild, *Improvised music, essays and interviews* (Copenhagen: Edition Wilhelm Hansen, 2011), 174 pp.

Pedersen, Birgitte Stougaard, 'At være eller ikke være "sort". En samtale med rapperen Per Vers', *Global Aesthetics* (Mar. 2011). Online publication: http://globalaesthetics.au.dk/fileadmin/www.globalaesthetics.au.dk/At_vaere_eller_ikke_vaere__sort_.pdf, 15 pp.

Pedersen, Birgitte Stougaard, 'Hvor blev beatet af? – Diskurser om rap og hiphop i populærmusikforskning', *Danish Musicology Online*, 3 (2011). Online publication: http://www.danishmusicologyonline.dk/arkiv/arkiv_dmo/dmo_03/dmo_03_artikel_01.pdf, 17 pp.

Pedersen, Peder Kaj, 'Hilsen til – og fra – Harlem. Den amerikanske forbindelse i dansk musikkultur i 1930'erne', in Peder Kaj Pedersen, Peter Stein Larsen, Steen Ledet Christiansen, Louise Mønster, and Kim Toft Hansen (eds.), *Kulturtrafik. Æstetiske udtryk i en global verden* (Interdisciplinære Kulturstudier, 2; Aalborg: Aalborg Universitetsforlag, 2011), 81–100.

Ravn, Thomas Bloch, 'Langhårede, bonderøve eller bøller fra København. En rockkoncert i Aarhus 1965', *Den Gamle By* (2011), 43–52.

Skousen, Niels, *Herfra hvor jeg står. Erindringer* (København: Gyldendal, 2011), 337 pp.

Smith-Sivertsen, Henrik, 'Om gartnere, måger og dejlige Angelique. Refræner, pop og populærmusikforskning – En kritisk gennemgang af *Ekstra Bladets* spørgeskemaundersøgelse om populærmusik, august 1961', *Fund og Forskning i Det Kongelige Biblioteks samlinger*, 50 (2011), 483–548.

Smith-Sivertsen, Henrik, 'Tjo och tjim og Karl Herman og jeg – Olrog i et dansk perspektiv', *Noterat* (Tema: Ulf Peder Olrog), 19 (2011), 35–58.

Steinskog, Erik, 'Hunting High and Low. Duke Ellington's *Peer Gynt Suite*', in Thomas Solomon (ed.), *Music and identity in Norway and beyond. Essays commemorating Edvard Grieg the humanist* (Bergen: Fagbokforlaget, 2011), 167–84.

Steinskog, Erik, 'Den androide siden. Interview med Janelle Monáe', *ENO Magasin*, 2 (2011), 73–80.

Strauss, Frithjof, 'Improkunstens værdi. Litterære jazzdiskurser i Norden', *Svensk tidskrift för musikforskning*, 92 (2010), 11–29.

Washburne, Christopher, 'Jazz Re-Bordered: Cultural Policy in Danish Jazz', *Jazz Perspectives*, 4/2 (2010), 121–55.

Wickström, David-Emil, *"Okna otkroi!" – "Open the Windows!" Transcultural Flows and Identity Politics in the St. Petersburg Popular Music Scene* (Soviet and post-Soviet politics and society, 101; Stuttgart: Ibidem-Verlag, 2011), 350 pp.

SOCIOLOGY

Ferland, Poul, *Rundt om Aalborg Symfoniorkester. En undersøgelse af relationer mellem ASO og publikum, interessenter, kulturen, samfundet, (ud)dannelsen, historien og fremtiden* (København: Books on Demand, 2011), 96 pp.

Jensen, Anne Ørbæk, 'Experiencing Materials and Knowledge: The Danish National Library's Music Collection', *Fontes Artis Musicae*, 58/3 (July-Sept. 2011), 253–59.

Jensen, Klaus Bruhn and Peter Larsen, 'The Sounds of Change. Representations of Music in European Newspapers 1960–2000', in Jostein Gripsrud and Lennart Weibull (eds.), *Media, Markets & Public Spheres. European Media at the Crossroads* (Bristol: Intellect, 2010), 249–66.

Killmeier, Matthew A. and Paul Christiansen, 'Wolves at the Door. Musical persuasion in a 2004 Bush-Cheney advertisement', *Mediekultur*, 27/50 (2011). Online publication: http://ojs.statsbiblioteket.dk/index.php/mediekultur/article/view/2857, 21 pp.

Larsen, Jakob Eg and Arkadiusz Stopczynski, 'A Festival-Wide Social Network Using 2D Barcodes, Mobile Phones and Situated Displays', *International Journal of Mobile Human Computer Interaction*, 3/3 (July-Sept. 2011), 14–30.

Mikkelsen, Line Fog, Mette Riis Sørensen, and Nicolai Abrahamsen, *Musikkens værdi* (København: Koda/Gramex, 2010), 87 pp.

ETHNOMUSICOLOGY

Andersen, Lene and Henriette Kragh Jacobsen, *Kildevæld – Viser & eventyr fortalt for 100 år siden* (København: Dansk Folkemindesamling, 2011). Online publication: http://www.kb.dk/da/nb/fag/dafos/kildevaeld/

Brewer, Jane, 'Waulking and waulking songs from the Outer Hebrides', *Kalliopes hjørne* (2010). Online publication: http://www.kvinderimusik.dk/kalliopes-hjørne-7.html, 13 pp.

Christensen, Anders Chr. N., *Vildspil og nodespil* (København: Kragen, 2011), 205 pp. and 2 CDs.

Fock, Eva, *På tværs af musik* (København: Wilhelm Hansen, 2011), 286 pp.

Grove, Arnaq, Michael Hauser, and Hivshu Robert Peary (eds.), *Christian Ledenip Uummannami Upernavimmilu 1909-mi 1912-imilu immiussai, ileqqorsuutit erinarsuutit taallallu, Christian Ledens lydsamlinger fra Uummannaq og Upernavik, fra 1909 og 1912, sange, vrøvlevers og digte, Christian Leden's audio collections from Uummannaq and Upernavik, from 1909 and 1912, songs, nonsense rhymes and poems* (København: Det Grønlandske Selskab, 2011), 72 pp.

Jensen, Ole, *På sporet af spillemanden Ole Jensen, Bakkerup 1840-1927. Ole Jensens erindringer – og breve mellem folkemindesamleren Chr. Olsen og Ole Jensen* (S.l.: S.n., 2011), 46 pp.

Kirkegaard, Annemette, 'Om at fare vild i verdensmusikkens budskab', *Danish Musicology Online*, 2 (2011), 53–78. Online publication: http://www.danishmusicologyonline.dk/arkiv/arkiv_dmo/dmo_02/dmo_02_artikel_03.pdf

Skriver, Niels, *Ali bali bi. Folk, fakta og anekdoter fra Storkespringvandet til Vise Vers Huset*, (Hvidovre: Prudentia, 2011), 154 pp.

Vang, Anne-Marie, 'Om tyrkisk folkemusik', *Kalliopes hjørne* (2010). Online publication: http://www.kvinderimusik.dk/kalliopes-hjørne-7.html, 12 pp.

DANCE RESEARCH

Aschengreen, Erik, *Forført af balletten. Ballettens klassikere set over 60 år* (København: Gyldendal, 2011), 256 pp.

Jürgensen, Knud Arne, 'Il balletto italiano nella Copenhagen del secolo XVII', in José Sasportes (ed.), *La danza italiana in Europa nel settecento* (La Danza Italiana quaderno, 3) (Roma: Bulzoni, 2011), 11–44.

Urup, Henning, 'Dansen reel i Danmark', *Meddelelser fra Dansk Dansehistorisk Arkiv*, 30 (2011), 5–10.

PHILOLOGY

Geertinger, Axel Teich and Laurent Pugin, 'MEI for bridging the gap between music cataloguing and digital critical edition', *Die Tonkunst*, 5/3 (July 2011), 289–94.

V. CRITICAL EDITIONS

Bing, Erik Henriques (ed.), *Jøden under træet. Beretninger om visesangeren Michel Levin på Dyrehavsbakken* (København: Tågaliden, 2011), 179 pp.

Christoffersen, Peter Woetmann (ed.), *The Complete Works of Gilles Mureau (c1440–1512) – poet-musician of Chartres*. Online publication: http://www.pwch.dk/chansonniers/Mureau/01Start. html (2011).

Christoffersen, Peter Woetmann (ed.), *The Uppsala Chansonnier, MS 76a*. Online publication: http://uppsala.pwch.dk/ (2011).

Fellow, John (ed., introduction and notes), *Carl Nielsen Brevudgaven, vol. 7: 1921-1923* (København: Multivers, 2011), 663 pp.

Fellow, John (ed., introduction and notes), *Carl Nielsen Brevudgaven, vol. 8: 1924-1925* (København: Multivers, 2011), 493 pp.

Frøhlich, Johannes Frederik, *Symfoni i Es-dur, opus 33 / Symphony in E Flat Major, Opus 33*, ed. Lisbeth Ahlgren Jensen (DCM 010; København: Dansk Center for Musikudgivelse, Det Kongelige Bibliotek, 2011), Score (162 pp.). Online publication: http://www.kb.dk/export/ sites/kb_dk/da/kb/nb/mta/dcm/udgivelser/download/froehlich/froehlich_opus_33.pdf

Gade, Niels W., *Concert Ouvertures, op. 37, 39, A Summer Day / Konzertouvertüren Op. 37, 39, Ein Sommertag*, ed. Peder Kaj Pedersen (Niels W. Gade Works / Werke, I/10; Copenhagen: Foundation for the Publication of the Works of Niels W. Gade / Stiftung zur Herausgabe der Werke Niels W. Gades, 2011), xxvi + 208 pp.

Hartmann, J.P.E., *Klaversonater og Klaverstykker*, ed. Niels Krabbe (DCM 009; København: Dansk Center for Musikudgivelse, Det Kongelige Bibliotek, 2011). Preprint for J.P.E. Hartmann, *Udvalgte Værker / Selected Works / Ausgewählte Werke*, 232 pp. Online publication: http://www.kb.dk/export/sites/kb_dk/da/kb/nb/mta/dcm/udgivelser/download/hartmann/ hartmann_klavermusik1.pdf

Langgaard, Rued, *Drapa (Ved Edvard Griegs Død)*, ed. Michael Fjeldsøe (Rued Langgaard Edition; København: Edition·S, 2011), 39 pp.

Sørensen, Inger (ed.), *Et venskab. C.F.E. Hornemans korrespondance med Edvard Grieg 1863-1898* (København: Museum Tusculanum, 2011), 166 pp.

Thielst, Peter (transl., ed. and introduction), *Friedrich Nietzsche, Tilfældet Wagner. Et musikant-problem* ([Helsingør]: Det lille forlag, 2011), 87 pp.

Publications received

PERIODICALS, YEARBOOKS ETC.

Carl Nielsen Studies 5 (2012), ed. David Fanning, Michael Fjeldsøe, Daniel Grimley, and Niels Krabbe, 393 pp., illus., music exx., ISSN 1603-3663.

Meddelelser fra Dansk Dansehistorisk Arkiv 30 (2011), ed. Henning Urup, 18 pp., illus., ISSN 0107-685X.

Mitteilungen der Paul Sacher Stiftung, 25 (Apr. 2012). 68 pp., illus., music exx., ISSN 1015-0536.

Svensk tidskrift för musikforskning. Swedish Journal of Musicology 93 (2011), ed. Tobias Lund, 141 pp., illus., ISSN 0081-9816.

BOOKS

Christiansen, Steen, Kim Toft Hansen, Peter Stein Larsen, Louise Mønster, and Peder Kaj Pedersen (eds.), *Kulturtrafik. Æstetiske udtryk i en global verden* (Interdisciplinære kulturstudier, 2; Aalborg: Aalborg University Press, 2011), 280 pp., illus., music exx., ISBN 978-87-7112-000-4, ISSN 1904-898x.

Erichsen, Jørgen, *Friedrich Kuhlau. Ein deutscher Musiker in Kopenhagen* (Hildesheim: Georg Olms Verlag, 2011), 416 pp., illus., music exx., ISBN 978-3-487-14541-9.

Gould, Elaine, *Behind Bars. The Definitive Guide to Music Notation* (London: Faber Music, 2011), 676 pp., music exx., ISBN 978-0-571-51456-4.

Graakjær, Nicolai Jørgensgaard, *Musik i tv-reklamer – teori og analyse* (Medier, kommunikation, journalistik, 4; København: Samfundslitteratur, 2011), 198 pp., illus., ISBN 978-87-593-1486-9, ISSN 1904-271X.

Hovland, Erland (ed.), *Vestens musikkhistorie. Fra 1600 til vår tid* (Oslo: Cappelen Damm Akademisk, 2012), 448 pp., illus., music exx., ISBN 978-82-02-27728-4.

Lohman, Laura, *Umm Kulthum. Artistic Agency and the Shaping of an Arab Legend, 1967–2007* (Middletown: Wesleyan University Press, 2010), 299 pp., illus., ISBN 978-0-8195-7071-0.

Lundberg, Mattias, and Sven-Åke Selander (eds.), *Melos och logos. Festskrift till Folke Bohlin* (Skellefteå: Artos & Norma bokförlag, 2011), 454 pp., illus., music exx., ISBN 978-91-7580-563-4.

Müller-Dombois, Richard, *Der deutsch-dänische Komponist Friedrich Kuhlau. Klassik und Frühromantik im Kontext der geistigen, sozialen und politischen Bewegungen Europas. Ein synchro-synoptisches Lese- und Nachschlagebuch* (Detmold: Syrinx Verlag, 2004), 119 pp., ISBN 3-00-014132-4.

Rasmussen, Per Erland, *Acoustical Canvases. The Music of Poul Ruders – up to and including The Handmaid's Tale* (Copenhagen: dmt publishing 2007, distributed by Syddansk Musikkonservatorium & Skuespillerskole, smks.dk), 439 pp., illus., music exx., ISBN 978-87-990266-1-6.

Studia Musicologica Regionis Balticae I, ed. Ole Kongsted (København: Capella Hafniensis Editions / The Royal Library, 2011), 304 pp., illus., music exx., ISBN 978-87-994281-0-6.

Sørensen, Inger (ed.), *Et venskab. C.F.E. Hornemans korrespondance med Edvard Grieg 1863-1898* (Danish Humanist Texts and Studies, 40; København: Det Kongelige Bibliotek & Museum Tusculanum Forlag, 2011), 166 pp., illus., ISSN 0105-8746, ISBN 978-87-635-3741-4.

Sørensen, Inger, *Horneman. En kunstnerslægt* (København: Museum Tusculanum Forlag, 2011), 397 pp., illus., ISBN 978-87-635-3740-7.

Troelsgård, Christian, *Byzantine Neumes. A New Introduction to the Middle Byzantine Musical Notation* (Monumenta musicae byzantinae, Subsidia, 9; Copenhagen: The Royal Danish

Academy of Sciences and Letters & Museum Tusculanum Press, 2011), 142 pp., illus., music exx., incl. Quick Reference Card, ISBN 978-87-635-3158-0, ISSN 0105-3566.

Ulrik Volgsten, *Musiken, medierna och lagarna. Musikverkets idéhistoria och etablerandet av en idealistisk upphovsrätt* (n.p.: Gidlunds förlag, 2012), 224 pp., ISBN 978-91-7844-853-1.

MUSIC EDITIONS

Langgaard, Rued, *Drapa (Ved Edvard Griegs Død) / Drapa (On the Death of Edvard Grieg)*, critical edition by Michael Fjeldsøe (Copenhagen: Rued Langgaard Edition / Edition S, 2011), 39 pp.

COMPACT DISCS

Anna Brożek, *Roman Maciejewski, Complete Piano Mazurkas / Wszystkie mazurki fortepianowe* (Warsaw: Sarton Records, 2011), 2 CDs.

Contributors to this issue

LARS OLE BONDE, professor, Ph.D., Department of Communication and Psychology, Krogh-stræde 6, DK-9220 Aalborg Ø, lobo@hum.aau.dk

MICHAEL FJELDSØE, associate professor, Ph.D., Section of Musicology, Department of Arts and Cultural Studies, University of Copenhagen, Klerkegade 2, DK–1308 Copenhagen K, fjeldsoe@hum.ku.dk

NIELS BO FOLTMANN, senior researcher, Danish Centre for Music Publication, The Royal Library, P.O. Box 2149, DK-1016 Copenhagen K, nbf@kb.dk

PETER HAUGE, senior researcher, Ph.D., Danish Centre for Music Publication, The Royal Library, P.O. Box 2149, DK-1016 Copenhagen K, ph@kb.dk

JENS HESSELAGER, associate professor, Ph.D., Section of Musicology, Department of Arts and Cultural Studies, University of Copenhagen, Klerkegade 2, DK–1308 Copenhagen K, hesselag@hum.ku.dk

THOMAS HOLME HANSEN, associate professor, Ph.D., Section for Musicology, Department of Aesthetic Studies, University of Aarhus, Langelandsgade 139, DK–8000 Aarhus C, musthh@hum.au.dk

TORE TVARNØ LIND, associate professor, Ph.D., Section of Musicology, Department of Arts and Cultural Studies, University of Copenhagen, Klerkegade 2, DK-1308 Copenhagen K, ttlind@hum.ku.dk

ANNE ØRBÆK JENSEN, cand.mag., Head of Department of Music and Theatre, The Royal Library, P.O. Box 2149, DK–1016 Copenhagen K, aoj@kb.dk

ANNEMETTE KIRKEGAARD, associate professor, Ph.D., Section of Musicology, Department of Arts and Cultural Studies, University of Copenhagen, Klerkegade 2, DK–1308 Copen-hagen K, kirkegd@hum.ku.dk

NIELS KRABBE, research professor, cand.mag., Danish Centre for Music Publication, The Royal Library, P.O. Box 2149, DK–1016 Copenhagen K, nk@kb.dk

BJARKE MOE, part-time lecturer, Ph.D., Section of Musicology, Department of Arts and Cultural Studies, University of Copenhagen, Klerkegade 2, DK–1308 Copenhagen K, bjarkemo@hum.ku.dk

STEEN KAARGAARD NIELSEN, associate professor, Ph.D., Section for Musicology, Depart-ment of Aesthetic Studies, University of Aarhus, Langelandsgade 139, DK–8000 Aarhus C, musskn@hum.au.dk

PETER E. NISSEN, research fellow, mag.art., College of the Resurrection (University of Sheffield), Stocks Bank Road, Mirfield, West Yorkshire, WF14 0BN, England, peteredlefnissen@gmail.com

PEDER KAJ PEDERSEN, associate professor, cand.mag., Department of Culture and Global Studies, Aalborg University, Kroghstræde 6, DK-9220 Aalborg Ø, pkp@cgs.aau.dk

KRISTIN RYGG, associate professor, Dr. art., Section of Musicology, Department of Music, Arts and Media, Hedmark University College, Holsetgt. 31, 2318 Hamar, Norway, kristin.rygg@hihm.no

HEINRICH W. SCHWAB, professor emeritus, Dr. phil., Dr. habil., Section of Musicology, Department of Arts and Cultural Studies, University of Copenhagen, Klerkegade 2, DK-1308 Copenhagen K, schwab@hum.ku.dk

JOHANNES FRANDSEN SKJELBO, Ph.D. fellow, Section of Musicology, Department of Arts and Cultural Studies, University of Copenhagen, Klerkegade 2, DK–1308 Copenhagen K, jfs@hum.ku.dk

ARNE SPOHR, assistant professor, Dr. phil., Department of Musicology, Composition and Theory, College of Musical Arts, Bowling Green State University, Bowling Green, OH 43403, aspohr@bgsu.edu

SØREN MØLLER SØRENSEN, associate professor, Ph.D., Section of Musicology, Department of Arts and Cultural Studies, University of Copenhagen, Klerkegade 2, DK–1308 Copenhagen K, sms@hum.ku.dk

ESBEN TANGE, editor, cand.mag., DR P2 Danish Broadcasting Company, Amalie Skrams Allé 7, 1, 2500 Valby, esbentange@tdcadsl.dk

Guidelines for authors

Danish Yearbook of Musicology is a peer-reviewed journal published by the Danish Musicological Society featuring contributions related to Danish music and musical research in the widest sense. The yearbook accepts articles in English, German, and Danish. All articles will be subjected to peer reviewing by the Editorial Board, the composition of which is 'dynamic' and may vary from year to year depending on the number and character of articles submitted. The submission of an article is taken to imply that it has not previously been published and has not been submitted for publication elsewhere. Proposals for articles, reviews and reports are welcomed, and submissions should be sent by e-mail to the editors, preferably in the form of an attached MS Word document, as well as a printout sent to the editorial office (see the colophon). All contributors are asked to state their name, academic position and degree, address and e-mail.

Articles consisting of more than 45,000 keystrokes including notes and spaces are not normally accepted. Musical examples and illustrations are to be provided by the author. Extensive musical examples and illustrations may only be included by prior agreement. Contributors are responsible for obtaining permission to reproduce any material in which they do not own copyright for use in print and electronic media, and for ensuring that the appropriate acknowledgements are included in their manuscripts. The full texts of articles published in *Danish Yearbook of Musicology* will be made available in electronic form.

In principle notes and references follow British practice as indicated in the *Oxford Style Manual*, with use of the author–title system in the event of repeated citations. In texts written in English, British quotation practice is to be used. Contributors from North America, though, may use North American spellings. In texts written in Danish the latest edition of *Retskrivningsordbogen* is to be used. The most recent issue of the Yearbook should be consulted for style, bibliographical citation practice, and general approach. Further information is available at www.dym.dk.

The deadline for proposals or contributions for Vol. 40 (2013) is 1 January 2013.

Danish Musicological Society

Danish Musicological Society was founded 1954. The society aims at addressing issues of musicological interest, that is, results that may be based on scholarly research as well as the conditions of musicological research. It holds meetings, arranges symposiums and conferences, as well as being a publisher of books, music, and the *Danish Yearbook of Musicology*. The society is member of the International Musicological Society.

Membership including a subscription to *Danish Yearbook of Musicology* can be obtained by anyone interested in supporting the aims of the Society. The fee is DKK 250 for individual members, DKK 100 for students and DKK 300 for couples. Application for membership and letters to the society should be mailed to Jens Hesselager, hesselag@hum.ku.dk, or sent to Danish Musicological Society, c/o Section of Musicology, University of Copenhagen, Klerkegade 2, DK–1308 Copenhagen K. Further information is available at www.musikforskning.dk.

PUBLICATIONS OF DANISH MUSICOLOGICAL SOCIETY

Dansk Årbog for Musikforskning, 1–30 (1961–2002).
Danish Yearbook of Musicology, 31– (2003 ff.).
Dania Sonans. Kilder til Musikkens Historie i Danmark:
  I *Værker af Mogens Pedersøn*, ed. Knud Jeppesen (København, 1933).
  II *Madrigaler fra Christian IV's tid* [Nielsen, Aagesen, Brachrogge], ed. Jens Peter Jacobsen (Egtved: Musikhøjskolens Forlag, 1966).
  III *Madrigaler fra Christian IV's tid* [Pedersøn, Borchgrevinck, Gistou], ed. Jens Peter Jacobsen (Egtved: Musikhøjskolens Forlag, 1967).
  IV *Musik fra Christian III's tid. Udvalgte satser fra det danske hofkapels stemmebøger (1541)*, part 1, ed. Henrik Glahn (Egtved: Edition Egtved, 1978).
  V *Musik fra Christian III's tid. Udvalgte satser fra det danske hofkapels stemmebøger (1541)*, part 2 and 3, ed. Henrik Glahn (Egtved: Edition Egtved, 1986).
  VI J.E. Hartmann, *Fiskerne*, ed. Johannes Mulvad (Egtved: Edition Egtved, 1993).
  VII J.E. Hartmann, *Balders Død*, ed. Johannes Mulvad (Egtved: Edition Egtved, 1980).
  VIII C.E.F. Weyse, *Samlede Værker for Klaver 1–3*, ed. Gorm Busk (København: Engstrøm & Sødring, 1997).
  IX C.E.F. Weyse, *Symfonier.* Vol. 1: *Symfoni nr. 1 & 2*; Vol. 2: *Symfoni nr. 3 & 4*; Vol. 3: *Symfoni nr. 5 (1796 & 1838)*; Vol. 4: *Symfoni nr. 6 & 7*, ed. Carsten E. Hatting (København: Engstrøm & Sødring, 1998, 2000, 2002, 2003).
Report of the Eleventh Congress, Copenhagen 1972, ed. Henrik Glahn, Søren Sørensen and Peter Ryom – in cooperation with International Musicological Society (Copenhagen: Edition Wilhelm Hansen, 1974).
20 Italienske Madrigaler fra Melchior Borckgrevinck »Giardino Novo I–II«, København 1605/06, ed. Henrik Glahn et al. (Egtved: Edition Egtved, 1983).
Die Sinfonie KV 16a »del Sgr. Mozart«. Bericht über das Symposium in Odense anlässlich der Erstaufführung des wiedergefundenden Werkes Dezember 1984, ed. Jens Peter Larsen and Kamma Wedin (Odense: Odense Universitetsforlag, 1987).
Heinrich Schütz und die Musik in Dänemark zur Zeit Christians IV. Bericht über die wissenschaftliche Konferenz in Kopenhagen 10.-14. November 1985, ed. Anne Ørbæk Jensen and Ole Kongsted (København: Engstrøm & Sødring, 1989).
13th Nordic Musicological Congress – Aarhus 2000, Papers and Abstracts, ed. Thomas Holme Hansen (Studies & Publications from the Department of Musicology, University of Aarhus, 7; Århus: Aarhus University, 2002).